THE UNITED STATES
AND ARMS CONTROL

THE UNITED STATES AND ARMS CONTROL

The Challenge of Leadership

Allan S. Krass

Westport, Connecticut
London

Library of Congress Cataloging-in-Publication Data

Krass, Allan S.
   The United States and arms control : the challenge of leadership /
Allan S. Krass
      p.   cm.
   Includes bibliographical references and index.
   ISBN 0–275–95947–3 (alk. paper)
   1. Arms control—United States.   2. Arms control.   I. Title.
JX1974.K79   1997
327.1'74'0973—dc21   97–8863

British Library Cataloguing in Publication Data is available.

Library of Congress Catalog Card Number: 97–8863
ISBN: 0–275–95947–3

First published in 1997

Praeger Publishers, 88 Post Road West, Westport, CT 06881
An imprint of Greenwood Publishing Group, Inc.

Printed in the United States of America

The paper used in this book complies with the
Permanent Paper Standard issued by the National
Information Standards Organization (Z39.48–1984).

10 9 8 7 6 5 4 3 2

For Dorothy and Caroline

With Love

CONTENTS

LIST OF ACRONYMS

ABM	Anti-ballistic Missile (Treaty)
ACCORD	Arms Control Community On-line Repository of Treaty Data
ACDA	Arms Control and Disarmament Agency
ACIS	Arms Control Intelligence Staff
ACIWG	Arms Control Interagency Working Group
ACRCC	Arms Control Research Coordinating Committee
AFTAC	Air Force Technical Applications Center
ARPA	Advanced Research Projects Agency
ATSD(NCB)	Assistant to the Secretary of Defense for Nuclear and Chemical and Biological Defense Programs
BDA	Bilateral Destruction and Non-production Agreement
BIC	Bilateral Implementation Commission (START II)
BL	Biosafety level
BW	Biological warfare
BWC	Biological and Toxin Weapons Convention
BXA	Bureau of Export Administration
CBM	Confidence-building measure
CBO	Congressional Budget Office
CFE	Conventional Forces in Europe (Treaty)
CFE-1A	Conventional Forces in Europe (troop levels)
CIA	Central Intelligence Agency
CIO	Central Imagery Office
COCOM	Coordinating Committee for Multilateral Export Controls
COMINT	Communications intelligence
CPPM	Continuous perimeter-portal monitoring
CSBM	Confidence- and security-building measure
CTBT	Comprehensive Test Ban Treaty
CTBTO	Comprehensive Test Ban Treaty Organization
CTR	Cooperative Threat Reduction
CW	Chemical warfare
CWC	Chemical Weapons Convention
DCI	Director of Central Intelligence

DIA	Defense Intelligence Agency
DOD	Department of Defense
DOE	Department of Energy
DOS	Department of State
DPRK	Democratic Peoples Republic of Korea (North Korea)
DSWA	Defense Special Weapons Agency
EIF	Entry into force
ELINT	Electronic intelligence
Enmod	Environmental Modification Convention
FMCT	Fissile Material Cutoff Treaty
FSC	Forum for Security Cooperation
GAO	General Accounting Office
GPS	Global Positioning System
HEU	High-enriched uranium
HUMINT	Human intelligence
IAEA	International Atomic Energy Agency
ICBM	Intercontinental ballistic missile
IDA	Institute for Defense Analysis
INF	Intermediate Nuclear Forces (Treaty)
IRBM	Intermediate-range ballistic missile
JCG	Joint Consultative Group (CFE)
JCIC	Joint Compliance and Inspection Commission (START I)
JCS	Joint Chiefs of Staff
LTBT	Limited Test Ban Treaty
M(B)FR	Mutual (Balanced) Force Reductions
MASINT	Measurement and signatures intelligence
MINATOM	Ministry of Atomic Energy (Russia)
MOU	Memorandum of understanding
MTCR	Missile Technology Control Regime
NATO	North Atlantic Treaty Organization
NFIB	National Foreign Intelligence Board
NIF	National Ignition Facility
NIMA	National Imagery and Mapping Agency
NNWS	Non-nuclear weapon state
NPAC TWG	Nonproliferation and Arms Control Technology Working Group
NPC	Nonproliferation Center
NPT	Non-Proliferation Treaty
NRDC	Natural Resources Defense Council
NRO	National Reconnaissance Organization
NRRC	Nuclear Risk Reduction Center
NSA	National Security Agency
NSC	National Security Council
NSG	Nuclear Suppliers Group
NTM	National Technical Means
NWS	Nuclear weapon state
OOV	Object of verification (CFE)
OPCW	Organization for the Prevention of Chemical Weapons
OSCC	Open Skies Consultative Commission
OSCE	Organization for Security and Cooperation in Europe
OSIA	On-site Inspection Agency
OTA	Office of Technology Assessment
PNE	Peaceful nuclear explosion
PNET	Peaceful Nuclear Explosion Treaty

R&D	Research and development
SALT	Strategic Arms Limitation Treaty
SCC	Standing Consultative Commission (ABM)
SFRC	Senate Foreign Relations Committee
SIGINT	Signals intelligence
SLBM	Submarine-launched ballistic missile
SSBN	Ballistic missile submarine
START	Strategic Arms Reduction Treaty
SVC	Special Verification Commission (INF)
THAAD	Theater High-Altitude Area Defense
TLI	Treaty-limited item
TTBT	Threshold Test Ban Treaty
TWG	Trilateral Working Group
UNSCOM	United Nations Special Commission on Iraq
USD(A&T)	Undersecretary of Defense for Acquisition and Technology
VCAWG	Verification and Compliance Analysis Working Group
VEREX	Verification Experts Group (BWC)
VTWG	Verification Technology Working Group

ACKNOWLEDGMENTS

Most of the research for this book was done while I was a visiting Science Fellow at Stanford University's Center for International Security and Arms Control. I want to express my gratitude to Michael May, David Holloway, and John Harvey for inviting me to Stanford and for providing me with generous support during the 1994-1995 academic year. I also want to thank my colleagues at CISAC for many hours of stimulating and helpful conversation about nuclear weapons, arms control and/or disarmament, proliferation, nonproliferation and counterproliferation, and many other related subjects. Herbert Abrams, David Bernstein, Cameron Binkley, Byron Bland, Lynn Eden, Jon Epstein, Sy Goodman, Jonathan Mercer, Bob Mozley, and Scott Sagan all helped to make my year more productive and enjoyable. Special thanks to Herb and Byron for many happy hours on the magnificent Stanford tennis courts. I also want to thank the friendly and competent staff at CISAC, especially Betty Bowman, Analia Bond for administrative support, Anca Ruhlen for her help in the library, and Megan Lauppe for editorial assistance. But I want to reserve a special place in this acknowledgment for George Bunn. His deep knowledge and understanding of both the theory and practice of arms control, and his constant support and encouragement throughout this project, both during my year at Stanford and since then, were, I believe, decisive in making it successful. The best of so many good things about my year at Stanford was the chance to get to know and work with George Bunn.

The initial stages of my research involved interviews with a substantial number of people involved in the day-to-day implementation of arms control. I want to thank all of them for giving me some of their valuable time and for providing much of the basic understanding of the way implementation really works (and sometimes doesn't work). At the Central Intelligence Agency I talked with Richard Haver, John Lauder, and Gordon Oehler; at the Pentagon I got help from Roland Lajoie, Gary Richardson, Steve Schleien, Mike Fitzgibbon and John Ruble; at the Arms Control and Disarmament Agency I interviewed Amy Sands,

O. J. Sheaks, Robert Rochlin, Lucas Fischer, and Mike Guhin; at the National Security Council I spoke with Anne Witkowsky and Elisa Harris; at the Department of Energy Jack Keliher, Notra Trulock, and Gail Bradshaw were helpful; and I was delighted to be able to talk with Frank von Hippel while he was still on duty at the White House Office of Science and Technology Policy. On Capitol Hill I was able to interview several staff members for key committees: David Barton of House Foreign Affairs, Monica Chavez of Senate Armed Services, and Ed Levine of the Senate Select Committee on Intelligence. At the On-Site Inspection Agency (OSIA) I received an informative briefing and was able to interview Director Gregory Govan, Principal Deputy Director Jeorg Menzel, and historian Pat Harahan. I want to express special thanks to Brinn Colenda for his help in setting up the briefing and doing so much to make my visit to OSIA both pleasant and productive. Finally, I want to thank Sidney Graybeal, Patricia Bliss McFate, and Lee Minichiello of Science Applications International Corporation for a helpful discussion of verification and implementation problems and for Lee's continued involvement with the project.

I have one more list of names of people that deserve special thanks: those who had the patience, fortitude, and generosity to read one or more draft chapters and provide comments and suggestions for improvement. They include David Bernstein, Sy Goodman, Cameron Binkley, Michael May, and Dick Gronet of CISAC, Amy Smithson of the Henry L. Stimson Center, Lee Minichiello of Science Applications International Corporation, and George Bunn. George again deserves special thanks for struggling through the entire manuscript, much of it in a dimly lit hotel room in North Korea. Last in this group, but far from least, is Dorothy Krass, who provided indispensable aid in the final editing and in preparing the camera-ready manuscript. Many of the comments and suggestions made by this group have been incorporated into the final version, but I am, of course, fully responsible for any errors or misjudgments that remain.

A final acknowledgment is owed to the Arms Control and Disarmament Agency, where I have been a William C. Foster Fellow in the Nonproliferation Bureau's Division of International Nuclear Affairs since September 1995. The fellowship has allowed me to observe and participate in some of the activities described in this book, and this experience has deepened and refined my understanding of the problems of implementing arms control agreements. I especially appreciate the efforts of my Division Chief, Susan Burk, in making sure that I became involved in useful and interesting work during my tenure at ACDA. At the same time I want to emphasize that the first draft of this book was completed before I began my fellowship, and that while much of it has been modified since then, the changes have been editorial rather than substantive. I have in no way used my official access to government documents or activities, classified or unclassified, to provide material for this book. All of the judgments and opinions expressed here are exclusively mine and do not necessarily reflect those of ACDA or the U.S. government.

1

INTRODUCTION

Arms control has undergone a revolutionary expansion in the past decade. Progress has been made in all areas of weaponry—nuclear, conventional, chemical and biological—in bilateral, multinational, and international treaties, informal agreements and collaborations, and unilateral initiatives. The massive arsenals of weapons that were accumulated during the Cold War have already been significantly reduced and show every prospect of even deeper reductions. The signing of the Chemical Weapons Convention and the Comprehensive Nuclear Test Ban and the indefinite extension of the Nuclear Nonproliferation Treaty represent significant progress in the battle against the spread of weapons of mass destruction. The Treaty on Conventional Forces in Europe, the Stockholm-Vienna Confidence and Security Building regime, and the Open Skies Treaty constitute the first major steps toward an international regime in which preparations for aggressive war can be detected at a relatively early stage, and in which the legitimate military activities of states can be monitored by neighbors and international organizations to prevent mistaken perceptions of threat.

That's the good news. The bad news is that the rate of progress in virtually all areas of arms control and nonproliferation has slowed noticeably since 1993, and persistent problems of implementation and compliance can be found in most of the agreements achieved in the 1987–1993 period. Russia and other former Soviet republics face difficult problems in implementing the Conventional Forces in Europe (CFE) Treaty, the Strategic Arms Reduction Treaties (START), and the Chemical Weapons Convention (CWC); and the United States and other Western countries are under great pressure to provide financial and technical aid in order to keep the treaties on schedule. START II and Open Skies face an uncertain future in the Russian Duma, and as of January 1997 neither Russia nor the United States had yet ratified the Chemical Weapons

Convention.[1] The Anti-ballistic Missile (ABM) Treaty, long seen as one of the essential foundations of U.S.-Soviet arms control, is under increasing pressure from missile defense advocates in the U.S. Congress, and plans to expand the North Atlantic Treaty Organization (NATO) to include former Warsaw Pact members has called into question future Russian adherence to several important agreements. Meanwhile, revelations of nuclear, chemical, or biological weapon proliferation, both demonstrated and suspected, continue to emerge with disturbing regularity. For all of the remarkable progress made in arms control during the past decade, there remains a substantial agenda of unfinished business, and its continued progress is by no means guaranteed.

THE CHANGING CONTEXT FOR ARMS CONTROL

Modern arms control was conceived in the context of a U.S.-Soviet rivalry dominated by the nuclear arms race and the prospect of nuclear war. Early attempts at nuclear disarmament were half-hearted and ineffectual (some would say cynical as well), and both sides built and deployed nuclear weapons during the 1940s and 1950s about as fast as their technical and financial resources allowed. The idea that there was a middle ground between all-out nuclear competition and total nuclear disarmament was born in the 1950s among a small coterie of scientists and academics. It emerged into public view with the attempts made by U.S. President Eisenhower and Soviet General Secretary Khrushchev to agree on a nuclear test ban in the late 1950s [1]. Arms control became theoretically respectable with the publication of two seminal works that defined its nature and purposes [2, 3], and it occupied an increasingly central role in the foreign and military policies of the Kennedy and Johnson administrations throughout the 1960s [4, 5, 6]. The Limited Test Ban Treaty (LTBT) achieved under the Kennedy administration and the Nuclear Nonproliferation Treaty (NPT) signed in the closing months of the Johnson administration were the two most prominent and lasting accomplishments of this period, although a less heralded achievement of the Kennedy administration—the so-called "hot line" installed after the Cuban Missile Crisis—turned out to be the harbinger of even more dramatic achievements in military transparency in the 1980s and 1990s. Today's Nuclear Risk Reduction Centers, whose terminals in Washington, Moscow, Kiev, Minsk, and Almaty carry the heavy volume of notifications and data exchanges for several major treaties, are direct descendants of the original hot line.

The Nixon, Ford, and Carter administrations made further advances with the ABM Treaty and the two Strategic Arms Limitation agreements (the SALT I Interim Agreement in 1972 and the SALT II Treaty in 1979) limiting offensive strategic weapon systems. But by the time of the signing of SALT II, political trends were undermining public and congressional support for arms control. The early 1980s witnessed a determined attack on the concept by the first Reagan administration [7]. Fortunately this was short-lived, to some degree because of the reluctance of the U.S. Congress to dismantle the foundations of U.S.-Soviet accommodation built by previous administrations, but primarily because of the

---

[1] On April 24, 1997, five days before the CWC's entry into force, the U.S. Senate approved its ratification by a vote of 74 to 26. See the afterword following chapter 8 for a brief comment on this and related developments.

emergence of Mikhail Gorbachev and his programs of *perestroika* and *glasnost* in the Soviet Union. The change induced in the Reagan administration was historic; Reagan was transformed by his interaction with Gorbachev from arms control's grand inquisitor to one of its most ardent advocates. The change was consummated in 1987 when Reagan and Gorbachev signed the Intermediate Nuclear Forces (INF) Treaty. It incorporated several previously unattainable innovations, such as detailed data exchanges and on-site inspections—not to mention actual eliminations of nuclear weapons—and these formed the basis for a spectrum of new agreements covering conventional, chemical, and biological weapons reached with almost breathtaking rapidity by the Bush administration. As one of the last acts of his administration U.S. President Bush joined Russian President Yeltsin in signing the START II agreement in January 1993.

Things slowed down considerably in the first Clinton administration. The indefinite extension of the NPT in 1995 and the opening for signature of the Comprehensive Nuclear Test Ban Treaty (CTBT) in 1996 were important symbolic achievements, but neither changed the actual situation with regard to nuclear weapons in any substantive way. The U.S. Senate did consent to ratification of START II, but the Russian Duma was still preventing the treaty from entering into force. Meanwhile, conservative opposition to the ABM Treaty, Chemical Weapons Convention, and very likely the CTBT as well, created considerable uncertainty about the level of commitment the United States would bring to these regimes.

The basic premise of this book is that the arms control achievements of the past decade have made a significant contribution to peace and stability in a rapidly changing world, and that they are well worth the effort and expense required to preserve and expand them. It is true that arms control no longer holds the central position in U.S. foreign policy that it did during the Cold War. It must now compete for attention and resources with many other political and economic interactions with other states and with international organizations. But this decline in visibility should not be confused with a decline in importance. It is largely the successes of U.S. arms control and nonproliferation policy that have created the context of stable international regimes in which these other interactions can flourish. As a result of these policies the United States finds itself committed to a wide range of agreements, most of which are intended to last in perpetuity and for many of which much work remains to be done to bring them into full force and effectiveness. In short, arms control is worth doing and is therefore worth doing well. The purpose of this book is to examine the strengths and weaknesses of U.S. implementation efforts and suggest some ways in which they might be more efficient and effective.

THE PROCESS OF ARMS CONTROL

The arms control process can be divided into five sequential stages. It begins with *negotiation,* in which states attempt to find an agreement that is consistent with their interests in both national security and international stability. Once an agreement is reached it must go through a process of *ratification* in which it is incorporated into the laws and practices of each of the parties. In the United States this process requires the advice and consent of the Senate and often includes the passage of implementing legislation by Congress. Once a treaty is in force it must be *implemented*. Obligations incurred in the treaty must be carried out by all parties, usually according to procedures and schedules agreed on in the treaty text or protocols. Implementation is typically subject to *verification*, which assumed an increasingly central role in U.S.-Soviet arms control agreements during the Cold War and has become an essential feature of international treaties as well. The Biological Weapons Convention (BWC) is unusual in post–World War II arms control for its lack of explicit verification provisions, and many of its parties are making a serious effort to give it an effective verification regime.

The fifth stage represents the long haul. It might be called "evolution," or one could use Charles Flowerree's phrase and call it the period of "tending arms control" [8]. In this study it will be called the *compliance* stage. Almost from the very day they enter into force, most treaty regimes are confronted with unexpected political developments, new technological possibilities, and unforeseen financial difficulties by one or more parties. The most obvious evidence for this proposition is provided by the breakup of the Warsaw Pact and Soviet Union, which created a host of unforeseen political and economic difficulties for a number of important treaties. Most treaties recognize the likelihood of such changes and have created consultative bodies or other mechanisms for dealing with them as well as with problems of implementation and compliance. The compliance stage therefore will be assumed in this book to include all of the formal interactions among parties directed toward maintaining and perpetuating the treaty regime.

This study will not concern itself with the stages of negotiation and ratification. They have been analyzed in many other works, some of which are listed in the bibliography. The focus here will be on the processes of implementation, verification, and compliance that begin after treaties enter into force. The problems of verification and compliance have been studied extensively in the U.S.-Soviet context. But the advent of treaties that call for actual eliminations of weapons, facilities, and equipment, and the introduction of notifications, data exchanges, and on-site inspections into verification, have substantially altered the context in which implementation and verification must be analyzed. There is now a growing body of empirical evidence on how arms control and disarmament treaties really work, and much of what was written about these stages needs to be looked at in light of this new evidence. A major objective of this study is to examine this evidence for treaties that have entered into force or for which significant preparations have been made prior to entry into force.

VARIETIES OF ARMS CONTROL

The rapid expansion of the scope and intensity of international agreements during the past decade has produced a wide variety of different kinds of agreements that are often referred to collectively as "arms control." This is convenient for general discussions, but for more careful analysis, and especially for purposes of comparison of different approaches, it is better to be more precise. There seem to be no universally recognized definitions for these types of agreements, and the following list makes no pretensions to universality. Its purpose is simply to clarify the meanings of each of the terms as they are used in this study.

Arms Control

Arms control agreements limit, reduce, or regulate arms or military activities. Arms control treaties are negotiated, signed, and ratified between sovereign states on a basis of equality and reciprocity. They are bargains struck in the name of national security and international stability, and they generally contain verification provisions by which the parties can monitor each other's compliance. Examples are: the START agreements that reduce strategic nuclear weapon systems, the INF Treaty that eliminates certain subclasses of nuclear missiles but not others, the ABM Treaty that limits ballistic missile defenses, and nuclear testing agreements that limit the yields of nuclear tests or the environments in which they can be conducted.

Nonproliferation

Nonproliferation implies that certain weapons may be possessed by some states but not by others. Arms control agreements are generally signed by states who possess the weapons in question, while nonproliferation agreements or regimes attempt to prevent acquisition by new states. The distinction made here between arms control and nonproliferation is not accepted by all analysts. For example, the nuclear Nonproliferation Treaty (NPT) fits both definitions to some degree. It is arms control in the sense that it is a bargain struck by sovereign states in the name of national security and international stability. But it differs from arms control in its creation of two classes of parties with different obligations and requirements, both for weapons acquisition and verification. Other nonproliferation arrangements (or "regimes") involve supplier groups like the former Coordinating Committee for Multilateral Export Controls (COCOM), the Zangger Committee and Nuclear Suppliers Group, the Australia Group, and the Missile Technology Control Regime.[2] These have limited memberships consisting of those states that possess or produce sensitive materials and technologies. The members collaborate much as international cartels used to do to control exports of those materials and technologies to potential "proliferants."

Disarmament

Disarmament agreements eliminate and prohibit particular classes of weapons universally and without discrimination. There is no distinction made in the Biological or Chemical Weapons Conventions between states permitted to retain these weapons, even temporarily, and states not permitted to acquire them. All parties renounce the weapons, even for deterrence or defense, and agree to destroy their existing production facilities and stockpiles as quickly as possible. In the CWC all parties will also agree to international verification to confirm their implementation of the treaty's requirements. The verification is carried out by a neutral international organization and is administered without prejudice to any party.

---

[2] For a comprehensive guide to international nonproliferation arrangements see Roland M. Timerbaev and Meggen M. Watt, *Inventory of International Nonproliferation Organizations and Regimes* (Monterey, CA: Center for Nonproliferation Studies, Monterey Institute of International Studies, February 1995).

Confidence-Building Measures

Confidence-building measures (CBMs) do not limit armaments or military activities but attempt to make them more "transparent" and less threatening.[3] They include several forms of communication among states that provide a clearer picture of military activities, weapons capabilities, deployment practices, doctrinal assumptions, and research and development efforts. CBMs can be part of arms control agreements; for example, advance notifications of flight tests can help in the verification of restrictions on ballistic missile capabilities. But CBMs can also be independent of any specific arms control or disarmament agreements, as they are in the observations of military maneuvers conducted under the Stockholm and Vienna Documents, or will be in Open Skies overflights. Other confidence building measures include, *inter alia*, the 1972 Incidents at Sea agreement between the United States and USSR, the United Nations Register of Conventional Arms, and the exchange of information on military biological research facilities and unusual outbreaks of disease associated with the BWC.

Laws of War

Laws of war control the use of weapons and techniques in actual combat. An example is the 1925 Geneva Protocols prohibiting the use of asphyxiating gases or biological agents or toxins in warfare. Others are the 1977 Environmental Modification Convention that prohibits "deliberate manipulation of natural processes [with] widespread, long-lasting or severe effects" on the environment, and the 1981 Inhumane Weapons Convention that prohibits "the use of certain conventional weapons which may be deemed to be excessively injurious or to have indiscriminate effects." Such conventions have signatories and states parties, but they are often considered to apply to all states whether or not they have ratified and become party to the convention, as long as most major states have become parties. A new candidate for an agreement of this type is a proposal to ban antipersonnel land mines, millions of which remain active and threaten injury or death to innocent civilians, often children, long after the war in which they were deployed is over [9].

ORGANIZATION OF THE BOOK

The United States is a party to all of these types of agreements and has been a leader in negotiating and implementing most of them. This leadership has been necessary in part because the United States and the former Soviet Union had by far the most weapons to eliminate, and in part because the United States possesses a unique combination of wealth, technical capabilities, operational expertise, and political interest in pressing international arms control. It is worthwhile, therefore, to examine how the United States is implementing and monitoring the several treaties it has become party to, what problems or obstacles it has encoun-

---

[3] "Transparency" is a relatively new word in the arms control lexicon. It suggests greater openness in national security policy and a willingness to reassure other states by opening military decision making to greater scrutiny by possible adversaries. It is a relative not an absolute concept., since military preparations can never be completely transparent if they are to be effective.

tered in the learning process, and how the lessons learned from this experience will affect the prospects for arms control and military transparency.

To address these questions the book is organized as follows. Chapter 2 briefly examines the history of arms control implementation, monitoring, and compliance in the first four decades of the Cold War. Chapter 3 describes developments since 1986 in nuclear, conventional, chemical, and biological arms control, and chapter 4 describes the bureaucratic apparatus the United States has created to carry out its obligations in these areas. Chapter 5 examines the costs of implementing and verifying treaties and compares those costs with the benefits to U.S. national security. Chapter 6 examines several persistent problem areas involving bureaucratic organization and the role of technology and research in verification. Chapter 7 examines the ever-present problem of noncompliance, and chapter 8 draws some general conclusions and looks at the implications of U.S. arms control experience for the stability of existing regimes and the prospects of new agreements.

REFERENCES

1. Jennifer E. Sims, *Icarus Restrained: An Intellectual History of Nuclear Arms Control, 1945–1960* (Boulder CO: Westview, 1990).

2. Thomas C. Schelling and Morton H. Halperin, *Strategy and Arms Control* (Washington, DC: Pergamon-Brassey, 1985).

3. Donald G. Brennan, ed., *Arms Control, Disarmament, and National Security* (New York: George Braziller, 1961).

4. Glenn T. Seaborg, *Kennedy, Khrushchev, and the Test Ban* (Berkeley: University of California Press, 1981).

5. Glenn T. Seaborg and Benjamin S. Loeb, *Stemming the Tide: Arms Control and the Johnson Years* (Lexington, MA: Lexington Books, 1987).

6. George Bunn, *Arms Control by Committee: Managing Negotiations with the Russians* (Stanford, CA: Stanford University Press, 1992).

7. Allan S. Krass, Death and Transfiguration: Nuclear Arms Control in the 1980s and 1990s, *World Security: Trends and Challenges at Century's End,* Michael T. Klare and Daniel C. Thomas, eds. (New York: St. Martin's Press, 1991), pp. 68–100.

8. Charles C. Flowerree, "On Tending Arms Control Agreements," *Washington Quarterly,* Winter 1990, pp. 199–214.

9. Michael J. Matheson, "New Landmine Protocol Is Vital Step toward Ban," *Arms Control Today,* July 1996, pp. 9–13.

2

COLD WAR ARMS CONTROL

The focus of this chapter is the period from the end of World War II to 1985, when Mikhail Gorbachev's accession to the leadership of the Soviet Union set in motion the chain of events leading to the end of the Cold War. It was a period during which progress in arms control could charitably be called glacial in most areas, but also during which important precedents were established and foundations laid for the spectacular breakthroughs of the late 1980s. The purpose of this chapter is to identify the most important of those precedents and foundations. Although the political, economic, and technical context for post–Cold War arms control is dramatically different from that of the earlier period, there are still some important lessons to be learned from the experiences of the Cold War. So it is worth spending a few pages reviewing that history.

Problems of negotiation and ratification dominated the arms control process during the Cold War period. The United States and Soviet Union had to learn how to talk to each other about issues that went to the heart of their national security concerns and their suspicion and fear of each other. On one hand, the two sides were developing and deploying massive nuclear arsenals aimed at each other and kept in high states of alert against surprise attack. On the other hand, they were attempting to reduce the tensions created by such preparations and gain some control over the enormous expenditures they required. Paul Warnke, a former Director of the Arms Control and Disarmament Agency and President Carter's chief SALT negotiator, once called arms control an "unnatural act, [which] requires countries to tear down what they have built up" [1]. Learning this unnatural act took a long time, and it was not until 18 years after the end of World War II that the first major arms control agreement, the Limited Test Ban Treaty (LTBT) of 1963, was signed and ratified. This treaty did nothing to halt, or even slow down, the testing of nuclear weapons. It simply moved them underground, causing many to characterize the LTBT as more environmental than arms control. However, it did teach the two sides a great deal about how to negotiate with each other and how to craft agreements that would give some reassurance to the anxious public while protecting what each side felt to be its legitimate interests in maintaining strong nuclear forces.

Some other important achievements of the Cold War era were the "Hot Line" Agreement of 1963, the nuclear Nonproliferation Treaty (NPT) of 1970, the Biological Weapons Convention (BWC) of 1972, the SALT Interim Agreement and ABM Treaty of 1972, the Threshold Test Ban (TTBT) and Peaceful Nuclear Explosion (PNET) Treaties of 1974 and 1976, the Helsinki Final Document of 1976, the SALT II Treaty of 1979, and the Inhumane Weapons Convention of 1981.[1] These were accompanied by a variety of relatively innocuous agreements on such things as the demilitarization of Antarctica (1959), banning deployments of nuclear weapons in outer space (1967) and on the ocean floor (1971), the Nuclear Accidents (1971) and Incidents at Sea (1972) Agreements, and the Environmental Modification (Enmod) Convention (1977) that prohibited military use of harmful environmental modification techniques like rain making or deforestation. Another development of this period was the concept of nuclear free zones or regional nonproliferation agreements. Two of these were successfully negotiated: the Treaty of Tlatelolco for Latin America (1967) and the Treaty of Raratonga (1985) for the South Pacific.

This list contains agreements of all of the five types defined in chapter 1 and makes clear that however slow and unsatisfying the pace of arms control may have appeared during the Cold War, a great deal was accomplished and a lot was learned about how to negotiate agreements and get them ratified. The latter process was much more of a problem for the United States than for the Soviet Union. The constitutional requirement of a two-thirds majority of the Senate to ratify a treaty is a major political obstacle for any president trying to get an agreement. Jimmy Carter learned this lesson the hard way when he had to withdraw the SALT II Treaty from the Senate in 1980. The Soviet invasion of Afghanistan late in 1979, while logically unrelated to the objectives of the SALT Treaty, made Senate approval of the agreement virtually impossible, and Carter had little choice but to withdraw it. Earlier in the 1970s it was Senator Henry Jackson of Washington who expressed grave reservations about the SALT I agreements and sponsored legislation that put future presidents on notice that they would face defeat in the Senate if terms more favorable to the United States were not negotiated.

A major U.S. innovation of the Cold War period was the creation of a new agency devoted explicitly to arms control and nonproliferation. Created in 1961, just six months after the inauguration of John F. Kennedy, the Arms Control and Disarmament Agency (ACDA) was given the lead responsibility for conducting arms control research, preparing for and conducting negotiations, operating verification and inspection systems, and informing the public about arms control [2]. Creation of ACDA represented an awareness by both the executive and legislative branches of government that arms control was an important new form of diplomacy in which political, military, and technical issues were combined. No existing agency of government had the expertise and administrative flexibility to deal effectively with arms control, and the rapidity and overwhelming support

---

[1] For a comprehensive chronology and analysis of the history of arms control developments, see Jozef Goldblat, *Arms Control: A Guide to Negotiations and Agreements*, Sage Publications (London: International Peace Research Institute Oslo,1994).

with which ACDA was created shows that the great majority of members of Congress understood the unique and important niche it was to fill.[2]

ACDA's first major achievement was the nuclear Nonproliferation Treaty (NPT), for which it was the lead negotiator representing the United States. Throughout the next 25 years ACDA managed U.S. participation in the NPT—helping the International Atomic Energy Agency (IAEA) with research and development on new safeguards technologies, preparing for and attending periodic review conferences for the treaty, participating in meetings of the Zangger and London export control groups (see below), and helping to recruit new parties to the treaty, which by 1995 had more signatories than any other arms control agreement [3, p. 842]. It was also ACDA that led the U.S. delegation to the review and extension conference in 1995, at which the treaty was extended indefinitely. The large majority for indefinite extension came as something of a surprise and owes much to the negotiating skills of the U.S. delegation, headed by ACDA's Ambassador Thomas Graham.

ACDA's record during the Cold War showed many positive achievements, but it also included some major disappointments against a background of more or less constant political controversy. Opposition to ACDA, so easily overcome at the time of its creation, grew stronger as arms control became a more salient feature of the U.S.-Soviet relationship. During the Nixon, Ford, and Carter administrations ACDA became a political whipping boy on which opponents of particular agreements could vent their wrath. The attitudes of Presidents Reagan and Bush toward the agency ranged from indifference to outright contempt. At the end of the Bush administration the agency survived an attempt to end its independence and absorb it into the State Department. But it was under fire again only two years later when a Republican-dominated Congress tried to do the same thing. At the end of 1996 ACDA's continued vitality, even its very existence, remained in doubt, as did the survival of several of its most prominent achievements. We will return to a deeper analysis of these difficulties in chapter 6.

Much more could be and has been said about the Cold War experience with negotiation and ratification. But I will have little more to say about these phases and instead will turn to implementation, verification, and consultation, about which less has been written. This is especially true for implementation, which was in most respects a nonissue during the Cold War. There has been more experience with the latter two phases, and there are some important lessons to be learned from that experience. The chapter ends with a list of those lessons.

IMPLEMENTATION

It is remarkable how little the United States had to do to implement its early arms control agreements. The limited and threshold nuclear test bans required only that the parties not do certain things or only do them within certain limits. But the TTBT and PNET were never ratified, so there was no need to assemble and exchange the geological and yield data that were to have been exchanged under them. The Antarctic, Seabed, and Outer Space treaties and the Biological Weapons Convention also required no positive actions by any of the parties.

---

[2] The legislation creating ACDA passed by votes of 73-14 in the Senate and 290-54 in the House. The entire process from introduction of legislation to final approval took only 65 days [2].

President Nixon did order the destruction of all U.S. military stocks of biological agents, but this was accomplished before the BWC was ratified. Nixon's order was not contingent on achieving a formal treaty. This is similar to the current situation with chemical weapons, where the United States is committed by presidential order and congressional legislation to destroy most of its chemical weapon stockpile whether or not the CWC is ratified. Strictly speaking, therefore, neither action should be considered as implementation of a treaty commitment. Indeed, it seems likely that a unilateral U.S. commitment to destroy these stockpiles was necessary to achieve the treaties in the first place.

The first SALT agreement set limits on intercontinental (ICBM) and submarine-launched (SLBM) ballistic missile launchers that were higher than the actual deployments on either side and therefore required no dismantlement or conversions. And while the ABM Treaty set many limits on development, testing, and deployment of ballistic missile defenses, it did not require either party to undo something it had already done. The United States did decide to mothball its single ABM site in North Dakota after the treaty was ratified, but this was a unilateral decision not mandated by the treaty.

The SALT II Treaty did require dismantlement of some systems by both the Soviet Union and the United States to make room for new deployments. The treaty was never ratified, but both parties observed its limits for several years after its signing in 1979. Ratification was opposed by many influential members of the Reagan administration, and decisions to remain in compliance by dismantling deployed systems were intensely controversial within the administration. A few systems, primarily Polaris submarines and B-52 bombers, were dismantled in the early 1980s, but the Reagan administration ultimately renounced SALT II, and U.S. deployments were allowed briefly to exceed the treaty's limits. Nevertheless, some important precedents were set during this time. Most important was the practice of dismantling weapon systems in a way that could be monitored by the other side's national technical means. Submarines or bombers were cut into pieces, which were left in the open for several weeks to allow the other side to photograph them with satellite cameras. This practice remains an important part of implementation procedure under more recent agreements.

Although there was little for it to do in the way of eliminating weapons or facilities, it was important that the United States act in compliance with the provisions of ratified treaties. Part of the ratification process often includes the passing of legislation by Congress that makes the treaty a part of U.S. law. As treaties grew more complicated it became necessary to give some agency the responsibility to ensure that the United States carried out its military activities in compliance with existing treaties. President Nixon chose the Department of Defense (DOD) for this task under the SALT and ABM Treaties. On June 16, 1972 he directed the Secretary of Defense to create a mechanism to review all U.S. military research and development (R&D) activities to make sure they were in compliance with the provisions of SALT, especially the ABM Treaty [4, 5]. Secretary of Defense Melvin Laird assigned the responsibility to the Director of Defense Research and Engineering (DDR&E) in the Office of the Under Secretary of Defense for Acquisition and ordered all other Pentagon agencies to report all activities relevant to implementation and compliance directly to that office. This basic arrangement has survived many bureaucratic reorganizations in the 23 years since its creation, although the office responsible for implementation is now called the Under Secretary of Defense for Acquisition and Technology.

The arrangement worked reasonably well until politics intruded during the Reagan administration. As part of its campaign to undercut the ABM Treaty and legitimize its Strategic Defense Initiative (SDI) the administration overruled DOD and National Security Council (NSC) advice and authorized the construction of two large radars in Thule, Greenland and Fylingdales, England [6]. These actions were violations of the ABM Treaty's prohibition against deploying early warning radars outside national territory, and both the Defense Department and NSC had warned against them. But the promotion of SDI took precedence, and the radars were deployed, even as the administration accused the Soviets of violating the treaty with their own construction of an ABM radar in Siberia.

Hopes for a nationwide defense against ballistic missile attacks, and problems with the ABM Treaty, did not end with the Reagan administration. This issue will be one of the central themes of my discussion of treaty compliance in chapter 7.

VERIFICATION

The closed nature of Soviet society and deep American distrust of Soviet intentions made verification the *sine qua non* of arms control during the Cold War. This can be seen in the very first arms control (or nonproliferation) proposal of the postwar period, the Baruch Plan for international control of atomic energy. The plan, placed before the United Nations in the months following the end of World War II, would have created an international authority to control all potentially threatening nuclear activities. It would have had all nuclear materials from uranium and thorium ore to weapon-grade fissile materials under its control and would have had the authority to carry out inspections in any nation suspected of pursuing development of nuclear weapons. The United Nations Security Council would have had the authority to punish any state caught violating the agreement, without being constrained by the veto power of permanent members.

The Baruch proposal reveals the complex mix of idealism, realism, and cynicism that marked the U.S. approach to arms control negotiations with the Soviet Union throughout the Cold War. On the idealism side there was a genuine desire for more openness in scientific and military activities and the desire to reach agreements that would reduce tensions and prevent a nuclear arms race. Realism dictated a recognition that the U.S.-Soviet rivalry would probably last a long time and that U.S. nuclear superiority was a potent antidote to Soviet conventional power on the European continent. Cynicism manifested itself most prominently in sweeping U.S. proposals for intrusive inspection and international control, which everyone knew would be unacceptable to the Soviet Union. Such proposals allowed the United States to claim the moral high ground by making demands that it would probably not be willing to accept itself [7, p. 70].

For its part, despite its repeated calls for "general and complete disarmament," the Soviet Union was determined to acquire nuclear weapons and to maintain sufficient conventional power to avoid what it saw as likely intimidation and coercion by the United States [8]. While it is hard to find evidence of idealism in Josef Stalin's approach to nuclear arms control, there was plenty of both realism and cynicism in Soviet policy.[3] Distrust of American motives and a deep sense of technological inferiority contributed to Soviet opposition to the transparency that the United States demanded. For most of the Cold War Soviet policymakers took the position that demands for on-site inspection or unrestricted aerial overflights like those in President Eisenhower's Open Skies proposal were thinly veiled attempts at espionage. In negotiations the Soviets often tried to exploit the U.S. interest in intrusive verification to extract concessions on substantive treaty provisions.

This was called "The Game of Disarmament" [9] and it went on for nearly 40 years until Mikhail Gorbachev rewrote the rule book. Despite the hostility, suspicion, and ambivalence on both sides, a surprisingly large number of agreements were achieved during these years, both bilaterally between the United States and Soviet Union and internationally under the auspices of the United Nations. There was also progress in verification, made possible in large part by the sophisticated monitoring technologies developed by the two superpowers as part of their military competition. It is one of the great ironies of the Cold War that techniques developed for threat assessment and war planning made it possible for the two bitter rivals to agree on limits to some of their more destructive and destabilizing weapons without the aid of on-site inspections.

These so-called national technical means (NTM) of verification[4] included a wide variety of satellite and aircraft imaging systems; extensive networks of satellites, seismographs, radiation monitors, and other sensors for detection and measurement of nuclear weapon tests; space-, land-, and sea-based antennas and sophisticated decryption and traffic analysis methods for communications monitoring; radars for tracking aircraft, ballistic missiles, and satellites; ground-based imaging systems for observing and identifying orbiting spacecraft; underwater sonar devices that could track submarines and surface ships and detect hydroacoustic waves at great distances; and many more. All of this capability, in which many billions of dollars and rubles were invested, gave each side a remarkably accurate picture of the military capabilities of its adversary.

Creation of all of these technologies required a sophisticated and expensive research and development effort carried out in a nationwide network of private and government laboratories. Most of the research on satellites and communications monitoring was directed and funded by the Intelligence Community, primarily through the CIA's Directorate of Science and Technology [10, pp. 17–19]. R&D related to nuclear test monitoring was done by the Atomic Energy Commission (later the Department of Energy) in the national laboratories at Argonne, Los Alamos, Sandia, and Livermore. The Advanced Research Projects Agency (ARPA) also played an important part in the R&D effort, sponsoring early exploratory research on some of the more esoteric technologies. At its creation in 1961 the Arms Control and Disarmament Agency was also expected to "conduct, support, and coordinat[e] . . . research for arms control and disarmament policy

---

[3] There certainly was idealism on the Soviet side, as the career of Andrei Sakharov makes clear. Much of this idealism came from the scientists who created the Soviet nuclear arsenal, just as it had on the U.S. side.

[4] The phrase "national technical means of verification" customarily used in treaty texts is not entirely consistent with U.S. terminology, which carefully distinguishes "verification" from "monitoring." This distinction will be made clear in chapter 4. For this chapter it will cause no confusion to use "verification" as the generic term for monitoring the activities and assessing the compliance of other parties.

formulation" [11, p. 1], but its focus was to be on implementation and cooperative inspection techniques, not secret monitoring technologies. The Intelligence Community and the Department of Defense have always maintained tight control over NTM research and development (see chapter 4).

ACDA's role in arms control R&D has been one of its major disappointments, and we will look more closely at it in chapter 6. However, during its early years ACDA did participate in some important R&D projects in collaboration with DOD and the Atomic Energy Commission. From 1962 to 1968 ACDA and DOD supervised a program, code-named Cloud Gap, which did research and field testing on techniques for aerial inspections, on-site inspections of conventional forces, identification of underground nuclear tests, and monitoring of nuclear weapons destruction [2, p. 14]. The last-mentioned project was called the FT-34 Experiment, and its purpose was to determine whether effective inspections of warhead dismantlement could be conducted without compromising sensitive design information.[5] In the 1970s, however, ACDA's research role diminished steadily as limited funding forced it to raid research budgets to support personnel and negotiation expenses [2, p. 18]. By 1989 ACDA's external research budget had declined to less than half a million dollars per year [14, p. 6].

From 1970 to 1987 all U.S.-Soviet agreements involved weapons and activities that could be monitored with remote observation systems, and there was little interest in cooperative verification techniques. The Limited Test Ban Treaty prohibited nuclear tests in the atmosphere, underwater, and in space, where they could be detected down to very small yields with the networks of sensors deployed by both sides. Verification is not even mentioned in the text of the LTBT, but it was understood by both sides that NTM would be used to monitor nuclear tests. The LTBT illustrates the principle followed in all treaties of the Cold War period: the capabilities of NTM set the limits for what could be controlled. The United States argued that a ban on underground tests could not be adequately verified without extensive on-site inspection rights, and the Soviet Union was just as adamant that at most only a very small number of inspections would be acceptable [15]. In 1974 the two sides agreed to limit the yields of underground tests to 150 kilotons, and two years after that they agreed to restrictions on peaceful nuclear explosions (PNE). These agreements required exchanges of information that had previously been treated as secret and even included an elaborate on-site inspection protocol for the PNET [16]. But the treaties were not ratified for more than 15 years, and then not until much more intrusive verification provisions were added to them at the insistence of the Reagan administration.

The capabilities of NTM were also an important factor in defining the limits of the ABM Treaty and the Strategic Arms Limitation Talks (SALT) pursued by the Nixon, Ford, and Carter administrations. The ABM Treaty prohibited development and deployment of nationwide antiballistic missile defenses, and the

---

[5] For a summary of the FT-34 experiment see Frank von Hippel, "The 1969 ACDA Study on Warhead Dismantlement," *Science and Global Security*, Vol. 2, No. 1, 1990, pp. 103–108. The FT-34 report itself was obtained by the Federation of American Scientists in 1990 under a Freedom of Information Act request as part of its campaign for a U.S.-Soviet warhead dismantlement agreement. [12] The agreement has still not been achieved, but the FT-34 report provides an interesting insight into the seriousness with which the idea was taken in the early years of arms control. [13]

SALT I Interim Agreement limited numbers of deployed launchers for intercontinental and submarine-launched ballistic missiles. It was possible to agree on these treaties without intrusive inspections because the critical components and activities for an ABM included construction of phased-array radars as big as football fields and deployment of hundreds of interceptor missiles in distinctive patterns. During the development of ABM systems, tests of interceptors against incoming missiles took place high in the atmosphere or in space. ICBM launchers generally took the form of large underground concrete and steel silos, and SLBM launchers were huge submarines that took years to build at shipyards that were impossible to hide completely. All of these objects and activities were observable from satellites and earth-based sensors, and there was no need to resort to on-site inspections to verify compliance with the limits negotiated in SALT I.

It was important that the existence and legitimacy of NTM were recognized in the SALT and ABM agreements. Although NTM were not specified or defined, remote sensing techniques that did not encroach on the territory of sovereign states were recognized as operating "in a manner consistent with generally recognized principles of international law" [17, pp. 379–80]. The parties agreed to prohibit interference with NTM and to refrain from deliberate concealment measures that "impeded" verification of compliance. The SALT II Treaty, negotiated by the Ford and Carter administrations and signed by Leonid Brezhnev and Jimmy Carter in 1979, pushed the practice of verification by NTM to new levels of both comprehensiveness and precision. Taking advantage of the ability of satellite cameras to resolve features only a few inches in size, of ground-based radars to accurately track missiles and their reentry vehicles, and of satellite and earth-based antennas to intercept telemetry signals broadcast during missile flight tests, the two sides were able to place qualitative as well as quantitative limits on bombers and missile systems. The noninterference and nonconcealment clauses were made somewhat more concrete by setting limits on the encryption of flight test telemetry. This last provision appeared to be another great step forward in cooperative use of NTM for verification, but it ended up causing more suspicion than reassurance in the 1980s. Accusations of excessive encryption of missile flight test telemetry were among the most important of the many charges leveled by the Reagan administration against the Soviet Union [18].

A third area in which verification played a critical role was the nuclear Nonproliferation Treaty (NPT), first signed by the United States, Great Britain, and the Soviet Union in 1968 and joined by a steadily increasing number of states throughout the 1970s and 1980s. This treaty recognizes five legitimate "nuclear weapon states" (NWS) and requires that all other parties renounce nuclear weapons and submit their commercial and scientific nuclear facilities to safeguards administered by the International Atomic Energy Agency (IAEA). Safeguards require that each state keep detailed records of its own nuclear energy activities and provide IAEA inspectors access to these records for verification. The IAEA is also permitted to use various kinds of containment and surveillance measures at facilities where fissile materials are processed or stored for the purpose of ensuring that no material is diverted to weapons programs. At the end of 1996 only five countries in the entire world remained outside the NPT regime, and more than 100 had negotiated safeguards agreements with the IAEA.

The NPT and its system of on-site inspections were unique in arms control for almost 20 years, and it is important to understand why such an unprecedented agreement was achievable during the Cold War. The most remarkable aspect of the treaty is its division of the world into two kinds of states subject to two different sets of obligations. The nuclear weapon states (NWS) were allowed to maintain nuclear arsenals and were not required to submit to safeguards, although some did so voluntarily in limited ways.[6] The non–nuclear weapon states (NNWS) were not permitted to have nuclear weapons and were required to submit all nuclear facilities to IAEA safeguards. Such an unsymmetrical agreement was possible only because the nuclear weapon states had for many years almost exclusive control over access to nuclear technology. At the same time many countries in the developing world had high hopes for both commercial nuclear energy and peaceful nuclear explosions, hopes encouraged by the advanced states looking for markets for their nuclear technologies. States that wanted to develop commercial nuclear facilities were usually forced to seek help from the advanced nuclear powers, and in return for that help the NWS could demand submission to safeguards. Articles IV and V of the NPT make clear the obligation of the NWS to provide the NNWS with access to the benefits of peaceful applications of nuclear energy (including peaceful nuclear explosions) in return for the acceptance of safeguards by the NNWS.[7]

This bargain was not the only reason why so many states accepted the status of NNWS. Many were convinced that they would be more secure in the long run if nuclear weapons did not proliferate to their neighbors, and the NWS also agreed to Article VI of the treaty, which commits them to good-faith negotiations toward ending the nuclear arms race and ultimate nuclear disarmament [20]. The discrimination in the treaty between two types of states was not intended to be permanent. Nevertheless, it was the guarantee of access to nuclear technology that attracted so many non–nuclear weapon parties to the NPT in the 1960s and 1970s. If nuclear technology had been cheaper and simpler to acquire, like chemical or biological technologies, it is difficult to believe that a nonproliferation treaty, especially one involving onsite inspections of only the non–nuclear states, would have been achievable. However, attitudes appear to have changed in the 25 years since the NPT's entry into force. The surprisingly strong reaffirmation of the treaty in 1995, at a time when most of the shine had worn off commercial nuclear energy, and when peaceful nuclear explosions had become virtually unthinkable, shows that security concerns had come to dominate the attitudes of most states toward the NPT. There was far more emphasis on Article VI (the promise of nuclear disarmament) at the review and extension conference than on Articles IV and V (technology sharing).[8]

These three areas—nuclear testing, strategic nuclear forces, and nuclear nonproliferation—formed the core of arms control and verification efforts during the Cold War. However, there is one other group of treaties that is worth examining briefly from the standpoint of verification. This group includes the Antarctic, Outer Space, Seabed, and Environmental Modification Treaties, and the Biological Weapons Convention (BWC). The first four are characterized by their

---

[6] All nonmilitary nuclear facilities in Great Britain were made subject to IAEA safeguards in 1968, and a similar arrangement involving facilities without "direct national security significance" was signed by the United States in 1970. The Soviet Union agreed in 1970 to permit safeguards at "designated peaceful nuclear facilities" [19, pp. 788–789]

[7] For a full text of the NPT see Goldblat, op. cit. or *Arms Control Today*, March 1995, pp. 24–26.

[8] George Bunn, Stanford University seminar, May 17, 1995.

relatively open verification arrangements, including on-site inspections, while the last is unusual for its total lack of any verification provisions, indeed any mention at all of verification in its text. The openness of the first group had more to do with the military uselessness or irrelevance of the environments and technologies controlled than it did with a genuine desire for military transparency by the parties. Still, there have been some positive effects even among these apparently innocuous treaties. Antarctica has been universally recognized as a nonmilitarized area, and all facilities on the continent are open to visits and inspections by all parties to the treaty. There has been an ongoing cooperative effort under the treaty to preserve Antarctica's environmental integrity, including a 50-year ban on mining signed in 1991. The treaty regime includes periodic consultative meetings of the parties, of which there had been 17 through 1992 [21].

The absence of verification in the BWC is also related to the lack of military utility of biological weapons, at least as perceived by the major powers in the early 1970s. Another important factor is the near impossibility of verifying with confidence the absence of such weapons in any state, even with extensive on-site inspections. The signing of the BWC was facilitated by the unilateral renunciation of biological weapons by the United States in 1969 and the destruction of its stocks of lethal organisms in 1970 [17, p. 93]. These actions were consistent with a determination by the Nixon administration that it saw little or no military value in biological weapons, and its willingness to sign a treaty with no verification provisions implied a judgment that the benefits of having a treaty outweighed the risks that some parties might be able to violate it without detection. These judgments were later called into question by the Reagan administration, which used alleged Soviet violations of the BWC to discredit both the Soviet Union and the treaty itself [22]. Recently there has been a resurgence of interest in adding verification to the BWC, and this will be dealt with in later chapters.

By the end of the 1970s national technical means were beginning to reach the practical limits of their capacity to monitor agreements with high confidence. The advent of smaller, more mobile, and more easily disguised nuclear weapons was causing NTM to fall behind in the relentless race between "hiders and finders," which characterized the nuclear arms race [23]. The early advantages of NTM for monitoring strategic weapons deployments derived from a unique set of technological factors that matched the capabilities of the sensors to the systems being observed. On both sides, large objects like strategic bombers, missile silos, or missile-carrying submarines were integrated into an extensive command, control, and communications system. All of these systems were distinctive and difficult to camouflage or hide. The SALT II Treaty went about as far as one could go in matching such objects of verification to the sensors that monitored them. But even as SALT II was signed, new weapons were approaching deployment for which NTM were bound to be much less effective. Mobile, multiple-warhead ballistic and cruise missiles were only a few of the systems on the horizon, and these made it clear to many that even if SALT II were ratified, further progress in arms control would require more intrusive forms of verification, including on-site inspection.

Another set of limitations associated with NTM derives from their high cost and technical sophistication. U.S. and Soviet reconnaissance satellites, communications monitors, and other surveillance devices are among the most sophisticated and expensive technologies developed in the Cold War. There is little likelihood that any but a handful of the most industrially advanced states will be able to acquire them. There have been proposals for an international satellite monitoring agency under the United Nations, and some collaborations among states have been launched to deploy imaging satellites in orbit. There is even the prospect that commercial satellite imagery will improve in quantity and resolving power to the point where less advanced states could do some of their own monitoring by purchasing images. One of the most important benefits of the Open Skies Treaty (see chapter 3) will be its potential for providing high-quality monitoring data to states without sophisticated NTM. But these efforts are unlikely to approach the comprehensiveness and quality of the imaging systems deployed by the two former superpower adversaries.

COMPLIANCE

The ink was barely dry on SALT I when U.S. critics of the agreement began to accuse the Soviets of cheating on it. The debate over Soviet compliance raged in U.S. politics for nearly 20 years, and it tells us much about how dependent the verification process is on the overall political relations among the parties to an agreement. During the Nixon, Ford, and Carter administrations, the relationship was basically cooperative, and compliance disputes were settled quietly in the Standing Consultative Commission (SCC), a forum created in SALT I precisely for this purpose. The SCC was one of the more important and successful innovations of the Cold War era, and it has provided a model for consultative groups in virtually all subsequent agreements.

The SCC was created in Article XIII of the ABM Treaty, and its mandate is to consider a wide range of questions that affect implementation and compliance with the Treaty [24]. The Commission meets regularly at least twice a year in Geneva and can also be called into special session by either of the parties. The U.S. delegation is led by a commissioner with the rank of ambassador who is nominally located in ACDA but who is chosen by consensus of the heads of the major agencies involved in national security and must be approved by Congress. Other members of the U.S. delegation represent interested agencies such as the State and Defense Departments and the Intelligence Community. Throughout the 1970s the SCC considered and resolved a wide range of implementation and compliance issues involving the dismantlement, deployment, and testing of strategic weapons systems and ballistic missile defense systems. Assessments of the performance of the SCC by the Nixon, Ford, and Carter administrations were consistently positive, and it was assumed that it would continue its deliberations under the SALT II Treaty signed in 1979.

This assumption did not reckon with the advent of the Reagan administration. During Reagan's first term the political atmosphere became charged with a new level of distrust and hostility toward the Soviet Union, and compliance issues became both more visible and more intractable. For several years charges of widespread Soviet cheating were used by opponents of arms control to attack agreements already reached and to prevent the achievement of new ones. The SCC was a major victim of the overall assault on arms control, and it barely survived the determined efforts of high-level Pentagon officials to discredit and weaken it. The intensity of the attack is best captured in Secretary of Defense Caspar Weinberger's characterization of the SCC as "an Orwellian memory hole into which our concerns have been dumped like yesterday's trash" [25]. Ultimately the Reagan administration decided as part of its abandonment of the SALT process to refrain from bringing any questions involving the SALT I or II agreements to the SCC. But it did continue to discuss ABM Treaty questions there, and that process is still going on. It is the SCC, whose membership is being opened to all former Soviet republics,[9] that is considering proposed U.S. "clarification" of the ABM Treaty to legitimate development of so-called theater missile defenses (see chapter 7).

The attack on the SCC was part of a much broader attack on arms control and on alleged Soviet violations of existing agreements. Secretary of State Alexander Haig made the first official accusation in 1981 with charges of use of biological toxins in Indochina and Afghanistan, and throughout the 1980s the list of alleged Soviet transgression grew steadily [18, 27]. In 1983, incensed by the shooting down of a civilian airliner by the Soviet Union,[10] Congress required the president to submit an annual report of "Soviet Noncompliance with Arms Control Agreements." These reports, initially issued directly from the White House, continued into the 1990s when they evolved into what is now the annual report on "Adherence to and Compliance with Arms Control Agreements" prepared by ACDA [28]. The accusatory tone of the early noncompliance reports has evolved into a more neutral and businesslike presentation of issues on which the United States feels it necessary to make a public statement of its concerns. Most questions that arise under existing treaties are dealt with confidentially in consultative commissions that are direct descendants of the SCC.

There are several lessons to be learned from the compliance battles of the 1980s. First, it is clear that the Soviet Union *did* violate treaty commitments (by their own subsequent admission) in at least two instances. In 1989 Foreign Minister Eduard Shevardnadze admitted that the large radar under construction near Krasnoyarsk was a violation of the ABM Treaty, and in 1992 Russian President Boris Yeltsin admitted that the Soviet government had for many years violated the Biological Weapons Convention by continuing research and development on biological weapons [17, p. 232]. Whether there are other cases of genuine violations among the many accusations made during the Reagan administration remains to be seen and is outside the scope of this discussion. What can be said is that even if more violations are authenticated there will still be no basis for a conclusion that there was a "pattern" of violations that proved Soviet intent to gain military advantage. The military significance of the whole list of violations did not amount to "a hill of beans" in the opinion of House Armed Services Committee Chairman Les Aspin and most other analysts [29].

There were patterns to Soviet compliance behavior, but their significance was more political and technical than military [18]. An analysis of the timing of a number of their actions shows that Soviet willingness to accommodate U.S. concerns or to abide by U.S. interpretations of ambiguous provisions depended most strongly on their assessments of the political prospects for improved rela-

---

[9] In December 1993, the Clinton administration accepted the principle of "multilateralization" of the ABM Treaty, which if successful will add as many as 12 new delegations to the SCC [26, p. 5].

[10] The Korean Airlines plane had strayed into Soviet airspace, probably because of a navigation error. It was mistaken by Soviet air defense forces for a U.S. spy mission and shot down, killing more than 280 passengers. For a full account of the incident see Seymour M. Hersh, *"The Target Is Destroyed"* (New York: Random House, 1986).

tions with the U.S. As relations deteriorated in the late 1970s and early 1980s, the Soviets appeared to become increasingly less concerned with U.S. interpretations of their behavior and increasingly willing to undertake activities that pushed close to or even beyond the limits set by treaties. Telemetry encryption, testing of the SS-25 ICBM, and a number of other decisions, including possibly the Krasnoyarsk radar, can be understood most clearly in this way. The lesson is that compliance behavior, like all other aspects of arms control, is a strong function of the overall political relationship, and that while treaties can help to cement and manage a good relationship, they can become a source of irritation and suspicion in a deteriorating one. A similar conclusion can be drawn for the SCC. When the two states approached their compliance questions in a businesslike and mutually respectful manner, resolution was always possible [24]. When they went public with accusations of bad faith and unilateral interpretations of ambiguous treaty provisions, progress stopped and tensions increased.

Another lesson follows directly from this one, i.e., that improved monitoring capabilities or tighter verification provisions would have had little if any effect on Soviet behavior. Clearly U.S. monitoring techniques were good enough to detect the activities that led to suspicions, and equally clearly, the Soviets knew this. No one could have imagined that the Krasnoyarsk radar, which was at least ten stories high and as long as a football field, would remain a secret for very long after its foundations had been poured. Similarly, after years of careful negotiations the Soviets had a good understanding of what information the U.S. wanted from missile telemetry and what level of encryption would upset them [30, pp. 194–202, 237–244]. In short, the ability to detect violations is not in itself a sufficient deterrent to violations. There must be costs associated with detected violations that exceed the benefits if a potential cheater is to be deterred.[11]

This result is hardly surprising; it was anticipated in the earliest analyses of arms control. In a widely quoted 1961 article Fred Charles Iklé pointed out that "a nation contemplating a violation will not be deterred if it thinks it can discourage, circumvent or absorb our reaction" [32]. To the Soviets the withdrawal of SALT II by President Carter and the arrival of President Reagan shortly thereafter made the prospects for arms control seem increasingly bleak. The Reagan administration added to this perception by its reaction to Soviet behavior. Instead of dealing firmly and constructively with the alleged violations, it responded with accusations of bad faith and a brief, confused, and ultimately ineffectual breaking of the SALT II limits on strategic weapons. In effect the Soviet Union had "absorbed" the U.S. reaction. If more vigorous reactions were "discouraged," they were discouraged more by factors internal to the United States than by anything the Soviets did or threatened to do. One Reagan administration official has revealed that even though many members of the administration wanted stronger responses to the alleged violations, political, economic, and bureaucratic obstacles prevented the administration from doing much more than protesting [33].

---

[11] This is an oversimplified shorthand for what is a far more complex and subtle phenomenon. It assumes that the "potential cheater" is a rational actor who makes each decision for compliance or noncompliance on the basis of a cost-benefit calculation. The real situation is much less "rational." States are not always rational actors, and costs and benefits are almost always incalculable. Abram and Antonia Chayes have provided a thoughtful analysis of compliance behavior, which I will examine more closely in chapter 7 [31]. Still, there is a kernel of truth in the cost-benefit model, and it will be sufficient for the purposes of this chapter.

As long as relations remained poor, these protests had no effect on Soviet actions. But in the late 1980s, as Gorbachev and Reagan began to make common cause against the nuclear arms race, the Soviet cost-benefit calculation changed. Now the political benefits of acknowledging the illegality of the Krasnoyarsk radar and dismantling it had increased and the military benefits of completing it had decreased. So the violation was acknowledged and the radar dismantled. This suggests that positive incentives are likely to be far more effective in encouraging compliance than threats of retaliation.

One more important lesson about the relationship between verification and compliance is illustrated by the infamous outbreak of anthrax in Sverdlovsk (now Ykaterinburg) in 1979. The Reagan administration concluded that the epidemic, which killed several dozen people, was the result of a release (presumably accidental) of airborne anthrax spores at a biological weapons production facility. If true, this would be strong evidence for a violation of the Biological Weapons Convention. The Soviets claimed, however, that the epidemic was the result of distribution of contaminated meat, and that the illnesses were intestinal rather than pulmonary, as they would have been if the organism had been distributed by air. A joint U.S.-Russian scientific team has now produced solid evidence that it was indeed the pulmonary form of the disease that killed the majority of victims [34, 35]. This establishes at least a *prima facie* case for a violation, although there remain ambiguities of interpretation. The facility from which the spores were released could have been used for vaccine production, which is permitted by the BWC [19, p. 720].

Whatever the final outcome of the legal question, there is an important lesson in this incident about verification and compliance. There are no verification provisions in the Biological Weapons Treaty, yet strong evidence for a violation was discovered by accident and coincidence. An American physician who happened to be visiting in Sverdlovsk at the time of the incident observed the increase in anthrax cases and passed this information on to U.S. authorities. Verification provisions are therefore not always necessary to detect violations, and states contemplating violations must consider the risk of accidental exposure as well as detection through espionage or defection.

Under the nuclear Non-Proliferation Treaty responsibility for managing the compliance process is vested in the International Atomic Energy Agency, based in Vienna. Every year, on the basis of its safeguards inspections and the containment and surveillance measures that supplement them at many facilities, the IAEA must certify that to the best of its knowledge there has been no diversion of fissionable material from civilian to military purposes. For most of its history the IAEA was able to make this certification, but events in Iraq and North Korea in the 1990s have called the effectiveness of traditional safeguards into question. Iraq was discovered to have an extensive and well-developed nuclear weapons program that it had created despite receiving repeated clean bills of health from the IAEA. In North Korea the IAEA was denied access to certain sites where data might have been obtained either to verify or to contradict statements by the North Korean government that it had extracted only minuscule quantities of plutonium from spent reactor fuel. These two incidents have caused the IAEA to begin a process of broadening and intensifying its safeguards system under its Program 93+2, a name that records both its beginning in 1993 that the hope that it would be completed by 1995. This hope was not realized, and at the end of 1996 significant parts of the program had not yet been institutionalized. I will have more to say about Program 93+2 in the next chapter.

A previous incident of nuclear weapon proliferation, the underground detonation of a nuclear device by India in 1974, led to another important innovation of the Cold War era—the formation by suppliers of nuclear technology of an informal export control group called the Nuclear Suppliers Group [36]. India had used heavy water from the United States in a reactor from Canada to make plutonium for its device, and the purpose of the group of seven states that met in London soon after the Indian test was to expand the list of nuclear-related technologies subject to strict export controls. The Indian experience had suggested that an earlier suppliers group, formed in 1971 under the chairmanship of Professor Claude Zangger of Switzerland, was not sufficient [37]. The Zangger Committee focused on the requirements of Article III.2 of the NPT, which forbids the transfer to any non–nuclear weapon state of "equipment or material especially designed or prepared for the processing, use or production of special fissionable material," unless either the source or the fissionable material are placed under IAEA Safeguards [17, p. 344]. To implement this provision the Zangger Committee produced a "trigger list," a list of items whose transfer to a NNWS would trigger the application of safeguards. The original trigger list, first issued in 1974, dealt primarily with complete fuel cycle facilities, such as enrichment or reprocessing plants and major reactor components [37]. The list was expanded during the 1980s and 1990s to include many new technologies and materials.

The Zangger Committee and the Nuclear Suppliers Group were not the first to attempt to control exports of technologies relevant to weapon proliferation. An earlier export control regime, the Coordinating Committee for Multilateral Export Controls (COCOM), was created in 1949 to prevent exports of sensitive military equipment from NATO countries to the Warsaw Pact. Its rationale collapsed with the end of the Cold War, and it was formally disbanded on 1 April 1994. But by then the practice of using export controls to assist nonproliferation had become institutionalized across the full spectrum of weapon types. Chemical and biological weapon proliferation are addressed by the Australia Group, founded in the 1980s in the aftermath of the use of chemical weapons by both sides in the war between Iraq and Iran. Another export control group, the Missile Technology Control Regime, seeks to limit the spread of ballistic and cruise missiles to more countries. Disbanding COCOM left conventional weapons transfers uncontrolled, so a new regime was created in 1996. It is called the Wassenaar Arrangement after the Dutch city in which it was negotiated.

These five groups have different memberships, different operating styles, and have experienced differing degrees of success. They form an important part of the worldwide nonproliferation effort, but they remain informal arrangements as opposed to international treaties or conventions. They are also becoming increasingly controversial as international regimes like the NPT and Chemical and Biological Weapons Conventions cause some states to see them as at best redundant and at worst a means for perpetuating discrimination in access to technology by the developed against the less developed countries. These are important issues and they deserve a far more detailed and careful analysis than space will permit in this book.[12]

CONCLUSIONS AND LESSONS

Post–World War II arms control efforts can be traced all the way back to the Baruch Plan for international control of atomic energy offered to the newly formed United Nations by the Truman administration in 1945. The 40 years that followed this initiative saw much failure and some success, and while the world of the 1990s looks very different from the world in which these efforts were made, there are still some lessons to be learned, both positive and negative, about how arms control can be made to work and how it can be made to fail.

The most important lessons learned in the 1945–1985 period relate to negotiation and ratification, subjects we have decided not to analyze in this book. Still, some lessons are too obvious to ignore. Negotiation works best when the parties perceive themselves to be equals and when agreements can be crafted that enhance the security of both (or all) simultaneously. Attempts to coerce, intimidate, or hoodwink negotiating partners are doomed to failure. As for ratification, the American system of division of powers makes it imperative that domestic politics be taken into account from the beginning of any negotiation. The President must lead, but the Senate and public must never be left too far behind. Public support is important for the ratification of any treaty, and it is incumbent on the President to ensure that its benefits to national security, as well as its cost-effectiveness, are made clear and compelling to opinion makers and the voting public. It is fascinating to watch the Russian leadership begin to learn these lessons as democratic institutions take hold in Russia. Ratification by the Supreme Soviet was always a rubber stamp operation, but the new Russian legislature is making it increasingly clear that Russian leaders are going to have to spend far more energy and political capital getting treaties ratified than they have in the past.

I have already noted that implementation was not a major feature of Cold War arms control and nonproliferation agreements in the United States. Few weapons were eliminated and there was little in the way of data exchange or notification of military activities. An apparatus was created by the Nixon administration to implement treaties and oversee U.S. compliance, but had little to do until the Intermediate Nuclear Forces Treaty of 1987 forced the U.S. to find a way to dismantle and destroy hundreds of missiles and their launchers and other supporting equipment. Most of the implementation infrastructure that exists today has been built since then, and I will analyze it in detail in chapter 4.

Verification was conducted entirely by national technical means (NTM): satellites, seismographs, radio antennas, code breaking, and any number of other technically sophisticated means of observing an adversary at a safe distance. NTM proved themselves extremely useful for monitoring certain kinds of objects, facilities, and activities, and they were essential in making early arms con-

---

[12] An annual compilation of international export control regimes is published by the Center for Nonproliferation Studies at the Monterey Institute of International Studies [38]. The seminal study of U.S. administration of export controls is National Academy of Sciences, *Finding Common Ground: U.S. Export Controls in a Changed Global Environment* (Washington, DC: National Academy Press, 1991).

trol agreements acceptable to both sides. They remain useful monitoring tools today, but they are no longer sufficient to verify modern arms control and non-proliferation agreements. They are also extremely expensive to build and operate and will never be available to more than a handful of states without arrangements for collaboration and sharing of data. The primary lesson of this experience is that greater voluntary transparency on the part of all states will be essential for further progress in arms control.

As for compliance, there is much to be learned from the Cold War experiences of the United States and Soviet Union, especially the acrimonious and counterproductive charges of violations that marked the 1970s and 1980s. The first lesson is that actions that amplify suspicion by stretching or unilaterally interpreting treaty restraints are more usefully seen as symptoms rather than causes of poor political relations. A second is that positive incentives for compliance are often a better means of preventing violations than are threats of sanctions or retaliation. A third is that even with no formal verification arrangements, there is always a risk of discovery through accident, espionage, or betrayal. Any state contemplating a treaty violation must take this incalculable risk into account. Finally, a consultative body with a non-ideological problem-solving approach to implementation and compliance disputes is essential for the successful functioning of any treaty.

REFERENCES

1. Leslie H. Gelb, Arms Agency: 25-Year Battleground, *New York Times*, September 27, 1986, p. 3.

2. Michael Krepon, Amy E. Smithson, and James A. Schear, The U.S. Arms Control and Disarmament Agency: Restructuring for the Post-Cold War Era, The Henry L. Stimson Center, 1992.

3. *Sipri Yearbook 1995* (London: Oxford University Press, 1995).

4. Michael Krepon, U.S. Government Organization for Arms Control Verification and Compliance, *Verification and Compliance: A Problem Solving Approach*, Michael Krepon and Mary Umberger, Eds. (Cambridge, MA: Ballinger, 1988), pp. 282–308.

5. Lee Minichiello, Implementing Arms Control Treaties (Briefing), Office of the Undersecretary of Defense for Acquisition, Department of Defense, March 1993.

6. Peter Zimmerman, "The Thule, Fylingdales, and Krasnoyarsk Radars: Innocents Abroad?" *Arms Control Today*, March 1987, pp. 9–11.

7. John Newhouse, *Cold Dawn: The Story of SALT* (New York: Holt, Rinehart & Winston, 1973).

8. David Holloway, *Stalin and the Bomb* (New Haven, CT: Yale University Press, 1994).

9. Alva Myrdal, *The Game of Disarmament* (New York: Pantheon Books, 1982).

10. Jeffrey T. Richelson, *The U.S. Intelligence Community,* 3rd ed. (Boulder, CO: Westview Press, 1995).

11. Sherman M. Funk, New Purposes and Priorities for Arms Control, U.S. Arms Control and Disarmament Agency, December 14, 1992.

12. Frank von Hippel, Ending the production of fissile materials for weapons; Verifying the dismantlement of nuclear warheads: The technical basis for action, Federation of American Scientists, June, 1991.

13. Field Test FT-34: Demonstrated Destruction of Nuclear Weapons, U.S. Arms Control and Disarmament Agency, Washington, DC, January, 1969.

14. *Verification Technologies: Managing Research and Development for Cooperative Arms Control Monitoring Measures*, OTA-ISC-488, U.S. Congress, Office of Technology Assessment, May 1991.

15. Glenn T. Seaborg, *Kennedy, Khrushchev, and the Test Ban* (Berkeley: University of California Press, 1981).

16. *Sipri Yearbook 1977* (London: Taylor & Francis, 1977).

17. Jozef Goldblat, *Arms Control: A Guide to Negotiations and Agreements* (London: International Peace Research Institute Oslo, Sage Publications, 1994).

18. Gloria Duffy, *Compliance and the Future of Arms Control*, Center for International Security and Arms Control, Stanford University, Global Outlook, 1988.

19. *Sipri Yearbook 1994* (Oxford: Oxford University Press, 1994).

20. George Bunn, Roland M. Timerbaev, and James F. Leonard, Nuclear Disarmament: How Much Have the Five Nuclear Powers Promised in the Nonproliferation Treaty? Lawyers Alliance for World Security, the Committee for National Security, and the Washington Council on Nonproliferation, June 1994.

21. *Arms Control Reporter*, 1994, p. 840.A.4.

22. Nicholas A. Sims, *The Diplomacy of Biological Disarmament* (London: Macmillan, 1988).

23. Amrom H. Katz, *Verification and SALT: The State of the Art and the Art of the State*, (Washington DC: Heritage Foundation, 1979).

24. Sidney N. Graybeal and Michael Krepon, "Improving the Utility and Effectiveness of the Standing Consultative Commission," *Verification and Compliance: A Problem Solving Approach*, Michael Krepon and Mary Umberger, Eds. (Cambridge, MA: Ballinger, 1988), pp. 239–259.

25. Caspar Weinberger, Responding to Soviet Violations Policy (RSVP) Study, Memorandum for the President, Department of Defense, November 16, 1985.

26. Keith B. Payne, Proliferation, Potential TMD Roles, Demarcation and ABM Treaty Compatibility, National Institute for Public Policy, September 1994.

27. Allan Krass and Catherine Girrier, *Disproportionate Response: American Policy and Alleged Soviet Treaty Violations*, (Cambridge, MA: Union of Concerned Scientists, 1987).

28. *Threat Control through Arms Control*, U.S. Arms Control and Disarmament Agency, July 13, 1995.

29. Charles Mohr, Soviet Arms Pact Breaches: Charges Questioned, *New York Times*, June 6, 1986, p. A6.

30. Strobe Talbott, *Endgame: The Inside Story of SALT II* (New York: Harper & Row, 1979).

31. Abram Chayes and Antonia Handler Chayes, "On Compliance," *International Organization*, Spring 1993, pp. 175–205.

32. Fred Charles Iklé, "After Detection—What?" *Foreign Affairs*, January 1961, pp. 208–220.

33. Kenneth L. Adelman, *The Great Universal Embrace: Arms Summitr—A Skeptic's Account* (New York: Simon & Schuster, 1989).

34. F. A. Abramova, et al., "Pathology of inhalational anthrax in 42 cases from the Sverdlovsk outbreak of 1979," *Proceedings of the National Academy of Sciences*, March 1993, pp. 2291–2294.

35. M. Meselson, et al., "The Sverdlovsk Anthrax Outbreak of 1979," *Science*, 18 November 1994, pp. 1202–1208.

36. Tadeusz Strulak, "The Nuclear Suppliers Group," *The Nonproliferation Review*, Fall 1993, pp. 2–10.

37. Fritz W. Schmidt, "The Zangger Committee: Its History and Future Role," *The Nonproliferation Review*, Fall 1994, pp. 38–44.

38. Roland M. Timerbaev and Meggen M. Watt, *Inventory of International Nonproliferation Organizations and Regimes*, (Monterey, CA: Center for Nonproliferation Studies, Monterey Institute of International Studies, February 1995).

3

THE ARMS CONTROL REVOLUTION

The Stockholm Document on Confidence- and Security-Building and Disarmament in Europe was signed on September 19, 1986 and the Chemical Weapons Convention on January 13, 1993. During this period at least ten major agreements were signed, along with a wide range of confidence and transparency enhancing measures, major unilateral reductions, and changes of alert status, targeting policies, and military doctrines. This period also saw a quantitative and qualitative leap forward in verification that was stunning in its contrast with the slow and fragile accomplishments of the preceding 30 years. In particular, the long-awaited achievement of on-site inspection in the Stockholm Document and the Intermediate Nuclear Forces Treaty (December 8, 1987) was followed by a veritable avalanche of increasingly intrusive and elaborate on-site inspection arrangements in subsequent treaties.

All of this progress was made possible by the end of the U.S.-Soviet confrontation and the dissolving of the East-West standoff that had defined European politics for 40 years. The initially rapid pace of agreement represented a pent-up backlog of treaties, some of which had been on the negotiating table for decades during the Cold War. Obviously this pace could not be sustained for long. In the four years after the signing of the Chemical Weapons Convention there were only two more significant achievements in arms control: the renewal and indefinite extension of the nuclear Nonproliferation Treaty in May 1995 and the signing of the Comprehensive Nuclear Test Ban Treaty in September 1996.

The implementation of these agreements will be a long-term, expensive, and in some cases technically challenging and politically controversial process. Thousands of nuclear warheads will be retired and their launchers and associated equipment and facilities dismantled or converted to peaceful uses. Tens of thousands of large conventional weapons will be destroyed by cutting torch, high explosive, or wrecking ball. Seventy thousand tons of lethal chemical agents and their associated munitions will be destroyed by incineration or chemical neutralization. Chemical weapon production facilities will be shut down or converted to other uses. All of this destruction, dismantlement, decommissioning, and conversion will cost many billions of dollars to accomplish and will continue well into the next century.

The burdens imposed by these requirements have been distributed quite unequally, in part because the Eastern Bloc had produced substantially larger stockpiles of all of these weapons, and in part because of the economic and political dislocations created by the collapse of the Warsaw Pact and Soviet Union. Former Soviet republics like Ukraine and Belarus inherited large numbers of tanks, artillery pieces, and combat vehicles from the Soviet Army as well as strategic nuclear weapons that must be returned to Russia or dismantled in place. Meanwhile these states and others throughout Eastern Europe and the former Soviet Union are facing severe economic and social problems, and the challenge of converting military industrial complexes to civilian production.

This situation has required an unprecedented response from the West, in particular from the United States. It has become obvious that unless substantial aid, both technical and financial, is provided to the former East Bloc states, they will not only be unable to meet their arms reduction commitments but may lose effective control of some of their most dangerous weapons and nuclear infrastructure. Since it is clearly in the security interests of the West to have these commitments met and strong control maintained, it makes sense to provide aid to states having difficulty implementing treaties. A number of Western states, including Germany, Sweden, France, and others, have offered some aid, but the largest contribution has come from the United States[1] under the Cooperative Threat Reduction Program. More than one billion dollars of Defense Department funds had been obligated to the program (usually referred to as the Nunn-Lugar Program after the two senators who sponsored the original funding legislation) in fiscal years 1993-1996, and the intention was to continue funding the program at about $400 million per year through the end of the decade [1]. However, continued funding at this or any level will depend on congressional support, and that support is by no means guaranteed. Fiscal restraints, impatience with Russian foreign and domestic politics, and a noticeably lessened commitment to arms control in general led to attacks on the Nunn-Lugar Program in the Republican-dominated 1995-1996 Congress, and the Clinton administration had to fight hard to keep appropriations even close to projected levels.

All of the new agreements constitute a historic breakthrough in the transparency of military affairs. They require detailed exchanges of information on force structures, deployments, infrastructure, and weapon characteristics. All involve advance notifications of military activities, including, *inter alia*, transport or destruction of weapons, troop exercises and maneuvers, and flight tests of missiles. And all involve on-site inspections to verify baseline data, observe destruction of weapons and bases, monitor production facilities and weapon characteristics, and check for the absence of prohibited weapons and activities. The Open Skies Treaty comes closer than anyone would have thought possible to

---

[1] This is a bit misleading. Germany has been forced to pay vast sums of money to support the evacuation of Soviet and Russian troops formerly deployed on its territory. One estimate puts these costs at nearly $25 billion. Germany has also paid all the costs of absorbing the former East Germany, including its demilitarization and industrial conversion. These investments far outweigh anything the United States has done or is likely to do to aid demilitarization in the former Soviet Union. Thanks to Annette Schaper for reminding the author of these German contributions.

breaking one of the oldest and strongest bastions of national sovereignty—the inviolability of a state's airspace to foreign surveillance. The verification provisions of the treaties listed in table 3.1 take up hundreds of pages of text, prescribing in excruciating detail where inspectors can go, the procedures they must follow, the objects and facilities they can observe, the instruments and techniques they can employ, and the data they can take away with them for analysis. There is far too much in all of this to permit a detailed analysis in a study of this length; this chapter will be able to provide only a general overview of the verification effort the United States will face in the coming years.

The last and longest phase of arms control is the compliance phase, and only some of the treaties considered here have entered it. As this is written (January 1997), START II and Open Skies are still waiting for full ratification and entry into force, and the Chemical Weapons Convention has just entered into force. START I has been in force for two years, and the Stockholm and Vienna Documents, the INF Treaty, and the CFE Treaty have been in force for several years. All of these latter agreements have accumulated significant experience with the compliance process, and the emphasis in this study will be on that experience and the lessons to be learned from it.

Most of the agreements (the only exceptions are the bilateral chemical weapon agreements) have created consultative bodies in which implementation and compliance questions are resolved (see table 3.1). The nuclear treaties have groups modeled on the SALT Standing Consultative Commission discussed in chapter 2. They are the Special Verification Commission (SVC) for the INF Treaty, the five-member Joint Compliance and Inspection Commission (JCIC) for START I, and the Bilateral Implementation Commission (BIC) for START II. The CFE and CFE-1A Treaties have a Joint Consultative Group (JCG), the Confidence- and Security-Building Measures (CSBM) agreements use the Forum for Security Cooperation (FSC) of the Organization for Security and Cooperation in Europe (OSCE). The Open Skies Treaty will use the Open Skies Consultative Commission (OSCC). Compliance questions arising under the Chemical Weapons Convention will be dealt with in the Technical Secretariat of the Organization for the Prevention of Chemical Weapons (OPCW), and the United States, United Kingdom, and Russia discuss their collaboration on biological weapon inspections in the Trilateral Working Group (TWG). The Comprehensive Test Ban Treaty will create its own international organization (CTBTO), modeled to a considerable degree on the OPCW. Some of these groups meet at specified intervals and others only when summoned by one or more parties. Geneva and Vienna are the usual venues for meetings, except for the OPCW Technical Secretariat, which is permanently based in the Hague, Netherlands, and the TWG, which rotates its meetings among the three participating states.

Table 3.1
Major Arms Control Agreements since December 1986

Weapon type	Treaty/ Agreement	Date signed	Signatories	EIF	Consultative Group
Nuclear	INF	Dec 8, 87	U.S.-USSR	Jun 1, 88	SVC
	START I	Jul 31, 91	U.S.,Russia, Ukraine, Kazakhstan, Belarus	Dec 5, 94	JCIC
	START II	Jan 3, 93	U.S.-Russia	—	BIC
	CTBT	Sep 24, 96	143 states*	—	CTBTO
Conventional	CFE CFE 1A	Nov 19, 90	30 states	Jul 17, 92	JCG
	CSBM	Dec 19, 86 Mar 24, 92 Nov 28, 94	52 states	Jan 1, 87 May 1, 92 Dec 6, 94	FSC
	Open Skies	Mar 24, 92	27 states	—	OSCC
Chemical	Wyoming MOU	Sep 23, 89	U.S.-USSR (Russia)	Sep 23, 89	none
	BDA	Jun 1, 90	U.S.-USSR (Russia)	—	none
	CWC	Jan 13, 93	162 states*	Apr 29, 97	OPCW
Biological	Trilateral	Sep 11, 92	U.S.,U.K.,Rus	Sep 11, 92	TWG

* As of April 15, 1997.

NUCLEAR WEAPONS

The complex of agreements controlling nuclear weapons encompasses two major groups, one essentially bilateral and the other fully international. The first includes a group of treaties between the United States and the former Soviet Union and its successors: the Anti-ballistic Missile (ABM) Treaty, the Intermediate and Shorter Range Nuclear Forces (INF) Treaty, and the Strategic Arms Reduction Treaty (START). Also included in this group are the withdrawals and deactivation of large numbers of nonstrategic nuclear weapons ordered by Presidents Bush and Gorbachev in the fall of 1991. These were reciprocal unilateral measures and have no formal implementation and verification requirements, but they do involve significant implementation activities by both sides which have led to serious questions about the safety and security of Russian tactical weapons. The second group comprises the international regime that includes the Nonproliferation Treaty (NPT) and the Comprehensive Test Ban Treaty (CTBT). As we saw in chapter 2, the NPT is the most widely adhered to of any of the international regimes, and its renewal and indefinite extension in 1995 ensure that it will continue to govern the nuclear activities of all but a handful of states for many years to come. The CTBT is of much more recent vintage, and while it attracted a substantial number of signatories in the months following its opening for signature in September 1996, its eventual entry into force remains highly uncertain as this is written. Nevertheless, the large number of states that have signed it (over 130 as of the end of 1996), and the strong international norm that has evolved in opposition to nuclear testing, suggest that noncompliance with the CTBT is likely to entail great political costs for any violator, signatory or not.[2]

Implementation

In the INF Treaty the United States and Soviet Union agreed to eliminate all land-based nuclear missiles with ranges between 500 and 5,500 kilometers, including both ballistic and ground-launched cruise missiles. In START I they agreed to reduce their strategic forces to a total of 6,000 "accountable" warheads,[3] and in START II they agreed to further reductions down to a level of 3,000–3,500 *actual* warheads.

To implement INF a total of 2,692 missiles had to be destroyed, 1,846 by the Soviet Union and 846 by the United States, along with all of their launchers, deployment bases, and other supporting equipment and facilities. The reductions were accomplished by May 31, 1991. The focus in START is on launchers rather than missiles, although some Russian mobile missiles will have to be eliminated. The United States plans to eliminate a total of 500 ICBM silos at three bases in South Dakota, Missouri, and Montana.[4] Twelve Trident I nuclear missile submarines are being retired, while three new Trident II boats will be added to the fleet, giving a post–START II total of 336 launchers on 14 subs. All B-52G bombers have already been deactivated and all B-1B bombers are being converted to carry conventional weapons. All of these destructions and conversions are to be carried out according to detailed procedures laid out in a protocol to the START I Treaty, and all are subject to verification by national technical means and/or on-site inspections.

Well before START I entered into force, the parties began retiring and dismantling weapon systems. According to the updated data exchanged in January 1995 the United States had already dismantled 41 ICBM silos, 15 ballistic missile submarines (SSBNs), and 230 heavy bombers, removing a total of 2,578 strategic warheads from accountability. Corresponding Russian numbers were 378 silos, 14 SSBNs, 37 heavy bombers, and 914 accountable warheads [2]. Dismantlements have continued at rates in excess of those demanded by the treaty, and in January 1997 both sides were well ahead of the pace necessary to achieve the full required reductions by the deadline at the end of 2001.

---

[2] The CTBT has superseded three other agreements that controlled aspects of nuclear testing since 1963. The Limited Test Ban, the Threshold Test Ban, and the Peaceful Nuclear Explosions Treaties have all been rendered obsolete by the CTBT. Therefore, I will have little to say about the earlier treaties except where they can provide useful historical lessons.

[3] The counting in START I depends on the assignment of nominal warhead loadings to missiles and bombers that may or may not equal the actual number they carry. The actual number of warheads allowed under START I has been estimated to be at least 9,000, but this number will be rendered moot when START II begins counting actual deployed warheads.

[4] The data on START are from Robert S. Norris and William M. Arkin, "U.S. Strategic Nuclear Forces, End of 1994," *Bulletin of the Atomic Scientists*, January/February 1995, pp. 69–71.

The unilateral reductions announced by Bush and Gorbachev in 1991 covered nonstrategic nuclear weapons. Bush declared the elimination of all theater nuclear weapons including artillery shells and short-range, ground-launched ballistic missiles. He also announced the withdrawal of all nuclear weapons from surface ships, attack submarines, and naval aircraft, ordered a stand-down from alert status of all ICBMs scheduled for elimination under START, and terminated the development of mobile ICBMs and the short-range attack missile for aircraft. In his response Gorbachev matched Bush's withdrawal of artillery, short-range missiles, and naval tactical weapons and added Soviet nuclear anti-aircraft weapons and land mines to the list of systems to be withdrawn and at least partially destroyed. He also canceled several development programs and reduced the alert status of many Soviet nuclear forces.

Because they were unilateral, these actions are not subject to formalized implementation procedures or verification. Each country is free to carry them out at whatever pace and by whatever methods it chooses, and neither party has any right to complain about that pace or those methods. Still, the two states, not to mention the rest of the world, have an obvious interest in the progress being made, and it is mutually understood that NTM will be used to whatever extent is feasible to monitor progress toward the declared objectives. This is not an entirely satisfactory situation however, since nondeployed tactical weapons cannot be counted accurately with satellite cameras. The safety and security arrangements for Russian nonstrategic weapons are of particular concern. It appears that all Russian tactical weapons deployed in former Soviet republics and Eastern Europe have been returned to Russian territory,[5] but there are many thousands of these weapons spread over a vast area, and there is considerable concern in the West over their ultimate fate.

Another important set of questions concerns the pace and methods of warhead dismantlement and the disposition and safeguarding of the nuclear explosive materials in them. According to one authoritative source, the United States had reduced its warhead stockpile from 23,400 in 1988 to 14,900 at the end of 1994 [4]. This represents an average dismantlement rate of about 1,400 per year at the single U.S. dismantlement facility, the Pantex Plant near Amarillo, Texas. The same source estimates that the Soviet/Russian warhead stockpile decreased from 42,500 to 29,000 over the same six-year period, which represents an average dismantlement rate of 2,250 per year. Russia is believed to have four dismantlement facilities [5], but since these have been kept off limits for inspection there is no way for the estimates to be confirmed. There are no treaties requiring the dismantlement of warheads and no formal controls over the disposal of weapon-grade fissile materials. Nevertheless, the United States has made a major effort in the form of the Nunn-Lugar Program to gain some access to and influence over these activities in Russia.

The Cooperative Threat Reduction Program

Even before the disintegration of the Soviet Union it had become clear that the economic problems created by Gorbachev's reforms were going to make it very difficult for the Soviets to meet their arms control commitments. After the

---

[5] According to declarations by all four former Soviet republics, all tactical nuclear weapons had been returned to Russia from Kazakhstan, Ukraine, and Belarus by May 6, 1992 [3].

collapse it was even more obvious that the United States was going to have to subsidize the weapon dismantlement and economic conversion processes in Russia, Belarus, Kazakhstan, and Ukraine. The first legislation authorizing the transfer of $400 million in Defense Department funds for this purpose was passed in November 1991. Its purpose, according to its sponsors Senators Sam Nunn and Richard Lugar, was to respond to the request of "key Soviet and republic leaders . . . to help them dismantle their massive military-industrial complex . . . [and] to help them destroy thousands of chemical and nuclear weapons." Anticipating criticism of such a large aid package when the United States was cutting back its own military spending, they emphasized that the program was "not foreign aid [but] a prudent investment to reduce a grave threat that we otherwise must be prepared to deter and, if need be, defend" [6]. In short, the program could provide more national security per dollar than any conceivable new weapon system.

The initial legislation authorized the Department of Defense to use the money to help former Soviet republics transport, store, safeguard, and destroy nuclear, chemical, and other weapons. Within these guidelines DOD had great freedom to spend the money as it saw fit, as long as the recipient states remained in compliance with their arms control commitments and fulfilled certain conditions consistent with U.S. arms control and nonproliferation objectives [7]. The slow start was not surprising given the difficulty of overcoming the suspicions and sensitivities of former Cold War adversaries, negotiating the details of dozens of project proposals, obtaining presidential certification of progress toward arms control objectives and congressional approval of specific projects, and, last but not least, getting competitive bids from U.S. contractors who would supervise or carry out the work [8]. These delays resulted in the expiration of $330 million in obligational authority from the first two years of the program, money that must now be made up from succeeding years' appropriations [9].

The situation improved considerably in 1994, in what the Cooperative Threat Reduction (CTR) Program calls its "Year of Implementation" [10]. Obligations (money approved and committed to actual projects) rose to $434 million by the end of September 1994 [11], to $950 million by April 1995 [10], and to almost $1.1 billion by September 1996 [12]. Of this last amount $75 million had been obligated to projects in Belarus, $107 million to Kazakhstan, $300 million to Ukraine, and $543 million to Russia. If fully funded, the CTR Program will ultimately cost at least $3 billion [1].

The money is being spent on three classes of projects: destruction and dismantlement, chain of custody, and demilitarization. Examples of the first class include the destruction of SS-19 missiles and silos in Ukraine and heavy bombers at the Engels Air Base in Russia [13]. Examples of the second include special containers, railroad cars, and bulletproof blankets for transporting warheads and fissile materials in Russia, and improved material control and accounting measures to be installed at Russian nuclear facilities. In the third class are the International Science and Technology Centers created in each of the four republics, designed to provide employment on nonmilitary projects for former weapon scientists and engineers, and a new housing development for former Ukrainian ICBM officers. Because all four republics are now parties to START I, they must participate in the data exchanges and notifications mandated by the treaty. To help them do this the CTR Program provided the three non-Russian states with their own Nuclear Risk Reduction Center terminals (see below).

There have been a number of other bilateral efforts by the United States and Russia to facilitate the disarmament process and to develop new transparency measures and channels of cooperation. Perhaps the most important of these is a commission headed by U.S. Vice President Albert Gore and Russian Prime Minister Viktor Chernomyrdin. They signed an agreement in June 1994 that offered both aid and reciprocal transparency measures in return for a commitment from the Russian Ministry of Atomic Energy (MINATOM) to stop making plutonium at its three remaining military production reactors [14]. The following September Presidents Clinton and Yeltsin agreed to "exchange detailed information . . . on aggregate stockpiles of nuclear warheads, on stocks of fissile materials and on their safety and security" [15]. To allow the exchange with a former enemy of such highly classified information the United States had to amend the Atomic Energy Act of 1954. But progress in Russia has been much slower, and almost two years later neither the reactor shutdown agreement nor the warhead transparency measures had been fully implemented [16].

Two other important developments fall under the general rubric of cooperative threat reduction, even though they are not part of the formal CTR Program. One is a February 1993 agreement for the United States to purchase 500 metric tons of high-enriched uranium (HEU) from dismantled Russian weapons. This agreement was followed by a Memorandum of Understanding (September 1993) and a Protocol (March 1994) specifying transparency arrangements. The protocols specify three facilities in Russia and six in the United States at which inspectors from the other side will monitor the processes of conversion, blending, and fuel fabrication [5]. By the end of 1996 most of these arrangements were in place and the agreement appeared to be functioning well [17].

The first $60 million spent by the United States on the HEU purchase agreement was not used to bring uranium to the United States but was used to compensate Russia for sending 100 tonnes of reactor-grade uranium to Ukraine, the first installment of Russian payment for the nuclear warheads Ukraine was returning to Russia. This three-way exchange was an important part of the Trilateral Agreement reached by the United States, Ukraine, and Russia in Moscow in January 1994. In effect, the United States used money committed to purchase uranium from Russia to help finance nuclear disarmament in Ukraine. This money, along with additional funds pledged to Ukraine for dismantlement of missiles and silos under the Nunn-Lugar program, was, in the opinion of the U.S. State Department, crucial in getting Ukraine to agree to join the Nonproliferation Treaty and get rid of all its nuclear weapons [1].

A second success in nuclear material management was the purchase of 600 kilograms of high-enriched uranium from Kazakhstan in November 1994. Inspired by information that Iranian agents were attempting to purchase the uranium, which was originally supposed to be fabricated into fuel rods for naval propulsion reactors, U.S. intelligence agents undertook a secret operation to purchase the material and get it to the United States [18]. Called Project Sapphire, the operation took several months and resulted in the transfer of the material from a poorly secured warehouse in Ust Kamenogorsk to the vaults at the U.S. Y-12 plant at Oak Ridge, Tennessee. The cost to the CTR Program was reported to be several tens of millions of dollars [19]. The operation's success has been a feather in the cap of the U.S. Intelligence Community, and much is made of it in congressional testimony and public defenses of administration nonproliferation policy. It is unquestionably better from the U.S. point of view to have the uranium at Oak Ridge than in Kazakhstan, let alone delivered to Tehran. But the quantity was small, the price was high, and the opportunity fortuitous. It is unlikely that any appreciable amount of the inventory of fissile materials in the former Soviet Union will be dealt with in this way.

Data Exchanges and Notifications

The first time the United States and the Soviet Union exchanged data on their strategic nuclear weapon deployments was in the last stages of the SALT II negotiations after long and difficult bargaining. The only information exchanged was a list of deployed strategic weapons that the U.S. already knew all about from its NTM monitoring. But it was a big deal to the Soviets, who saw it as a major departure from their traditional military secrecy [20, pp. 96–98]. Unfortunately, this historic exchange didn't become the official "agreed data base" it was intended to be because SALT II was never ratified.

The major breakthrough for data exchanges, as for so many other aspects of nuclear arms control, came in the INF Treaty. A Memorandum of Understanding (MOU) not only specified the numbers and locations of all intermediate and shorter-range missiles, but also included those physical characteristics, such as lengths, diameters, and weights of launchers and missile stages, needed to permit unambiguous identification. The original data base was verified by baseline inspections, and as missiles and launchers were deactivated and destroyed, the base was updated by notifications using the Nuclear Risk Reduction Centers (NRRC) established in an agreement reached earlier in 1987 [21, pp. 514–518]. The process ended in May 1991 when the last of the INF missiles had been eliminated and both sides had verified this to their satisfaction.

If INF was a breakthrough, then START I could be called an avalanche of data exchanges and notifications. The MOU establishing the data base takes up 126 pages of the 280-page published version of the treaty [22]. The data include numbers of warheads and throw-weight of all ICBMs, SLBMs, and strategic bombers and the total number of each system deployed; locations of all deployment bases with numbers of each type deployed at each base; locations of production, storage, and repair facilities and test ranges; dimensions and weights of each stage for each missile; distinguishing features of bombers equipped for nuclear bomb or cruise missile delivery; characteristics of long-range air-launched cruise missiles; and even the locations of missiles and bombers displayed in museums, such as a Minuteman at the Air and Space Museum in Washington.

Another START protocol is devoted to notifications, starting with the data just described and also including notifications of any changes in weapon characteristics or warhead loadings, movements of any treaty limited items (TLI), throw-weights of any new types of ICBM or SLBM being developed, conversion or elimination of any systems or facilities covered by the treaty, requests for displays in the open of TLI for observation by national technical means, flight tests of ICBMs or SLBMs, production and tests of prototypes of new missiles, and dispersals of mobile missiles and bombers from their regular bases. Even more remarkable, especially in light of the intense debates over telemetry encryption in the 1980s, is a protocol on exchange of telemetry tapes. Not only are the two sides forbidden to encrypt this information, which is crucial for diagnostic purposes in the testing of any missile, but each side is required to supply the other with a full, unedited tape recording of all telemetric data collected during the flight.

All of the data and notifications under START are communicated via the Nuclear Risk Reduction Centers (NRRCs).[6] NRRCs use computers and satellite links to store and transmit data in much the same way as the Internet transmits electronic mail. When Ukraine, Kazakhstan, and Belarus became parties to START I under the Lisbon Protocol of 1992 they also became responsible for notifications and data exchanges concerning weapons and facilities on their territory. This has required that the original NRRC connection between Washington and Moscow be supplemented with terminals in Kiev, Almaty, and Minsk, and these were installed in time for entry into force (or shortly thereafter) with the aid of Nunn-Lugar funds. U.S. NRRC terminals are located in the State Department and at the On-Site Inspection Agency's Dulles Airport office.

Inspections and Observations

The first U.S.-Soviet agreement on a form of on-site inspection was in the Peaceful Nuclear Explosion Treaty (PNET) of 1976. The inspection protocol to this treaty went into considerable detail in laying out the kinds of data and notifications to be provided, the rights and obligations of inspectors, and the kinds of equipment that could be used to gather data [23]. The original protocol was replaced in 1990, and the new version was at least as detailed as the original one. The PNET inspection protocol provided a preview of the elaborate protocols that were to follow in future treaties, but none of its procedures was ever carried out. By the time the treaty was ratified, both sides had abandoned PNEs.

The first true on-site inspections to be implemented in a U.S.-Soviet agreement began in June 1988 under the Intermediate Nuclear Forces (INF) Treaty.[7] The treaty had been signed in December, and in the six months between December and June the United States had to create a new agency, the On-Site Inspection Agency (OSIA), to do the inspections. An indication of the surprise Soviet acceptance of on-site inspections created in Washington is given in Joseph Harahan's history of the OSIA. Harahan quotes Brigadier General Eugene L. Daniel, head of a ten-person task force hastily assembled in December to plan the new agency: "There was no money, no people for a new agency, no structure, just an operational concept embedded in the INF Treaty" [24, p. 15]. I will return to the remarkable story of OSIA's creation in chapter 4.

Article XI of the INF Treaty specifies the kinds of inspections that can be carried out: baseline inspections to verify the original data exchanged at entry into force; closeout inspections to verify the closing and retirement of bases and support or production facilities; elimination inspections to verify the destruction of missiles, launchers, and support equipment; "short notice" or "quota" inspections to look again at bases and facilities that are supposed to be shut down to

---

[6] Pronounced "nerks" by the people who use them every day.

[7] The first on-site inspections under the Stockholm CSBM agreement were conducted in August 1987. See chapter 4.

verify that no treaty-limited items have been reintroduced; and continuous perimeter-portal monitoring (CPPM) at one production facility in each country. Baseline, closeout, and short-notice inspection teams are made up of a maximum of ten inspectors, who are transported to the inspection site, escorted, and returned to their point of entry by the host country. Elimination inspection teams could have up to 20 members, and the CPPM teams have 30 members who live in the host country near the monitored facility for their entire tour of duty.

The two facilities subject to CPPM until May 31, 2001 under the INF Treaty are the Votkinsk Machine Building Plant, located about 600 miles east of Moscow, and the Hercules Plant Number 1 at Magna, Utah, near Salt Lake City. The Votkinsk plant manufactured missile stages for the SS-20 and still produces stages for the SS-25 and other missiles not eliminated under the INF Treaty. Monitors at the plant's perimeter must be able to inspect missiles that leave the plant and verify that they are not forbidden SS-20s. The Hercules Plant once produced rocket motors for the Pershing II and still makes motors for other missiles, but there is much less similarity between these and the Pershing II than between the SS-20 and SS-25. Russian inspections at Magna are less intrusive than American inspections at Votkinsk, and the latter have been a source of friction because of the sophisticated technology used by U.S. inspectors (see chapter 6).

All INF baseline inspections were completed by August 31, 1988 and all closeout and elimination inspections by May 31, 1991. The United States conducted a total of 354 inspections under these categories and the Soviet Union 170 [25]. The disparity in numbers between the two sides reflected the much greater number and wider dispersal of Soviet bases and support facilities. Quota inspections will continue until 2001, with an allowance of 20 per year in the first three years, 15 per year for the next five, and 10 per year for the final five years. It has so far been the practice of both sides to use their full quotas [25].

The START inspection regime builds on the foundation created by INF. START covers more types and larger numbers of weapons, and inspections must be done at a greater number and variety of facilities. The treaty mandates 12 types of inspections in contrast to INF's five. Baseline, data update, conversion or elimination, closeout, and formerly declared facility inspections, as well as continuous monitoring, are similar in purpose and procedure to their counterparts in INF. Under START, some bombers and missiles can be converted to peaceful or nonnuclear missions, and these conversions must be verified by inspection. The data update inspections in START are similar to the quota or short-notice inspections in INF, but in START the quota remains fixed at 15 per year for the full duration of the treaty, which is 15 years (until December 2009) unless it is superseded by another treaty. Formerly declared facility inspections are postcloseout checks on retired facilities, and there is a quota of three per year of these for each party.

There are several new types of inspections in START. New facility inspections are needed because the development, production, and deployment of weapons covered by the treaty are expected to continue. Suspect site inspections and special access visits are important new departures in START and are as close as the treaty comes to including challenge inspections. Suspect site inspections can be conducted at three missile production plants that each side has specified in an annex to the Memorandum of Understanding. Other facilities can be added later if they produce missiles as large as or larger than the mobile missiles covered by the treaty. Special access visits (more precisely, "visits with special right of access") can be requested in circumstances where either side raises an "urgent concern relating to compliance" in the Joint Compliance and Inspection Commission [22, p. 118]. However, the provision allowing such visits is carefully crafted to say that the "response of the requested Party *may* . . . include acceptance of the proposed . . . visit." In other words, the request does not have to be accepted, and other methods may be found to satisfy the requesting party.

Reentry vehicle inspections are one of the more remarkable features of START. After years of wrangling about "counting rules" for multiple warhead missiles, the two sides finally agreed to allow inspectors to observe and count the number of warheads on randomly selected ICBMs or SLBMs at their deployment sites. The inspection protocols are designed to allow protection of secret design information, but inspectors are given sufficient access to ensure that the inspected missile is carrying only the number of reentry vehicles it is allowed. For years people tried to think of sophisticated detectors that could count the number of warheads on a missile without removing the shroud that covers them. One such method is used in the INF Treaty to distinguish three-warhead SS-20 intemediate-range ballistic missiles (IRBMs) from single-warhead SS-25 ICBMs in the field [24, pp. 145–146]. It is a measure of the political progress made between 1987 and 1991 that under START the host country will simply remove the shroud from ICBMs and SLBMs in situ and allow inspectors to count the warheads directly.

Postdispersal inspections are conducted at Russian mobile ICBM bases to ensure that the proper number of launchers, either road- or rail-mobile, are returned to the base after a dispersal exercise. Since the United States has no mobile ICBMs, this is not a reciprocal obligation, clear evidence of the lengths to which Gorbachev was willing to go to reach an agreement. A final type of onsite inspection involves "technical characteristics exhibitions" of each separate type of ICBM, SLBM, and long-range bomber. These are intended to verify the descriptions exchanged in the original data base notifications and were not supposed to begin until the treaty entered into force. However, the two sides agreed soon after the signing ceremony to allow inspections of individual weapons even before ratification. By August 1994, 20 such exhibitions had taken place, 16 of Russian weapons and 4 of American [25].

National Technical Means

Russian strategic nuclear weapons remain the most dangerous and readily mobilizable military threat to American security, so keeping track of their numbers, locations, and states of readiness remains a high priority for U.S. intelligence agencies. U.S. satellites are used to photograph missile, submarine, and bomber bases, as well as to monitor communications between them. Satellite sensors are used along with Earth-based radars and receivers to monitor testing activities, both for missiles covered by INF and START and for ballistic missile defense developments covered by the ABM Treaty. NTM remain the only way the United States can monitor the Russian ABM system around Moscow and the two test ranges where research and development are conducted.

Another constellation of satellites, and worldwide networks of seismic, hydroacoustic, and nuclear radiation sensors, watch, listen, and "sniff" for possible underground, atmospheric, or underwater nuclear tests. Major portions of the land- and sea-based networks will become part of the International Monitoring System of the Comprehensive Test Ban if and when it enters into force. NTM also monitor states such as Israel, South Africa, India, Pakistan, Iraq, and Iran for nuclear activities. With the shift of emphasis on threat assessment away from the former Soviet Union to so-called "rogue states and nuclear outlaws," the selection of targets for NTM has become more complex and demanding [26]. Efforts by the International Atomic Energy Agency to improve its inspection activities rely on information from U.S. and other states' NTM to provide clues to facilities or sites that may require special inspections.

Compliance

The consultative body with the oldest and richest tradition is the Standing Consultative Commission (SCC) created for the SALT and ABM Treaties. It was the venue for many productive interactions between the two sides in the early years of SALT/ABM but became the target of attacks by influential members of the Reagan administration and barely survived the compliance controversies of the 1980s. Most recently it has been restored to its proper function as the place where U.S. and Russian negotiators are attempting to agree on more precise definitions of the ABM Treaty's distinctions among strategic, theater, and tactical defense systems. The SCC has met regularly at least twice a year for the 23 years since the ABM Treaty was ratified, and it has served as the model for similar bodies set up under many other agreements.

In INF the consultative body is called the Special Verification Commission (SVC). It is "special" (as opposed to "standing") because it meets only at the request of one of the parties. Otherwise its task is the same as that of the SCC: to "resolve questions relating to compliance" and to "agree on measures that will improve the viability and effectiveness" of the treaty. This latter role has been particularly important because of the unprecedented reliance on on-site inspections in the INF Treaty. The detailed rules and procedures for all types of inspections, and especially for the continuous perimeter-portal monitoring, could only be worked out while the treaty was in force and being implemented. It was not until December 21, 1989, nearly a year and a half after ratification, that the two sides signed a Memorandum of Agreement specifying the details of on-site inspections, and even then a serious disagreement over the use of an X-ray system at Votkinsk had to be resolved by Secretary of State Baker and Foreign Minister Shevardnadze [24, pp. 90–93].

The consultative body for START is called the Joint Compliance and Implementation Commission (JCIC). It has two kinds of meetings: "sessions" and "special sessions," with the latter intended only for "urgent concern(s) relating to compliance." The START Treaty is an exceptionally complex document, and its implementation was further complicated by the breakup of the Soviet Union and the inheritance by four newly independent states of its strategic nuclear weapons. This required extensive renegotiation, leading finally to the Lisbon Protocol, which was signed in May 1992. Under this protocol the membership of the JCIC was expanded to include Belarus, Kazakhstan, and Ukraine as well as Russia and the United States. During the nearly three and one-half years between START's signing and ratification, the JCIC met frequently, indeed almost continuously, to resolve a wide variety of issues. In all, 27 agreements and 18 joint statements clarifying implementation ambiguities were produced by the JCIC in the period preceding entry into force [27, p. 10]. Since then the JCIC has been resolving ambiguities identified at inspections and clarifying nterpretations of treaty provisions, such as those governing the exchange of telemetry tapes.andconversion of ICBMs to space-launch vehicles.

Nuclear Testing

The Comprehensive Test Ban Treaty (CTBT) was opened for signature on September 24, 1996, and U.S. President Clinton was the first to sign it. When it enters into force, an event which all observers agree is by no means inevitable and at best some years in the future, it will supersede both the Limited Test Ban Treaty of 1963 and the Threshold Test Ban and Peaceful Nuclear Explosion Treaties of 1991. Meanwhile, the latter treaties remain in force, but there are unlikely to be any tests conducted, at least by the recognized nuclear powers, during the long ratification process. All five nuclear weapon states have declared moratoria on testing and have signed the CTBT. If any of them were to conduct a nuclear explosion prior to ratification, it would undercut the basic objectives of the treaty and in effect be tantamount to a violation. In practice, therefore, there is no implementation to be done for the CTBT, and verification and compliance activities associated with the existing treaties will continue as before. These have already been described in chapter 2.

Meanwhile the work necessary to create the new CTBT framework had just begun at the end of 1996. The main tasks will be to secure ratification of the treaty by all 44 states, including India, Pakistan, and Israel, over the next several years and to create the international organization, the CTBTO based in Vienna, that will administer the treaty. The form of the CTBTO specified in the treaty mimics in almost every detail the Organization for the Prevention of Chemical Weapons (OPCW), which will be described in the next section. The Preparatory Committee for the CTBTO held its first meetings at the end of 1996 and began what promises to be a long and contentious process of setting up a viable international monitoring and verification regime. As the leading nuclear weapon state and the state with the most widespread and sophisticated nuclear explosion monitoring capabilities, the United States will have much to say about the form and substance of the CTBTO, and the interagency collaboration of ACDA and the State, Energy, and Defense Departments in this process promises to be at least as difficult as it has been for the Chemical Weapons Convention.

CONVENTIONAL WEAPONS

There are four major agreements that form the framework for conventional arms control in Europe and a confidence-building measure that is international in scope. The first group includes the Conventional Forces in Europe (CFE) Treaty, which mandates reductions in five types of major conventional armaments; the CFE-1A Agreement, which sets limits to active-duty military personnel on the continent; the Stockholm-Vienna Documents on Confidence and Security Building Measures (CSBM), which create a military transparency regime; and the Open Skies Treaty, which will permit overflights by participating states to observe the military activities of other states. The regime created by these agreements is complex—for example, the CSBM and Open Skies treaties have different memberships from each other and each has a different membership from the CFE and CFE-1A treaties. Nevertheless, they form a tightly integrated regime of transparency covering the entire European continent from the Atlantic to the Urals. The international arrangement is the United Nations Register of Conventional Arms, a confidence-building measure designed to make the international trade in large conventional weapons more transparent and eventually to create an open record of the full conventional weapons capabilities of member states.

The CFE Treaty was signed on November 19, 1990 after less than two years of negotiations—a remarkably short time for a complex agreement involving 22 states parties.[8] But in reality it was the culmination of a 17-year process that began with the M(B)FR negotiations in 1973. The strange acronym is symbolic of the frustrating lack of agreement in those negotiations—the two sides could not even agree on their name! To the Warsaw Pact states they were the Mutual Force Reduction Talks, but to the NATO participants they were the Mutual and *Balanced* Force Reduction Talks. The word "balanced" was more than the Soviet bloc could swallow for 16 years, until this venue was shut down in February 1989, just before the CFE talks began. The rapid progress toward agreement that followed was a result of the political changes in Europe and the Warsaw Pact that accelerated in 1989 with the unification of Germany and the release of the Soviet grip on Eastern Europe. Nevertheless, the M(B)FR negotiations laid much of the groundwork for the CFE Treaty, and the latter could not have been achieved so quickly without that foundation.

The CFE Treaty limits five categories of military equipment deployed in the region between the Atlantic Coast of Europe and the Ural Mountains in Russia: tanks, artillery, armored combat vehicles, helicopters, and combat aircraft.[9] The treaty was originally negotiated between two alliances, so the limits on each category were fixed at equal levels for the 16-member NATO group and the six-member Warsaw Pact group. Members of each group decided among themselves how to allocate weapons to individual states within the group, limited only by the requirement that no single state could have more than approximately two-thirds of the allotment of its own alliance. The breakup of the Soviet Union and the subsequent split of Czechoslovakia into two states led to further intra-alliance negotiations on allocations.[10] The states formed from the former Soviet Union met in Tashkent in May 1992 to settle matters among themselves, and these new arrangements were incorporated into the treaty at an "extraordinary conference" held in Oslo in June [28, pp. 671–683]. The dissolution of Czechoslovakia into the Czech Republic and Slovakia on January 1, 1993 was

---

[8] The original negotiations involved the 16 NATO members and 6 Warsaw Pact members. With the breakup of the Soviet Union and Czechoslovakia and the unification of Germany, the number of parties has increased to 30.

[9] For detailed listings of CFE Treaty limits in the five categories and for annually updated tables of progress toward those limits see either the *Sipri Yearbooks* (Stockholm International Peace Research Institute, Oxford University Press) or the *Arms Control Reporter* (Institute for Defense and Disarmament Studies, Cambridge, Massachusetts).

[10] Latvia, Lithuania, and Estonia opted to stay out of the treaty by joining the neutral and nonaligned group that includes Sweden, Finland, Switzerland, Austria, Ireland, Albania, and the states of the former Yugoslavia.

incorporated at a special meeting of the CFE Joint Consultative Group the following month [29, p. 576].

Although it took until February 1993 to complete all of these arrangements, the treaty entered into force provisionally on July 17, 1992, initiating a 120-day baseline validation period during which inspections were carried out to confirm the numbers of weapons declared by each state. The three-year period of reductions ended on November 17, 1995, and, after another 120-day validation period, the treaty settled into its final compliance phase in which inspections continue indefinitely to ensure that no country rebuilds forces that exceed its limits. More adjustments to the zonal limits were made at the May 1996 review conference in response to Russian and Ukrainian protests against the so-called "flank limits" (see chapter 7). Commitments were also made at that conference to a full-fledged reform of the treaty to reflect the new post–Cold War security structure of Europe [30].

As its name implies, CFE-1A supplements the CFE treaty by doing for military personnel what CFE does for large combat weapons. It is not a treaty, but a politically binding agreement that does not require formal ratification. It is also structured differently from CFE, with maximum troop levels set for individual countries rather than aggregated by alliance. This reflects the fact that both the Warsaw Pact and the Soviet Union had been dissolved by the time the agreement was signed in July 1992. CFE-1A is closely tied to CFE in its schedule of implementation. It entered into force simultaneously with CFE, and its final mandated troop levels were achieved in November 1995, the same time that CFE completed its reductions.

The Stockholm-Vienna Confidence and Security Building Measures (CSBM) agreements include all of the CFE parties as well as the 23 other members of the Organization for Security and Cooperation in Europe (OSCE) that were not members of either Cold War alliance or, like the Baltic states, have chosen to stay outside the CFE Treaty. The process is descended from the first set of transparency measures included in the Helsinki Final Act of 1975. These were greatly expanded in the Stockholm Document of 1986 and further still in the Vienna Documents of 1990, 1992, and 1994. All of these declarations have as their basic objective "to give effect and expression to the duty of States to refrain from the threat or use of force in their mutual relations" [31, p. 355]. The fundamental difference between the CSBM process and the arms control process of the CFE Treaty is the former's "operational" emphasis [32]. It focuses on measures to increase transparency and dispel unjustified fears, while CFE focuses on weapons and troop levels. During the Cold War the CSBM approach was generally associated with Soviet foreign policy, while NATO advocated the MBFR/CFE approach. The two processes were intimately linked, since this was the only way to get East and West to sit down at the same table. They remain linked now that they are in force and, along with Open Skies, form the basis for a full-fledged "cooperative security regime" in Europe [33, p. 790].

The Helsinki agreement was the first to require advance notification of large military exercises (more than 25,000 troops) and to recommend the invitation of observers to these exercises. The Stockholm Document expanded these requirements, reduced the size of notifiable maneuvers to 13,000 troops, made invitation of observers to notifiable activities mandatory, and introduced on-site inspections [31, pp. 355–369]. The three Vienna Documents expanded the

Stockholm CSBMs even further, adding annual exchanges of calendars of planned military activities; mechanisms for risk reduction, including the use of a Conflict Prevention Center created by the 1990 Document; military contacts, including visits to air bases, exchanges and visits between military institutions, and demonstrations of new types of weapons and equipment; prior notification of concentrations of forces, maneuvers, or exercises; observations of major military activities; and limits on the size and frequency of military activities [28, pp. 635–653]. All of this is to be verified by a system of inspection and evaluation, communicated via an international computer network, and discussed at an annual implementation assessment meeting of the OSCE.

The Open Skies Treaty was signed on March 24, 1992 by 25 European states. By September 1995 the number had risen to 27, with 22 ratifications, including the United States [34]. But at the end of 1996 neither Russia nor Ukraine had ratified the treaty, and it had still not entered into force. The slow pace of ratification is due to several factors: domestic politics in Russia and Ukraine, a reduced sense of urgency, and the difficulty of some states in finding funds for the reconnaissance flights [29, pp. 601–603]. The opening up of the former Eastern Bloc and the implementation of CFE and CSBMs has created much of the transparency that was the original objective of Open Skies, and the squeeze on military budgets in many European states and former Soviet republics has made it difficult for many of them to find adequate funding for overflights. There has been some success in forming groups of states to share expenses, and there have been a number of trial flights between Russia and Great Britain, the United States and Ukraine, and Hungary and Canada among others. But 1996 ended with little prospect of early entry into force.

While these four treaties represent an impressive achievement, they will not bring about the demilitarization of the European continent. In November 1995, when all the CFE and CFE-1A reductions were completed, there were still 5.6 million full-time, active-duty military personnel and 154,000 pieces of heavy combat equipment permitted in the region covered by the treaties. Neither CFE nor CFE-1A places any restrictions on naval weapons or personnel. The zonal limits on deployment of heavy combat equipment and the transparency regime of notifications and inspections under the CSBM agreements will virtually eliminate the prospect of surprise attack in Europe, but few serious analysts ever suspected that a massive surprise attack could be launched in Europe anyway [35, p. 458]. The problems in ratifying Open Skies show that perceptions of threat have declined and concerns for cost have increased, and the conflict in the former Yugoslavia has shown that much of this painstakingly negotiated transparency regime may be irrelevant to the new problems emerging in Europe. Still, it would be foolish to argue that because a regime does not solve all possible problems it is no longer to be valued for the problems it does solve. The creation of a set of institutions through which Europeans and North Americans can reassure each other of their nonaggressive intentions and nonthreatening military capabilities is no mean achievement when viewed against the background of European history. The United States is an active participant in all of these treaties because it has wanted to remain involved in the affairs of Europe. That interest has not been diminished by the events of the past several years, so it is as important as ever that the United States exercise its responsibility to implement and monitor these treaties fully and effectively.

The United Nations Register of Conventional Arms is intended to be an international clearing house for data on conventional arms transfers.[11] There is a long history of attempts to control the international arms trade, going all the way back to the League of Nations, but the end of the Cold War and the 1991 Gulf War catalyzed the first successful steps, not so much to control the trade but to make it more transparent. The end of the Cold War drastically reduced the demand among the militarily advanced states for high-technology weaponry, and the Gulf War pointed up the dangers inherent in the proliferation of such weapons to developing states in conflict-prone areas. An initial attempt by the five permanent Security Council members to establish guidelines for conventional arms transfers failed when the U.S. sale of 150 F-16 fighters to Taiwan caused China to suspend its participation [36, p. 3]. The resulting impasse led to the UN General Assembly taking up the issue and ordering the Secretary General in 1988 to study ways of "promoting transparency in international transfers of conventional arms on a universal and non-discriminatory basis" [36, p. 4]. The result, which required several years of difficult negotiations to achieve, was the Arms Register, which came into effect in January 1992. Its reporting requirements are discussed below under data exchanges and notifications.

Implementation

Of all the conventional weapon agreements considered in this section the only one that needs to be "implemented" in the sense we are using that word is the CFE Treaty. Only CFE requires the actual reduction of weapons, and this can be done in a number of ways, including destruction, conversion, and transfer to other states or, in certain limited cases, to military, domestic security, or law enforcement units not covered by the treaty. Reduction procedures specified in the treaty allow four basic methods for destroying tanks, armored combat vehicles (ACVs), artillery, planes, and helicopters: severing, explosive demolition, smashing, and deformation. The items to be reduced are first displayed for inspection at a reduction site, and then the chosen procedure is executed. The destroyed, dismantled, or deformed weapon is then inspected again to verify that it is no longer capable of carrying out or being restored to its original function.

Some states, especially Soviet successor states, have complained about the cost of implementing CFE reductions. Belarus is the most prominent of these, and its President Alexander Lukashenko announced in February 1995 that he was suspending implementation of CFE reductions both because of the economic burden they imposed on his country and also because NATO's tentative expansion plans would bring it, "right up to Russia's borders and . . . at the western boundaries of Belorussia" [37]. The United States has contributed $10 million to Belarus under Project Peace [33, p. 767], to aid in weapon

---

[11] This brief discussion of the UN Register is based on the following references, in which more extensive description and analysis can be found: Malcolm Chalmers, Owen Greene, Edward J. Laurance, and Herbert Wulf (eds.), *Developing the UN Register of Conventional Arms* (Bradford, UK: University of Bradford,1994); Hendrik Wagenmakers, "The UN Register of Conventional Arms: A New Instrument for Cooperative Security," *Arms Control Today*, April 1993, 17–19; Hendrik Wagenmakers, "The UN Register of Conventional Arms: The Debate on the Future Issues," *Arms Control Today*, October 1994, 8–13; Edward J. Laurance, "The UN Register of Conventional Arms: Rationales and Prospects for Compliance and Effectiveness," *Washington Quarterly*, Spring 1993, 163–172.

dismantlement,[12] but Lukashenko claimed that $33 million would be needed [38]. Destruction resumed in the fall of 1995 but the long hiatus made it impossible for Belarus to complete its scheduled eliminations by the November 17 deadline. Ukraine had similar difficulties in meeting the costs of its CFE reductions, but appears to have met its obligations with only minimal ($5 million) aid from the United States [33, p. 767].

Any state can reduce its holdings by transferring, or "cascading," excess equipment to other states in its group. NATO took early advantage of this option, with the United States, Germany, and Netherlands transferring over 4,500 weapons to other NATO states. Small transfers went to Denmark, Norway, Portugal, and Spain, but by far the largest number went to Greece and Turkey. Greece received 916 tanks, 343 artillery pieces, and 350 ACVs, and Turkey got 922 tanks, 634 artillery pieces, and 350 ACVs [39, p. 283]. These transfers, far from representing a reduction in conventional military power for the two Mediterranean rivals, actually strengthen them substantially. Before the CFE Treaty, Turkey's tank force was made up primarily of obsolete M-47 and M-48 tanks. After cascading they now have 658 M-60s, the same type used by U.S. forces in the Gulf War. Greece received 671 M-60 tanks, increasing its numbers by 16 percent [40].

Not to be outdone, the former Warsaw Pact states are also trying to unload excess weapons on the international market. The Czech Republic sold 40 T-55 tanks to Cambodia in November 1994, and Poland sold another 50 to the same customer. Yemen purchased 56 T-62 tanks from Bulgaria. Former East German equipment acquired by Germany in the unification has been sold to countries in Africa, the Middle East, and Latin America, as well as some to former Warsaw Pact states like Hungary and Lithuania. More disturbing from the U.S. point of view was the sale by Poland of 100 tanks to Iran, reported in the UN Conventional Arms Register in May 1995 [41].

Data Exchanges and Notifications

Most notifications and data exchanges will be conducted over a computer network created by the OSCE countries in 1991 and mandated for use in all communications by the 1992 Vienna Document [28, p. 651]. By the end of 1994 the network comprised 38 end-user stations located at three OSCE institutions and in 35 states parties. Data are transmitted from individual stations to a central computer switch in the Netherlands' Foreign Ministry and from there to all participating stations. An enormous amount of information is exchanged over this network, including a full description of each state's military organization and the total number of weapons held in each category; the detailed distribution of these weapons among individual units and those not associated with particular units; and specification and location of all declared sites, objects of verification (see below), and reduction sites.

Information exchanges under the CSBM agreements include much of the same data as in CFE but for nearly twice as many countries. In addition, the CSBM process requires exchange of information on military budgets and ad-

---

[12] This is independent of the Nunn-Lugar program, from which no funds have so far been used to support CFE implementation.

vanced notification of military exercises involving more than 9,000 troops or 250 battle tanks, or only 3,000 troops if the exercises are amphibious landings or parachute drops. An annual calendar of all such activities with a detailed description of each one must be supplied by each state party to all other states parties. Not surprisingly the number of notifiable activities has declined substantially in the past few years. In the 1980s the annual list of such exercises took up several pages in the *Sipri Yearbook*. But there were only six in 1992 [28, p. 620], four in 1993 [29, p. 596], and seven in 1994 [33, p. 792]. All of the notifiable activities for the past several years have been conducted by NATO or other West European states. Russia and the former Warsaw Pact states no longer carry out any exercises on a scale large enough to require notification.[13]

When Open Skies flights begin, their data will be recorded on photographic film or magnetic tape, and all states parties will be entitled to first-generation duplicate copies of these records. In principle, therefore, any state party to the Open Skies Treaty could acquire a full set of data gathered on all flights conducted by all parties. This provision goes at least part of the way toward equalizing access to high-quality imagery between smaller states and larger, wealthy states who operate satellites and other sophisticated sensors.

Data submitted by states to the UN Register of Conventional Arms fall into two main categories: "requested" and "invited." All data submissions are voluntary, and there is no formal verification provision in the agreement, but a "request" for data is considered a stronger requirement ("a higher level of political obligation") than an "invitation" [42, p. 9]. Requested data include exports and imports of seven classes of heavy conventional weapons: battle tanks, armored combat vehicles, large-caliber artillery systems, combat aircraft, attack helicopters, warships, and missiles and their launchers.[14] The first five classes are essentially the same as those in the CFE Treaty, but the last two are unique to the UN Register. In addition to the raw numbers, states are also requested to supply background data, such as descriptions of the weapons, ranges, tonnages, etc. [43, p. 16]. States are also "invited" to submit information on their arms import and export policies and legislative and administrative procedures relevant to arms transfers [43, p. 18].

All of this information is collected and stored in a computer data base by the UN Office for Disarmament Affairs in New York. The data are open to all member states and are made public in an annual report from the secretary-general [43, p. 17]. The first data reported for the Register was for the year 1992 and was due on 30 April 1993. But despite efforts to make the process as simple as possible (data are reported on a one-page standardized form), many states had difficulty meeting this deadline. Some states were still reporting 1992 data in the autumn of 1994 [42, p. 10]. There were also problems in reconciling the numbers submitted by exporters with those submitted by importers. These problems appear to have been largely the result of misunderstandings of requirements and

---

[13] The Russian intervention in Chechnya involved forces much larger than the minimum requiring notification, and many feel that the operation constituted a violation of the CSBM agreements. I will return to this question in chapter 7.

[14] The U.S. report for calendar year 1995 can be found in *Arms Control Today*, May/June 1996, pp. 28–29, and a detailed analysis by Tracy M. Keith of the first four years of implementation is published in *The Nonproliferation Review*, Winter 1997, pp. 82–103.

bureaucratic delays, and there is no reason to suspect that there have been any deliberate falsifications or attempts to mislead [42, p. 10].

Inspections and Observations

The basic unit of verification in the CFE Treaty is the object of verification (OOV), defined in the inspection protocol as a military unit, typically of brigade or regimental size (or wing size if aircraft are involved), or a site used for storage, training, or maintenance of equipment covered by the treaty. These OOVs are located at "declared sites," and since more than one OOV might be located at a declared site, the number of the former generally exceeds the latter. For example, at one point the United States listed 80 OOVs at 50 declared sites, and Russia 378 OOVs at 244 declared sites [44]. These numbers change as military units are relocated or reorganized. Such changes are part of the information exchanged over the communications network described above.

Two types of inspections contribute to the yearly quota: declared-site and challenge. The former are visits to declared sites for the purpose of inspecting OOVs. Declared-site inspections cannot be refused and can be delayed only by *force majeur,* that is, events or circumstances such as weather or accident clearly beyond the control of the inspected party. The annual quota that a state must accept is limited to a fixed percentage of the number of OOVs on that state's territory. That percentage is 20 percent during the two 120-day validation periods, 10 percent during the three-year reduction period, and 15 percent during the indefinite residual period after all reductions have been completed. For example, in the baseline validation period from July 17 to November 14, 1992 Russia had to accept 75 declared site inspections (20 percent of 378) and the United States 16. States with smaller numbers of OOV (Canada, for example, has only one) must accept a minimum of one declared-site inspection per year.

Challenge inspections are not conducted at declared sites but at "specified areas," defined as any area within the Atlantic to the Urals region that is smaller than 65 square kilometers and on which no straight-line distance is longer than 16 km. Any state party can request a challenge inspection on such an area but the inspected party has the right to refuse it. If it does refuse, the challenged party is required either to "provide all reasonable assurance" that no limited items are present on the area, or, if some are present but serving permitted internal security functions, to "allow visual confirmation of their presence" by the inspecting party. There is a limit on challenge inspections to 15 percent of the quota of passive declared site inspections during the validation and reduction periods. This fraction increases to 23 percent during the residual period. Challenge inspections, when accepted, count toward the overall quota of passive inspections for the inspected party. Using the numbers from the previous paragraph, Russia would have been subject to 11 challenge inspections (15 percent of 75) during the initial validation period and the United States only two.

The destruction of weapons is verified by "reduction" inspections. The inspecting state is entitled to observe the entire destruction process if it chooses to do so, but in practice reduction inspections usually involve an initial inspection in which the weapons to be destroyed are identified by factory serial number, followed by a close-out inspection of the remnants of the destroyed equipment at the end of the reduction process. Reduction inspections are carried out at declared sites, but they do not count toward the quota of declared-site or challenge inspections. Nor are they refusable. The number of inspections carried out under CFE is remarkable. By the end of 1995 more than 2,300 on-site inspections had been conducted [45], and through August 15 of that year the United States had participated in over 450 active and 55 passive inspections.[15]

The CSBM Documents provide for a wide variety of visits, inspections, and observations, some voluntary and some mandatory.

- States are encouraged to invite observers from other states to military activities that might be cause for concern.
- At least once every five years each state with declared air combat units must invite all other parties to send representatives to a 24-hour visit to an operating airbase.
- States are encouraged to engage in a variety of military-to-military contacts.
- Any state introducing a new weapon system into the OSCE region must arrange a demonstration of it for representatives of the other states.
- A state conducting any military activity involving more than 13,000 troops or 300 battle tanks, or amphibious or airborne exercises with more than 3,500, must invite observers from all other participating states to view the exercise.
- Challenge inspections of any specified area can be demanded by any state party.

The Open Skies Treaty assigns a passive quota of overflights to each party, which is the maximum number it must accept in any year.[16] The quota will be 42 for the United States and Russia; 12 each for Canada, France, Germany, Italy, Turkey, Ukraine, and the United Kingdom; and lesser numbers for smaller states ranging from 7 for Norway to 2 for Portugal [44]. Sensors are limited to four types: optical panoramic and framing cameras, video cameras with real-time display, infrared line-scanning devices, and sideways-looking imaging radars. At the request of many of the less technically advanced states, the resolution of these instruments was limited to 30 centimeters for optical and video cameras, 50 centimeters for infrared sensors, and 3 meters for radar. The limitation to 3 meters resolution for radar imaging was unfortunate because this device is capable of producing much higher quality images and is useful in weather conditions that make optical or infrared imaging impossible.

An Open Skies overflight will be conducted either by a single state or a group of states and will take off from a designated "Open Skies airfield" on the territory of the observed state. A detailed notification of intention to conduct a flight is required, down to the genders and passport numbers of the personnel involved. If the aircraft is brought into the inspected country by the inspecting state, all of its sensor windows must be covered during transit to the Open Skies airfield from which it will start its inspection flight. The inspected state must provide calibration targets near the initial airfield to allow verification that the sensors do not exceed the allowable resolution.

The complexity of all these arrangements makes clear that Open Skies inspections will be expensive and sometimes unpredictable. They will require a

---

[15] Personal communication from On-Site Inspection Agency. The United States participated in these inspections both on its own and in collaboration with other states.

[16] The quotas mentioned here are the final steady-state values. For the first three years after entry into force no state need accept more than 75 percent of its final quota.

great deal of cooperation and good will between the inspecting and the inspected parties to avoid friction and even danger to the aircraft crews. They will also require frequent practice to produce crews that are capable of dealing with unanticipated situations. There have been a substantial number of practice flights since the treaty's signing in 1992, and more will be required if the process is to work smoothly. This is expensive, and many states do not have the resources to do much of it on their own. A number of collaborations (e.g., Benelux, Russia/Belarus, United States/Canada) have already sprung up, and more can be expected to form as the treaty nears entry into force.

Compliance

The CFE and CFE-1A treaties share a consultative body called the Joint Consultative Group (JCG). The Treaty requires it to have two four-week meetings a year in Vienna, but during the first four years of the Treaty's implementation it met much more frequently, indeed almost continuously. The Treaty also provides for special sessions to be held within 15 days of the request of any state party. One such special session was held in February 1993 to accept the division of Czechoslovakia and the new assignments of weapon limits, troop ceilings, objects of verification, and declared-site allocations. The chairmanship of the group rotates among the members, and its proceedings are confidential unless the entire group votes to make them public.

NATO has created its own Verification Co-ordinating Committee to schedule inspections more efficiently and to encourage joint inspections. The Committee held a two-day verification seminar in January 1993 to which all parties were invited, and there had been three more seminars by September 1994 [33, p. 765]. As a result, states from the former Eastern Bloc were invited to conduct collaborative inspections with NATO members, and NATO decided to devote up to 20 percent of its inspection quotas to such collaborations. The first one, in March 1993, involved a team of Azeri, Hungarian, Italian, and Polish inspectors at a site in Romania [28, p. 613].

The CSBM process is subject to annual Implementation Assessment Meetings, which until 1994 were organized by a Consultative Committee of the Conflict Prevention Center in Vienna. Now this task has been given to the Forum for Security Cooperation, which is also responsible for implementing CSBMs, preparing military doctrine seminars, and providing the venue for discussion and clarification of information exchanged under CSBMs [29, p. 595].

The Open Skies Treaty created an Open Skies Consultative Commission, based in Vienna. It began meeting after the treaty was signed to establish procedures for calibrating and operating sensors, define resolution limits, establish information exchange formats and procedures, and deal with many other technical and administrative problems raised by the treaty. During most of 1993 the Commission met weekly in Vienna, but meetings have become progressively less frequent as entry into force has been postponed.

CHEMICAL WEAPONS

The nuclear and conventional agreements considered so far have provided examples of arms control, nonproliferation, and confidence building. The first genuine disarmament agreements are those dealing with chemical and biological weapons. If they are successful, all such weapons and the facilities that produce them will be eliminated from the planet. In the entire history of arms control there has never been such an ambitious and all-encompassing disarmament effort. Its success or failure will have important implications for the future progress of efforts to control the production, proliferation, and use of conventional and nuclear weapons as well.

Chemical and biological arms control began in Geneva in 1925 when, with the horrors of World War I gas attacks still fresh in their minds, the nations of the world outlawed "the use in war of asphyxiating, poisonous or other gases" [21, p. 277]. In the 66 years since its entry into force in 1928 the Geneva Protocol has acquired 132 parties, placing it third after the Nuclear Nonproliferation Treaty and Biological Weapons Convention in the number of adherents [33, p. 842]. Unfortunately, it has also been violated a number of times in that same period. The most notable violators included Italy and Japan in the 1930s[17] and Iraq and Iran in the 1980s. Many other states, including the Soviet Union in Afghanistan and the United States in Vietnam, have been accused of violations, and such accusations, while unproved and generally unaccepted by world opinion, have called attention to ambiguities in the interpretation and verification of the convention, as well as its enforcement.[18]

The Geneva Protocol prohibited the use in war of certain kinds of weapons but said nothing about their production and stockpiling. As long as some states possessed chemical arsenals, they could be tempted to use them if the opportunity or necessity presented itself, while others could justify their own possession of them on the grounds of self-defense or deterrence. Historical evidence suggests that Germany, which produced and stockpiled prodigious quantities of chemical warfare agents during World War II, did not use them primarily out of fear of retaliation in kind. More recently Iraq has admitted to stockpiling and weaponizing both chemical and biological agents prior to the 1991 Gulf War. The weapons were not used, in part because Iraq feared massive retaliation [46].

The use of riot control agents and herbicides by the United States in the Vietnam War stimulated a resurgence of efforts in the late 1960s to strengthen the Geneva Convention [21, pp. 91–93]. Negotiations took place under UN auspices and rather quickly led to a complete ban on the development, production, and stockpiling of biological and toxin weapons, whose use in war had already been prohibited by the Geneva Convention (see below). But a chemical weapons ban proved far more difficult to achieve. Negotiations continued for more than 20 years until the Chemical Weapons Convention (CWC) was presented for signing in January 1993. It was signed by 130 countries at that time, and 30 more had signed on by the end of 1996. The treaty requires 65 ratifications before it can enter into force, and the 65th ratification (by Hungary) was recorded on October 29, 1996. That began the six-month preparation for entry into force, scheduled to take place on April 29, 1997. At the end of 1996 neither

---

[17] Japan was not a party to the Geneva Protocol when it used chemical and biological weapons in China and Manchuria in the 1930s. It did not ratify the Protocol until 1970 [33, p. 850].

[18] The United States was not a party to the Protocol during the war in Vietnam and did not ratify it until 1975. For a thorough analysis of the relationship between the United States and the Geneva Protocol see George Bunn, "Banning Poison Gas and Germ Warfare: Should the United States Agree?" *Wisconsin Law Review*, Vol. 1969, No. 2 (1969), pp. 375–420.

Russia nor the United States, the only two states acknowledged to possess chemical weapon arsenals, had ratified the Convention, and there was reason to doubt that either would ratify it before it entered into force. In Russia the concerns are mainly with cost and intrusive verification, while in the United States the treaty fell victim to 1996 election politics and continued to face powerful conservative opposition as the second Clinton administration began.

Meanwhile the United States and Russia were struggling with their bilateral chemical disarmament process. It was begun with two agreements: a Memorandum of Understanding (MOU) signed by Secretary of State James Baker and Soviet Foreign Minister Eduard Shevardnadze in Jackson Hole, Wyoming in September 1989, and a Bilateral Destruction and Nonproduction Agreement (BDA) signed by Presidents Bush and Gorbachev in June 1990. Although these were bilateral agreements, they were explicitly formulated to provide leadership and practical experience in implementing the international CWC. The MOU and the BDA were supposed to be implemented before the CWC entered into force, and the CWC was to benefit from the experience gained in implementing and verifying them. These expectations were not met, primarily because of the enormous problems associated with disposing of chemical weapons, especially in the former Soviet Union, but also because of political problems associated with the end of the Cold War and the collapse of the Soviet Union.

Implementation

The Wyoming MOU was divided into two phases [47]. In the first phase the parties exchanged data on amounts and types of chemical weapon agents and the locations of production, storage, and destruction facilities. They also hosted visits to some of their storage and production facilities and to two nonmilitary chemical production plants by teams from the other side. In the second phase more detailed data on chemical weapons (CW) stockpiles were exchanged, along with preliminary plans for how these weapons and their production facilities would be destroyed under the CWC. Phase II also involved on-site inspections, both declared-site and challenge, to verify the data exchanged in both phases. There were originally supposed to be at least five declared-site inspections and up to ten challenge inspections before the CWC entered into force.

The Bilateral Destruction and Nonproduction Agreement (BDA) was signed on June 1, 1990 while Phase I of the MOU was still proceeding smoothly [48]. In the BDA the two sides agreed to end all production of chemical weapons and to cooperate regarding their destruction. They agreed to reduce their stockpiles to a maximum of 5,000 tons by the end of 2002, with this limit to be reduced to 500 tons eight years after the CWC entered into force. The latter provision, which would have allowed the two major chemical weapon states to retain a CW arsenal until all other states had eliminated theirs, caused serious problems at the CWC negotiations in Geneva. Consequently, 11 months after signing the BDA, the Bush administration announced a major shift in U.S. policy, "formally forswearing the use of chemical weapons for any reason, including retaliation" and promising to eliminate its entire stock of chemical weapons within ten years of the CWC's entry into force [49]. This declaration committed the United States to not using chemical weapons under any circumstances, implying that there is no need for the United States to maintain a stockpile of them. But Congress went only partway toward implementing this policy, requiring only that the United States unilaterally eliminate its entire stocks of *unitary* chemical weapons [50]. The Defense Department has been ordered only to *plan* for the destruction of binary weapons.[19] Congress has therefore not fully embraced the Bush administration's renunciation of chemical deterrence, and given the political makeup of the present Congress, it is unlikely to do so until it is assured that Russian binary weapons are fully accounted for and subject to destruction. Unfortunately, concerns about the Russian binary weapons program have not been laid to rest [33, pp. 742; 751].

Even if these concerns are unfounded, there are going to be severe problems with Russian implementation of its commitments under the BDA and CWC [52]. Perhaps the most important problem is lack of funds, and it is precisely for problems like this that the Nunn-Lugar Cooperative Threat Reduction program was created, and the United States had committed $55 million for chemical weapon elimination by the end of 1994. The first $25M was offered in an agreement reached on July 30, 1992 and was intended primarily to help Russia develop a comprehensive plan for CW destruction [11]. It also provided for various kinds of hardware to aid the process of transportation or destruction of chemical weapons and to bring Russian scientists and engineers to U.S. CW facilities to learn U.S. elimination techniques [53].

In June 1993 the United States set up a Chemical Weapons Destruction Support Office in Moscow and staffed it with members of the U.S. Army Chemical/Biological Defense Command, the Army Corps of Engineers, the On-site Inspection Agency, and some private contractor personnel. In May 1994 the Bechtel Corporation was selected to work with the Russians in developing their destruction implementation plan. Earlier, in March 1994, another $30 million was approved to build an analytical laboratory in Russia to be used to do the research necessary to prepare for the destruction process. In August an eight-member delegation of Russian technicians visited an analytical lab in the United States to familiarize themselves with U.S. techniques. So, one can point to some progress in U.S.-Russian cooperation on chemical weapon elimination, but it is minuscule in comparison to the overall task.

Data Exchanges and Notifications

In Phase I of the Wyoming MOU each side was to present the other with data on the aggregate quantity of its chemical weapons, the types of chemical agents it had stockpiled, the percentage of each agent in the form of weapons, the locations of all of its CW storage facilities and the amounts and kinds of weapons stored in them, the locations of all of its CW production facilities along with the types of weapons produced there, and the locations of its chemical weapon destruction facilities. In these initial exchanges the United States declared 31,200 tons of chemical warfare agents at eight locations, and the Soviet

---

[19] Unitary chemical weapons are those that employ a single lethal chemical agent such as chlorine gas or nerve agents like sarin or tabun. Binary weapons use two chemicals that are not individually lethal but which create a lethal agent when combined. Binary agents were developed by both the United States and USSR for use in bombs and artillery shells.

Union declared 40,000 tons at seven locations [29, pp. 330–337]. Phase II data exchanges were more detailed and included general plans for the destruction of chemical weapons and their production facilities. These declarations were to be made at least four months before signing the CWC. But the CWC was signed in January 1993, and the Phase II declarations did not take place until January 1994 [54, p. 27]. Nor did they eliminate the large discrepancies between Russian data declarations and U.S. intelligence estimates of Russian CW stockpiles and production capability. According to one analyst, "The 40,000 agent tons the Soviet Union has formally declared is only the tip of the iceberg" [52, p. 17]. A Russian environmental official estimates the total production to have been 100,000 to 200,000 tons, but it is not clear how much of this total remains in the weapon stockpile and how much has been destroyed or disposed of prior to the Soviet declaration. Russian officials have announced what sound like relatively firm and detailed plans for destruction, but the government appears to have made little progress in laying the groundwork for implementing these plans [52].

Data exchanges under the CWC will be the most extensive ever attempted. All parties will be required to report annually on a wide range of activities in their domestic chemical industries, and all of these data will be collected and collated by the Organization for the Prevention of Chemical Weapons (OPCW) in the Hague. The lists of chemicals for which reporting is necessary include many that are used extensively for nonmilitary purposes, and the number of individual plants that must keep careful records and report periodically to their national authorities runs into the tens of thousands. One of the major tasks of the OPCW Preparatory Commission has been to design the management information system that will handle this flood of data [55].

An aspect of the CWC that makes it different from other agreements is the extensive involvement of private industry in both the data reporting and on-site inspection provisions. The Office of Technology Assessment estimates that between 200 and 300 U.S. chemical plants produce, process, or consume more than threshold quantities of Schedule 2 chemicals, and that about 1,000 produce more than the threshold quantity of Schedule 3 chemicals.[20] In addition, at least 10,000 plants produce more than the threshold quantity of "discrete organic compounds," which will require them regularly to report data on production, inventory, and sales and be subject to possible challenge inspections. The extent of the reporting requirements can be appreciated by noting that this represents over half of the entire U.S. chemical industry, which comprises some 20,000 plants, employs 846,000 people, and generates about $300 billion in annual shipments [56]. The chemical industries of other states are not as large as this, but nevertheless the U.S. reporting requirements will be only a fraction of the entire OPCW data management effort.

---

[20] Schedule 1 chemicals are chemical warfare agents such as mustard gas, lewisites, or nerve agents.

Schedule 2 chemicals are agents that are not generally produced in large quantities for nonmilitary purposes and that have not been traditionally used as chemical weapons, but which might be so used or might serve as key precursors in the production of chemical weapons.

Schedule 3 chemicals are dual-use agents that are generally produced in large quantities for nonmilitary purposes but which might be (and have been) used as chemical weapons or CW precursors. Eamples are phosgene, hydrogen cyanide, and some phosphorous and chlorine compounds.

Inspections and Observations

The Wyoming MOU mandated a total of 15 on-site inspections by each side, to begin four months before the signing of the CWC and end four months after it. The CWC was signed in January 1993, so MOU Phase II inspections should have started in September 1992 and been completed by May 1993. But no bilateral inspections had yet been conducted by the time the convention was signed. Shortly thereafter, in March 1993, the United States and Russia agreed to reduce the number of inspections from 15 to 10, partly in an attempt to "jump-start" the Phase II process and partly because legal advisors had warned the administration that inspector access to private firms in the United States could not be guaranteed in the absence of implementing legislation that specifically provided for it [54, pp. 28–29]. Then, in November 1993, the number of Phase II inspections was again reduced, this time to only five. According to the agreement reached in January 1994, these would include two "routine" declared-site inspections, one trial challenge inspection, and two challenge inspections of declared facilities.

All of these inspections, including the challenge, were to take place at declared facilities, which means that no experience would be gained in the delicate matter of inspecting sites not already acknowledged to be producing controlled chemicals. The first trial inspection by the United States was conducted on August 26–27, 1994 at the Pochep Storage Site 250 miles southeast of Moscow. A Russian team inspected the Tooele Storage Depot in Utah two months later [44]. The remaining inspections were completed by the end of the year [51].

On-site inspection plays a key role in the CWC, and the working out of its organization and implementation constituted the major reason why the Convention took so long to negotiate. Approximately 60 practice inspections, both routine and challenge, at both civilian and military facilities, were conducted by more than 30 countries in preparation for the Convention [35, pp. 183–186]. Most of these inspections were conducted unilaterally by states on their own facilities, but five were multinational efforts. The United States did four of them in the period from June 1989 to August 1991, two routine inspections at Schedule 2 facilities and one challenge inspection each at a civilian plant and a military installation. Reports of all 60 trial inspections were filed with the Conference on Disarmament in Geneva and were used in designing the inspection system for the Convention. Many more details remained to be worked out, however, and this task was assigned to the OPCW Preparatory Commission.

The Convention allows both routine and challenge inspections and specifies the conditions under which both types are to be conducted. Routine or "systematic" inspections will take place at storage and destruction facilities, production facilities, and facilities engaged in nonprohibited activities at which scheduled chemicals are present. CW production facilities are supposed to be shut down as soon as the treaty enters into force, or as soon as a country adheres to the Convention. They are then to be subjected to systematic verification until they are completely destroyed. Systematic inspections at storage and destruction sites are similar to the safeguards inspections carried out by the International Atomic Energy Agency under the nuclear Nonproliferation Treaty. They include on-site verification of inventory declarations and the use of tags, seals, and continuous monitoring (what the IAEA calls containment and surveillance) to constrain, observe, and record ongoing activities at the facility.

Each party is allowed to retain a single small-scale production facility for Schedule 1 chemicals that it intends to use for research on CW defenses or medical and pharmaceutical purposes. Possession of small quantities of Schedule 1 chemicals is necessary for such research, and this is permitted in aggregate amounts not exceeding one metric ton. The Schedule 1 facility will be subject to systematic verification, with the scale and intensity of the inspection to be based on the "risk to the object and purpose of the Convention" posed by the particular chemicals produced there. These details must be negotiated for each individual facility by the state party and the OPCW.

Facilities that produce, process, or consume Schedule 2 chemicals are subject to on-site inspections but not to systematic verification in the sense used above. The purpose of the inspections is to verify the absence of Schedule 1 chemicals at such facilities, to verify declarations of inventories and throughputs, and to verify the nondiversion of the chemicals to military purposes. No facility in this category can be inspected more than two times per year, and the inspections are to be scheduled in a way that the inspected party cannot predict when they will take place. Plant operators must be notified at least 48 hours in advance of the arrival of an inspection team. Inspections for Schedule 3 chemicals are restricted to facilities producing large quantities of these materials. Facilities must be declared only if they produce more than 30 metric tons per year, and they are subject to inspection only if they produce more than 230 metric tons per year. When inspections are conducted, however, they are as detailed and intrusive as those under Schedule 2, except that notice for a Schedule 3 facility must be given at least 120 hours in advance of the inspectors' arrival.

The Convention also provides for challenge inspections at any location specified by the challenging party. The challenging party must show evidence to the Director-General of the OPCW justifying a challenge inspection, and the challenge can be rejected only if three-quarters of the Executive Council determines within 12 hours that it is "frivolous, abusive, or clearly beyond the scope of this Convention." The inspected party must be notified at least 12 hours before the arrival of the inspection team at the point of entry designated for that country. Another 36 hours are then allowed to pass before the inspected party must deliver the inspection team to the perimeter of the inspection site. Monitoring and sample taking may begin outside the perimeter at this point, but further negotiations may ensue between the inspection team and the inspected state concerning access within the perimeter. Meanwhile the inspected party is free to make arrangements inside the perimeter to prevent inspectors from seeing or sampling anything that is not relevant to the treaty. This is called "managed access" and it allows the plant operator to shroud equipment, turn off computers, hide instrument readings, or take other measures to protect classified or proprietary information. Negotiating the details of the managed access regime was one of the most difficult challenges of the CWC, and it is still not finished. No one can predict how it will actually work until the Convention enters into force and the first challenge is made. All inspections under the CWC will be carried out by international teams chosen by the Technical Secretariat of the OPCW. When inspections are conducted in the United States, the On-Site Inspection Agency will be responsible for hosting the inspection team and making all necessary arrangements with the facility to be inspected.

The use of national technical means (NTM) is not mentioned in the CWC, but the existence of such means is recognized implicitly in the requirement that a challenging state provide evidence of suspicious or ambiguous behavior to justify an inspection. Just how such evidence might be used in practice remains to be seen. It has a high potential for creating political problems since it gives a clear advantage to states with sophisticated monitoring capabilities. Similar concerns were raised during negotiation of the Comprehensive Test Ban Treaty, where the legitimacy of NTM was one of the last issues settled before the treaty was opened for signature and under which the conditions of their use also remains to be determined by experience.

Compliance

The Organization for the Prevention of Chemical Weapons will be the largest and most expensive arms control organization ever constructed. It will be responsible for all administrative tasks associated with implementing and verifying the CWC, and estimates of its annual operating budget range from $50 to $200 million [57]. States parties will contribute to the support of the organization in the same proportion as they contribute to the United Nations, which commits the United States to paying approximately 25 percent of the OPCW's budget. This is in addition to each party's responsibility for the costs of destroying all its CW stocks and production facilities and having those destructions verified. Estimates of these costs to the United States had reached $12 billion and continue to rise with each passing year.

The OPCW will be made up of three organs: the Conference of States Parties, the Executive Council, and the Technical Secretariat.[21] The Conference is made up of representatives of all states parties and meets annually to conduct the overall business of the organization, to elect members of the Executive Council, and to consider questions of noncompliance. The Executive Council will have 41 members selected according to quotas from various regions. The quotas are designed to ensure that the major chemical weapons states and states with substantial chemical industries will always be represented on the Executive Council. Its members will be elected by the Conference from a list of nominees presented by the different regions. Its responsibilities, among others, are to make up the annual budget, to arrange sessions of the Conference, and to handle requests for challenge inspections and deal with other compliance concerns of states parties. The Technical Secretariat will be led by a Director General and will be responsible for managing the data declarations and supervising the Inspectorate, which will conduct all inspections under the Convention.

BIOLOGICAL AND TOXIN WEAPONS

The 1925 Geneva Protocol also bans the use of "bacteriological methods of warfare." In 1972 the Biological and Toxin Weapons Convention (BWC) ex-

---

[21] As noted above, the structure of the Comprehensive Test Ban Treaty Organization will be virtually identical to that of the OPCW.

tended the prohibition to the development, production, stockpiling, and acquisition of biological warfare (BW) agents. These include both living organisms, like bacteria, rickettsias, and viruses, and biologically produced toxins, such as those produced in many kinds of animals and plants. Examples of living organisms that have been extensively experimented with for military purposes are anthrax and plague. Examples of biological toxins include botulism, ricin (derived from castor beans), and trichothecene mycotoxins (produced by a mold that grows on wheat, millet, or barley) [58, p. 80].

There have been many allegations of use of such agents in warfare but few documented instances. *Arms Control Reporter* flatly asserts that "BW has never been successfully used as a military weapon" [59], but at least one instance, the use of plague by the Japanese Army in 1941 against Chinese civilians, has been documented. Documents uncovered by a Japanese researcher reveal that at least 300 Chinese died of plague as the result of the release by Japanese aircraft of mice carrying plague-infected fleas [29, p. 718; 60]. Many in the U.S. Intelligence Community still believe that tricothecine toxins were used in Indochina in the 1970s in the form of so-called "yellow rain." This accusation has been discredited by research showing that the phenomenon was associated with feces dropped by swarms of bees, but the U.S. government has never retracted the charge that it was biological warfare sponsored or approved by the Soviet Union [58, pp. 81–82].

While actual use of biological agents in warfare has been difficult to authenticate, it is not difficult to document the great interest shown by many states in research and development in the area of biological warfare. The United States had an offensive BW program until President Richard Nixon stopped it in 1969, paving the way for U.S. adherence to the 1972 Convention. The change of policy by the United States was crucial to the achievement of the BWC, and the United States joined the Soviet Union and United Kingdom as depositary governments for the Convention. The United States did not ratify the 1925 Geneva Protocol until it ratified the BWC. The Soviet Union also ratified the BWC in 1975, but mounting evidence indicates that their BW research and development program did not stop then and continued at least until 1992. U.S. analysts, relying on the testimony of defectors from the Soviet and Russian program, are concerned that it may have continued even beyond 1992 despite assurances by President Yeltsin that he had finally put a stop to it [29, pp. 716–718].

Yeltsin's assurances were made at the same time that he admitted that an anthrax epidemic in Sverdlovsk in 1979 (see chapter 2) was connected with Soviet violations of the BWC. The Sverdlovsk incident illustrates both the possibilities and limitations of biological arms control. Excellent scientific detective work done by two teams of Russian and American investigators showed what can be accomplished when inspectors have the freedom to gather and analyze evidence. On the other hand, even the apparently damning case made by these investigations cannot be taken as proof of a violation, since research on BW agents for *defensive* purposes is not prohibited by the BWC. Indeed, Defense Department–funded research on anthrax is still conducted in the United States and justified on defensive grounds.[22] A second disturbing aspect of the Sverdlovsk case is the small quantity of biological material that was actually released. All of the Sverdlovsk fatalities resulted from the release of at most *one gram* of anthrax spores and possibly as little as a few milligrams [61]. This shows how small the quantities are that could do serious damage to human populations and how difficult it would be to verify their nonexistence or to detect them without some visible incident like the Sverdlovsk release. The experience of the United Nations Special Commission (UNSCOM) in Iraq is also instructive in this regard. Despite a level of access far beyond anything that might be achievable in an international treaty, UNSCOM is still not certain that it has uncovered and eliminated all of Iraq's biological warfare program or that the program will not resume after it leaves [62].

According to the Office of Technology Assessment, "Weight-for-weight, BTW [biological and toxin weapon] agents are hundreds to thousand of times more potent than the most lethal chemical-warfare agents, making them true weapons of mass destruction with a potential for lethal mayhem that can exceed that of nuclear weapons" [58, p. 73]. This makes their elimination by an international treaty with effective verification highly desirable. But "effective verification" of such a treaty is at best problematic and at worst an oxymoron. Because of the small scale of the facilities required and the widespread availability of necessary materials and technology, the monitoring and inspection effort required would be enormous, intrusive, and expensive.[23] In addition, as the Sverdlovsk incident illustrates, even if activities involving BW agents were discovered, there would usually be no way to tell if they were offensive (prohibited) or defensive (permitted).

On the other hand, despite their repugnant and frightening image, the military effectiveness of biological weapons has never been demonstrated, and several features common to most of them, including unpredictability of effects, difficulty of distribution in combat environments, and instability in long-term storage, make their military utility dubious at best. Despite claims that advances in biotechnology may solve some of these difficulties [35, pp. 174–175], it is not at all clear that the true level of military risk posed by biological weapons can justify massive expenditures for a verification regime that could never be highly effective no matter how much money was spent on it.

It was this combination of low military utility and difficulty of verification that convinced the Nixon administration that it should sign and ratify a biological warfare convention with no verification provisions. The treaty does not permit challenge inspections, so when questions about Soviet activities in Sverdlovsk or Indochina arose there was no legal mechanism to allow the international community to find out what was really going on. This severely undermined respect for the BWC in the West and led many who wanted to strengthen the convention to suggest that verification and enforcement mechanisms be

---

[22] According to Michael Moodie of the Chemical and Biological Arms Control Institute, the United States produced a larger inventory of anthrax spores in its preparation of vaccine for personnel in the Gulf War than Iraq did in its entire BW program (Stanford University seminar, April 21, 1995).

[23] It is possible to manufacture lethal BW agents in any facility containing a simple fermenter. Examples of such facilities would be breweries or yogurt manufacturers, as well as agricultural ethanol, biotechnology, or pharmaceutical plants [58, pp. 84–87; 63]. However, the use of such facilities for producing lethal agents would be likely to involve special safety and security precautions that might be detectable in short-notice inspections.

added to it. At the Convention's Second Review Conference in Geneva in 1986 a suite of confidence building measures was created that included exchanges of data on high-safety research facilities and unusual outbreaks of infectious diseases, open publication of all research related to BW agents, and active promotion of scientific contacts between researchers engaged in this kind of work [64, p. 112]. Exchanges have been going on since 1987, but participation has been disappointing [33, p. 743]. Parties like India, Indonesia, and Pakistan have not participated at all, and Iraq and South Africa did not participate until 1993 [29, pp. 725–727]. Even when a state does participate, the absence of any verification makes such declarations problematic. For example, in 1987 the Soviet Union declared five military BW facilities, and then Russia added two to the list in 1992. But the United States believes it has identified more than 20 sites in the former Soviet Union that were engaged in BW work, one of which has been identified by defectors as continuing to conduct BW research even after Yeltsin's 1992 order to stop it [29, p. 725]. These shortcomings have led many states to believe that the Convention requires a full-fledged verification regime, and work is going forward on one in an Ad Hoc Group of Experts created by the Conference of States Parties in 1991 (see below).

Data Exchanges and Notifications

Formal data exchanges under the BWC were initiated in 1987. They require that all states parties submit annual reports (due on April 15) to the United Nations Department for Disarmament Affairs, which is then supposed to make the information available to all other states parties. The reports include four kinds of information [65]:

- Information on high-risk laboratories
  These are laboratories with biosafety level (BL) containments rated 3 or 4.[24] For example, one of the five BL4 facilities reported by the United States is at the Army Medical Research Institute of Infections Diseases in Frederick, Maryland. It does both molecular biology and toxin research and is funded by the Department of Defense.

- Information on unusual outbreaks of infectious diseases
  Most states already provide such information to the World Health Organization, and some have felt it unnecessary to provide it to the United Nations as well. When it is provided it is sometimes incomplete, as illustrated by U.S. reporting of an outbreak of a new disease called hantavirus pulmonary syndrome in the Southwest United States in 1993. There were 53 reported cases of the disease resulting in 27 deaths. However, the report of this outbreak to the UN lacked important details and did not comply fully with reporting requirements [33, p. 744].

- Information on publication of research results and on relevant conferences
  During the first three years of operation of CBMs there appeared to be little uniformity in the scope and quality of the information exchanged in this category. Many states simply provided lists of articles and/or journals, and others omitted publications of military institutions. This provision has been criticized for having "created reams of

---

[24] In a BL3 facility all personnel have been immunized against the agents they work with and also wear protective clothing, goggles, and face masks. All manipulations of infectious microorganisms are done in special safety cabinets maintained at negative pressure to prevent leakage. Air exchanged with the outside is filtered and incinerated. A BL4 facility has all of these features and adds others whose effect is to completely isolate workers from the organisms they work with [58, pp. 91–92].

paper filled with information that is unlikely to ever include activities that present a risk to the convention" [66].

• Additional information on activities "which might be of relevance to the Convention" This has included, inter alia, declarations of compliance with the Convention and of intention to continue to comply, information on work with animal pathogens, reports of laboratory accidents involving organisms relevant to the Convention, and work on vaccine development and usage [65, pp. 131–133].

These four confidence-building measures constituted the full list until 1991, when the Third Review Conference added three more. Facility declarations were expanded to include national biological defense research and development programs, and the states parties were also required to report on any legislation they enacted relevant to the BWC, to declare any past activities in offensive and defensive BW R&D, and to declare their human vaccine production facilities [66]. In their first three years of implementation these new CBMs did not appear to have generated any more enthusiasm than the old ones [29, pp. 727–728].

Inspections and Observations

There are no provisions for inspections or observations in the Biological Weapons Convention. To some countries, the United States in particular, this is seen as an unfortunate but unavoidable limitation of the Convention forced on it by the essential nature of the activities it is supposed to control. In the words of former Arms Control and Disarmament Agency Director Ronald F. Lehman, "The [BWC] is not effectively verifiable, and we do not know any way to make it so" [67, p. 39]. Other states agree that the lack of verification provisions is unfortunate, but are less convinced that this situation is inevitable. There has been a strong push in successive review conferences, especially since the compliance disputes of the 1980s, to examine ways in which inspections, observations, and other monitoring techniques could be added to the BWC. Official U.S. attitudes have evolved since Lehman made his remark, and the Clinton administration has taken a more positive position on BWC verification and played an active role in the Ad Hoc Group process [45]. Meanwhile, the United States and other countries with the necessary motivation and capability have relied on national intelligence methods to monitor developments in biological weapons. The nature of the activity pretty much rules out the use of satellite imagery, so the effort has been devoted more to communications interception and human intelligence, predominantly the latter. Testimony of defectors has been instrumental in raising suspicions of Soviet and Russian BW activity, and it is likely that human intelligence has been the major factor in producing the list of countries that the United States claims are working on biological weapons (see chapter 7).

There have been on-site inspections, both voluntary and coerced, to check for military biological activities. After President Yeltsin's 1992 order to end all Russian BW activities, there were visits by U.S. and British experts to three Russian facilities. These were included in a tripartite agreement signed in September 1992 by the United States, United Kingdom, and Russia, in which two visits by combined expert teams would be made to biological research facilities in each country, one military and one civilian. In October 1992 experts from the three countries examined the Institute of Specially Pure Biological

Preparations in St. Petersburg, a facility at which defectors had said BW research was being conducted. The inspectors determined that the institute was connected with bacteriological weapons only "indirectly, in the most general way" [28, p. 288]. Later visits to two other Russian facilities were made by U.S.-U.K. teams of experts [44]. The results of these inspections are secret, but it appears that the inspectors were satisfied that the inspected facilities (but not necessarily the full Russian BW program) were now in compliance with the Convention [29, p. 718]. The program of reciprocal inspections continued into 1994 with Russian visits to three U.S. facilities: the Pfizer pharmaceutical manufacturing plant in Terre Haute, Indiana; a Pfizer research lab in Groton, Connecticut; and the Plum Island Animal Disease Center on Long Island [44].

Highly intrusive surprise inspections have been conducted in Iraq by the United Nations Special Commission (UNSCOM). In two inspections looking for biological weapons activity, inspectors found "conclusive evidence" of an Iraqi military BW research program but no evidence of production and stockpiling of actual biological weapons [28, p. 701]. Of course, the Iraqis had considerable opportunity to dispose of such weapons prior to any inspections, and UNSCOM discovered that Iraq had destroyed the facility at which the research took place. Several undeclared sites "known to have been related to BW research" have also been inspected but have added no new information. The UNSCOM inspections in Iraq far exceed the limits of intrusiveness that one could hope for under the BWC, and there still remains a great deal of ambiguity about the extent and level of achievement of the Iraqi BW program.[25]

Alarmed by accusations against Russia and the reality of Iraqi violations, and dissatisfied with the response by states parties to existing confidence building measures, the 1991 BWC Review Conference convened an Ad Hoc Group of Governmental Experts to Identify and Examine Potential Verification Measures from a Scientific and Technical Standpoint. The group, generally known as the verification experts, or "VEREX," met four times in 1993 and 1994 and examined a list of 21 possible measures for their potential costs and benefits if added to the BWC. Various combinations of measures were also explored with a view toward exploiting synergism among them [29, pp. 729–734]. The VEREX group presented their report to a special BWC Conference in Geneva in September 1994, and the 80 states parties attending the conference agreed to create yet another committee, called the Ad Hoc Group, to draft a proposed verification regime. It is hoped that this group will eventually be able to recommend a workable verification regime, but progress through 1996 continued to be slow.

Compliance

There is no consultative body associated with the BWC, and the Convention provides only for parties to "consult one another and to cooperate in solving problems." If this process does not resolve compliance concerns, then parties can lodge a complaint with the United Nations Security Council and submit whatever evidence they have. The Security Council can then order an investiga-

---

[25] It was not until a high military official and son-in-law of Saddam Hussein defected to Jordan and began talking to Western intelligence agents that the Iraqi government turned over to UNSCOM extensive data on its biological and other weapons programs [46].

tion with which all parties are required to cooperate. Results of the investigation are to be communicated to all parties to the Convention.

The U.S.-U.K.-Russia Tripartite Agreement has created a Trilateral Working Group which meets to evaluate the results of the visits to biological research facilities. It met twice in 1994, in London in April and in Moscow in October, but its deliberations are secret, so little is publicly known about them [68, p. 26]. It will suffice to note that they have not yet succeeded in satisfying the United States that Russia is in full compliance with the BWC. I will return to a full discussion of this and other compliance concerns in chapter 7.

REFERENCES

1. Weapons of Mass Destruction: Reducing the Threat from the Former Soviet Union, GAO/NSIAD-95-7, U.S. General Accounting Office, October 1994.

2. "U.S.-Russian Strategic Weapons Dismantlements," *Arms Control Today*, May 1995, p. 32.

3. "Chronology of U.S.-Soviet-CIS Nuclear Relations," *Arms Control Today*, June 1994, pp. 32–33.

4. Robert S. Norris and William M. Arkin, "Estimated U.S. and Soviet/Russian Nuclear Stockpiles, 1945–94," *Bulletin of the Atomic Scientists*, November/December 1994, pp. 58–59.

5. Oleg Bukharin, "Nuclear Safeguards and Security in the Former Soviet Union," *Survival*, Winter 1995, pp. 53–72.

6. Sam Nunn and Richard Lugar, Dismantling the Soviet Arsenal: We've Got to Get Involved, *Washington Post*, November 22, 1991, p. A25.

7. Dunbar Lockwood, "Congress Approves $500 Million in Soviet Aid," *Arms Control Today*, December 1991, pp. 19, 25.

8. U.S. Bilateral Program Lacks Effective Coordination, U.S. General Accounting Office, GAO/NSIAD–95–10, February 1995.

9. Remarks of Harold Smith, Assistant to the Secretary of Defense for Atomic Energy, Stanford University, May 30, 1995.

10. Cooperative Threat Reduction, CTR Program, U.S. Department of Defense, April 1995.

11. Second FY 1994 Semi–annual Report on Program Activities to Facilitate Weapons Destruction and Nonproliferation in the Former Soviet Union, Department of Defense Cooperative Threat Reduction Office, October 30, 1994.

12. "U.S. Security Assistance to the Former Soviet Union," *Arms Control Today*, September 1996, pp. 25–26.

13. Bill Gertz, "Perry Sees U.S. Aid's Use in Russia," *Washington Times*, April 3, 1995.

14. Dunbar Lockwood, "U.S., Russia Agree to Phase-out of Nuclear Weapons Reactors," *Arms Control Today*, July/August 1994, p. 24.

15. "Joint Statement on Strategic Stability and Nuclear Security by the Presidents of the United States and Russia," *Arms Control Today*, November 1994, p. 31.

16. Evan S. Medeiros, "Gore–Chernomyrdin Commission Expands Nuclear Security Cooperation," *Arms Control Today*, July 1996, pp. 25, 29.

17. Wilson Dizard III, "Transparency Monitors in Place," *Nuclear Fuel*, November 18, 1996, pp. 3–4.

18. David Albright, "An Iranian Bomb?" *Bulletin of the Atomic Scientists*, July/August 1995, pp. 21–26.

19. "U.S. Removes Kazakhstani HEU in Secret Operation," *Arms Control Today*, January/February 1995, p. 27.

20. Strobe Talbott, *Endgame: The Inside Story of SALT II* (New York: Harper & Row, 1979).

21. Jozef Goldblat, *Arms Control: A Guide to Negotiations and Agreements* (London, International Peace Research Institute Oslo, Sage Publications, 1994).

22. START Treaty between the United States of America and the Union of Soviet Socialist Republics on the Reduction and Limitation of Strategic Offensive Arms, U.S. Arms Control and Disarmament Agency, 1991.

23. *Sipri Yearbook 1977* (London: Taylor & Francis, 1977).

24. Joseph P. Harahan, *On-site Inspections under the INF Treaty* (Washington DC: On–Site Inspection Agency, 1993).

25. Fact Sheet, On–Site Inspection Agency, August 1994.

26. Michael Klare, *Rogue States and Nuclear Outlaws* (New York: Hill and Wang, 1995).

27. *Adherence to and Compliance with Arms Control Agreements*, Arms Control and Disarmament Agency, May 30, 1995.

28. *Sipri Yearbook 1993* (Oxford: Oxford University Press, 1993).

29. *Sipri Yearbook 1994* (Oxford: Oxford University Press, 1994).

30. Sarah Walkling, "CFE Treaty Review Completed; Parties Agree on Flank Resolution," *Arms Control Today*, May/June 1996, p. 18.

31. *Sipri Yearbook 1987* (Oxford: Oxford University Press, 1987).

32. Richard E. Darilek, "The Future of Conventional Arms Control in Europe, A Tale of Two Cities: Stockholm, Vienna," *Sipri Yearbook 1987*, (Oxford: Oxford University Press, 1987), pp. 339–354.

33. *Sipri Yearbook 1995* (London: Oxford University Press, 1995).

34. States Parties to the Open Skies Treaty, U.S. Arms Control and Disarmament Agency Fact Sheet, Office of Public Affairs, September 28, 1995.

35. *Sipri Yearbook 1991* (Oxford: Oxford University Press, 1992).

36. Malcolm Chalmers, et al., Eds., *Developing the UN Register of Conventional Arms* (Bradford, U.K.: University of Bradford, 1994).

37. Aleksandr Koretsky, "Door Slamming as a Means of Persuasion," *Kommersant–Daily* (translation in *Current Digest*, Vol. 47, no. 8, pp. 25–26), February 21 1995, p. 4.

38. Sarah Walkling, "Belarus Suspends CFE–Required Weapons Reductions," *Arms Control Today*, April 1995, p. 19.

39. Richard A. Falkenrath, *Shaping Europe's Military Order: The Origins and Consequences of the CFE Treaty* (Cambridge, MA: MIT Press, 1995).

40. Lee Feinstein, "CFE: Off the Endangered List?" *Arms Control Today*, October 1993, pp. 3–6.

41. Theresa Hitchens and Brendan McNally, "European Nations Sell Arms to Comply with CFE," *Defense News*, June 19–25, 1995, p. 44.

42. Hendrik Wagenmakers, "The UN Register of Conventional Arms: The Debate on the Future Issues," *Arms Control Today*, October 1994, pp. 8–13.

43. Hendrik Wagenmakers, "The UN Register of Conventional Arms: A New Instrument for Cooperative Security," *Arms Control Today*, April 1993, pp. 16–21.

44. *Arms Control Reporter*, 1994, pp. 409.A.5–6, 1994.

45. *Threat Control through Arms Control*, U.S. Arms Control and Disarmament Agency, July 26, 1996.

46. Evan S. Madeiros, "Iraq Provides IAEA with Significant New Information," *Arms Control Today*, September 1995, p. 27.

47. "Chemical Weapons: Verification and Data Exchange," *Arms Control Today*, October, 1989, pp. 23–24.

48. "Chemical Weapons: Agreement between the United States of America and the Union of Soviet Socialist Republics on Destruction and Non–production of Chemical

Weapons and on Measures to Facilitate the Multilateral Convention on Banning Chemical Weapons," *Arms Control Today*, June 1990, pp. 23–25.

49. Lee Feinstein, "U.S. Shifts Position in CW Talks," *Arms Control Today*, June 1991, p. 29.

50. John D. Holum, "The Clinton Administration and the Chemical Weapons Convention: Need for Early Ratification, *"Ratifying the Chemical Weapons Convention*, Brad Roberts, Ed. (Washington, DC: Center for Strategic and International Studies, 1994), pp. 1–10.

51. Thomas W. Lippman, "Administration Voices Concern on Russian Treaty Compliance," *Washington Post*, December 11, 1994,

52. Igor Khripunov, "The Human Element in Russia's Chemical Weapons Disposal Efforts," *Arms Control Today*, July/August 1995, pp. 16–21.

53. Roland Lajoie, "Cooperative Threat Reduction Support to the Destruction of Russia's Chemical Weapons Stockpile," *Chemical Weapons Disarmament in Russia: Problems and Prospects* (Washington, DC: Henry L. Stimson Center, 1995).

54. U.S. Capability to Monitor Compliance with the Chemical Weapons Convention, Senate Select Committee on Intelligence, September 30, 1994.

55. Robert Mikulak, "The Chemical Weapons Convention Preparatory Commission: A First–Year Status Report," *Ratifying the Chemical Weapons Convention*, Brad Roberts, Ed. (Washington, DC: Center for Strategic and International Studies, 1994), pp. 85–92.

56. *The Chemical Weapons Convention: Effects on the U.S. Chemical Industry*, OTA-BP-ISC-106, U.S. Congress, Office of Technology Assessment, August 1993.

57. Amy Smithson, "Chemicals Destruction: The Work Begins," *Bulletin of the Atomic Scientists*, April 1993, pp. 38–43.

58. *Technologies Underlying Weapons of Mass Destruction*, OTA-BP-ISC-115, U.S. Congress, Office of Technology Assessment, December 1993.

59. *Arms Control Reporter*, 1992, p. 701.A.2.

60. Patrick E. Tyler, "Germ War, a Current World Threat, Is a Remembered Nightmare in China," *New York Times*, February 4, 1997.

61. M. Meselson, et al., "The Sverdlovsk Anthrax Outbreak of 1979," *Science*, November 18, 1994, pp. 1202–1208.

62. Christopher S. Wren, "UN Expert Raises Estimates of Iraq's Biological Arsenal," *New York Times*, June 21, 1995, p. A6.

63. Terence Taylor and L. Celeste Johnson, The Biotechnology Industry of the United States: A Census of Facilities, Center for International Security and Arms Control, Stanford University, July 1995.

64. *Sipri Yearbook 1988* (Oxford: Oxford University Press, 1988).

65. Erhard Geissler, Ed., *Strengthening the Biological Weapons Convention by Confidence–Building Measures* (SIPRI Chemical & Biological Warfare Studies, no. 10) (Oxford: Oxford University Press, 1990).

66. Graham S. Pearson, "Forging an Effective Biological Weapons Regime," *Arms Control Today*, June 1994, pp. 14–17.

67. Countering the Chemical and Biological Weapons Threat in the Post–Soviet World, House Armed Services Committee, February 23, 1993.

68. *Threat Control Through Arms Control*, U.S. Arms Control and Disarmament Agency, July 1995.

4

MANAGING ARMS CONTROL

The 1995 Annual Report of the Arms Control and Disarmament Agency lists a total of 75 different treaties, conventions, protocols, minutes, supplementary agreements, memorandums of understanding, agreed statements, and common understandings to which the United States is party [1]. All of these agreements place obligations on the U.S. government: to ensure U.S. implementation and compliance, to verify the compliance of other parties, and to participate in consultations and periodic review conferences to manage and amend the agreements and resolve implementation and compliance questions. The other parties range from a single partner in bilateral agreements (usually Russia) all the way to the more than 130 parties to the Biological Weapons Convention and the 184 parties to the nuclear Nonproliferation Treaty.

The purpose of this chapter is to describe how the United States manages all of these responsibilities. Governments do their work through bureaucracies, and arms control is no exception to this rule. During the Cold War the bureaucratic process of managing arms control evolved into a relatively stable form in which the Intelligence Community, the Departments of State, Defense, and Energy, and the Arms Control and Disarmament Agency played reasonably well-defined roles. The treaties signed and ratified since 1987 have modified and greatly expanded that process but have not changed its essential structure, which is still based on the division of labor among implementation, monitoring, verification, and compliance. This chapter is organized around those tasks and how they are carried out for the treaties discussed in the previous chapter.

For the purposes of this chapter *implementation* will be assumed to include the following activities: collecting information on U.S. activities and communicating it to other parties or to international organizations; destroying, converting, or transferring treaty-limited equipment or facilities; preparing U.S. facilities for inspections by foreign inspection teams as well as escorting those teams during their visits; and reviewing U.S. military activities to ensure that the U.S. remains in full compliance with all of its treaty obligations.

In previous chapters the term "verification" was used to describe the process of gathering information on the activities of other states and evaluating it to establish their compliance or noncompliance. In actual practice the process consists of two separate stages carried out by different groups of agencies. The first stage, usually called *monitoring*, consists in gathering, processing, and analyzing information on the treaty-limited equipment and treaty-relevant activities of other states.[1] The raw data are gathered by a variety of means, including data exchanges and notifications, on-site inspections and surveillance, national technical means, open sources, and human intelligence. Information from these sources is processed and analyzed by the intelligence community to put it into a form usable by policymakers in making compliance judgments.

Verification is the process of determining the compliance of treaty partners based on the results of monitoring and on judgments of their significance in the existing military and political context.[2] Rarely does the monitoring process produce a clear-cut violation, and even when it does, political judgment is still required to decide how and when to respond. Two complementary paths are generally taken if the monitoring process generates ambiguities or suspicions. One goes back to the Intelligence Community with requests for further information. Such requests lead to the "tasking" of intelligence "assets," which are directed at "targets" requiring closer surveillance or more focused inspection. The other path leads to consultations with the suspected party, what I have called the *compliance* process. Consultations usually take place in the consultative body with which each treaty is equipped, but they can also be kicked upstairs to much higher political levels, up to and including the President.

BUREAUCRATIC EVOLUTION

Arms control is a unique kind of diplomacy that combines military, technical, and political dimensions in what former negotiator Jonathan Dean calls "a 'culture' of friendly suspicion" [5]. It attempts to enhance mutual security by eliminating weapons that states have traditionally relied on to preserve their security. It attempts to increase transparency while at the same time protecting the sources and methods of the intelligence community, the secrets of the military establishment, and the proprietary information of private industry. In view of these complex and often contradictory demands, it is not surprising that it has taken a long time for the United States to evolve an effective bureaucratic mechanism for arms control implementation. The first major innovation was the creation of the Arms Control and Disarmament Agency (ACDA) by the Kennedy administration in 1961. For the first 25 years of its life ACDA focused primarily on negotiation of agreements and the education of Congress necessary to gain

---

[1] The monitoring process is primarily an intelligence function, and its stages of "collection, processing, integration, analysis, evaluation and interpretation" are essentially the same as those of the normal intelligence process [2, p. 2].

[2] There is no consensus on the distinction between monitoring and verification. Mark Lowenthal uses "verification" to refer to "the process of making policy decisions" and "monitoring" for "the actual gathering of intelligence" [3, p. 155]. Paula L. Scalingi's definition of monitoring is quite similar to Lowenthal's, but she defines verification as "procedures such as on-site inspections, data exchanges, exhibitions, and other force transparency measures that policymakers incorporate in a treaty to help ascertain or encourage compliance" [4, fn. 6]. This distinction makes good semantic sense, but I will not adopt it here. I will include all forms of information gathering under the rubric of "monitoring" and reserve "verification" for the political evaluation process.

political support for ratification. There was little implementation to be done, and the agency's efforts were directed toward negotiating with the Soviet Union on the SALT process and nuclear testing limits and with the international community on chemical weapons and nuclear nonproliferation. The Non-Proliferation Treaty, which entered into force in 1970 and was renewed and extended indefinitely in 1995, was ACDA's first major success and remains the hallmark of its contribution to arms control.

During the Nixon, Ford, and Carter administrations negotiations were limited to systems that could be monitored with U.S. national technical means. Limits on strategic ballistic missile launchers and ballistic missile defense systems in the SALT negotiations were set by the detection capabilities of U.S. remote sensing devices. Close communication between the Intelligence Community and policymakers was essential and helped determine the organization of the arms control bureaucracy in the Nixon administration. An important innovation was the Verification Panel, created in 1969 under the chairmanship of National Security Advisor Henry Kissinger.[3] Its membership included representatives of both the civilian and uniformed military branches of the Department of Defense: the deputy secretary of defense and the chairman of the Joint Chiefs of Staff. The Director of Central Intelligence (DCI) represented the Intelligence Community. On the diplomatic side were representatives of the State Department (under secretary) and the Arms Control and Disarmament Agency, whose director, Gerard Smith, was also the head of the U.S. SALT delegation. Rounding out the panel was the Attorney General. It is remarkable how stable this structure has remained over time. Except for the Attorney General, membership of the top-level arms control policymaking panel has remained essentially the same. The one major addition has been the Department of Energy, which became involved as negotiations began to include nuclear testing and controls on nuclear materials. Under President Carter the Verification Panel became the Special Coordinating Committee, but it had basically the same structure and functions. Overall direction for the panel was provided by the National Security Council (NSC), and leadership of working groups was exercised by NSC staff.

The Reagan administration made substantial changes in the process, considerably reducing the role of the NSC and decentralizing arms control policymaking to the point where its "organization chart resembled a Jackson Pollock painting" [6, p. 287]. The closest thing under Reagan to the centralized policymaking function of the Verification Panel and Special Coordinating Committee was the Arms Control Verification Committee, which was supposed to assess the verifiability of proposed arms control agreements, but it ended up dealing almost entirely with compliance issues, which came to dominate much of Reagan's approach to arms control during his first term. In the second term, INF and START verification issues were dealt with by the Consolidated Verification Group, whose membership looked more like the Nixon, Ford, and Carter groups.

The Bush administration returned to a structure similar to the one employed by earlier presidents. The top level panel was reconstituted and renamed the Arms Control Policy Coordinating Committee. The Clinton administration has changed the name to Arms Control Interagency Working Group (ACIWG), but

---

[3] The following description of arms control organization during the Nixon, Ford, Carter, and Reagan administrations relies primarily on the work of Michael Krepon [6].

its essential structure and function remained the same (see figure 4.1). The group includes the Departments of Defense (DOD), State (DOS), and Energy (DOE), as well as the Joint Chiefs of Staff (JCS), ACDA, and the Director of Central Intelligence (DCI). Leadership has been returned to the president's national security advisor, and the NSC staff members again chair the interagency working groups dealing with specific issues and treaties.

Implementation of each treaty is supervised by a subcommittee of the ACIWG, and each of these in turn has working groups devoted to equipment and procedures (usually led by DOE or DOD) and backstopping of delegations (led by ACDA). The INF Treaty, for example, has three such working groups. One provides guidance to the Special Verification Commission delegation through a Support Group chaired by ACDA; another (the Equipment and Procedures Working Group chaired by the Undersecretary of Defense for Policy) evaluates on-site inspection equipment and operating procedures; and a third (the Basing Country Working Group chaired by State) deals with U.S. allies on whose territories inspections are conducted. Also directly under the ACIWG is the Verification and Compliance subcommittee, which is supported by a Verification and Compliance Analysis Working Group (VCAWG) chaired by ACDA. The latter group is responsible for preparing the administration's annual report on compliance with arms control agreements. During the Reagan and Bush administrations the report dealt only with Soviet noncompliance, but it has been expanded under the Clinton administration to include all parties to treaties currently in force.

On the same level as the VCAWG is a group that monitors the government's research and development activities for arms control and nonproliferation. For many years it was called the Verification Technology Working Group (VTWG) and was chaired by ACDA. However, it never had sufficient authority to set priorities or direct arms control research, and a 1992 General Accounting Office critique noted that, "individual agencies are making independent judgments as to future research efforts" [7, p. 21]. These included the Departments of Defense, Energy, and State as well as ACDA and the Intelligence Community. Within DOD alone there are at least eight different offices with responsibility for verification technology development [8, p. 5]. In 1995 the old VTWG was replaced by a new Nonproliferation and Arms Control Technology Working Group (NPAC TWG), cochaired by ACDA, DOD, and DOE, with ACDA as Executive Secretary [9, p. 107]. I will return later in the chapter to a more detailed analysis of the verification R&D enterprise.

During the Cold War arms control and nonproliferation were seen as essentially independent activities, and the bureaucratic structure, with the exception of ACDA, reflected that independence. With the end of the U.S.-Soviet competition the focus of U.S. security concerns has shifted from a preoccupation with arms control to a broader emphasis on both arms control and nonproliferation. There is an emerging tendency to see these two activities as different aspects of the same problem, and this tendency is increasingly reflected in bureaucratic and policymaking structures. At the top levels, however, the areas remain separate,

Figure 4.1
Arms Control Policy Process

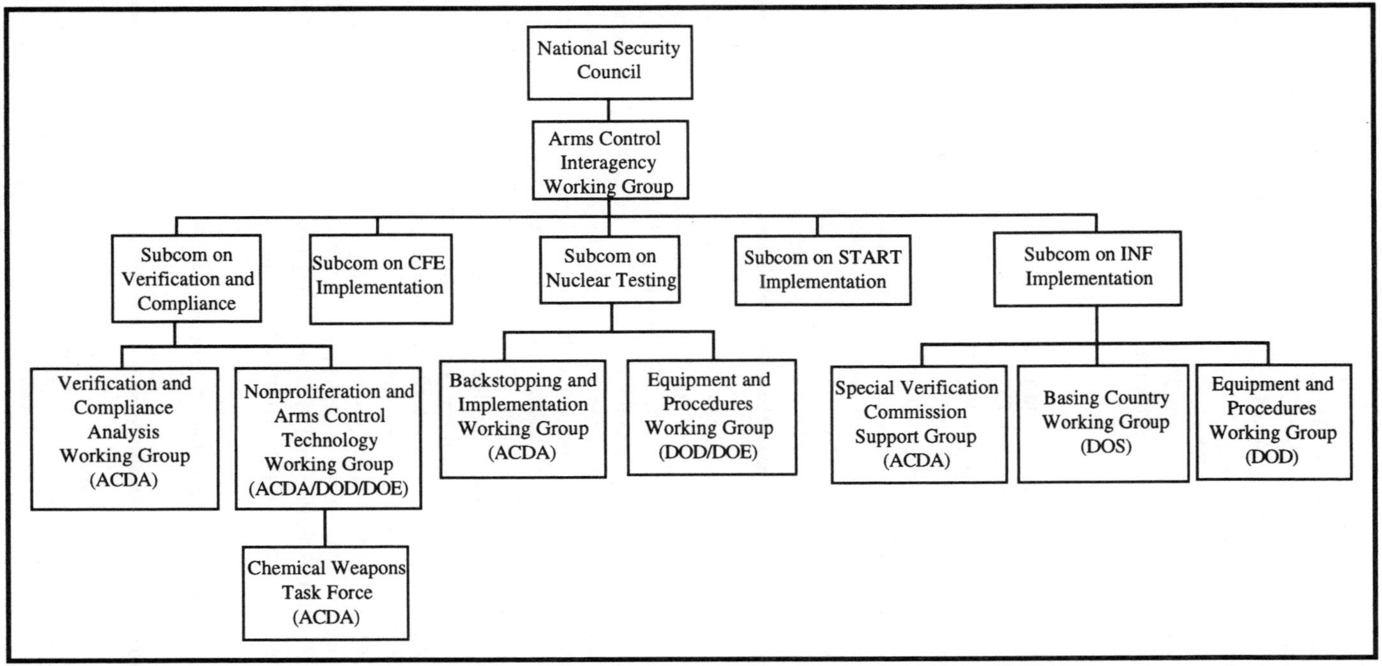

Source: Adapted and updated from ref. 7, p. 14.

and at the NSC level there are separate collections of interagency groups devoted to arms control and nonproliferation. The same actors—DOD, DOS, DOE, ACDA, and the Intelligence Community—participate in nonproliferation policymaking, but there are different emphases and different bureaucratic chains of command. Important examples of this continued separation are the Arms Control Intelligence Staff (ACIS) and the Nonproliferation Center (NPC). Both are based in the Central Intelligence Agency (CIA) but draw their personnel from the entire Intelligence Community. Despite very similar sizes and missions, and despite congressional interest in unifying the two bodies, they remain separate for reasons that are not entirely clear to an outside observer (see below).

IMPLEMENTATION

Implementation of arms control agreements is primarily a job for the executive branch of government, but Congress also plays an essential role. In addition to the constitutional obligation of the Senate to advise and consent to the ratification of treaties, Congress must often pass legislation that enables or legally mandates their implementation. For example, Congress passed a law prohibiting domestic activities in violation of the Biological Weapons Convention and will do the same once the Chemical Weapons Convention is ratified. Congress was also required to pass an amendment to the Arms Export Control Act to enable the United States to transfer (or "cascade") military equipment to NATO allies to comply with the CFE Treaty [10]. Amendment of the 1954 Atomic Energy Act was necessary to permit the exchange of nuclear weapons–related data with Russia in an agreement between the U.S. Department of Energy and Russia's Ministry of Atomic Energy [11]. Congress also appropriates funds for treaty implementation and exercises fiscal oversight of the process. The Cooperative Threat Reduction program was the product of an initiative by Senators Nunn and Lugar, and its success depends on continued congressional support. Appropriations of many billions of dollars over a period of at least ten years will be needed to implement the Chemical Weapons Convention, and to help Russia implement it as well. Oversight is maintained by the foreign relations, armed services, and intelligence committees of both houses. The General Accounting Office and Office of Technology Assessment, both arms of Congress, have also played important roles in monitoring the implementation process and providing technical analyses to support or improve it.[4]

In the executive branch the primary responsibility for carrying out U.S. arms control obligations is in the Department of Defense. It has been there since the Nixon administration and is now administered by the Office of the Under Secretary of Defense for Acquisition and Technology (USD[A&T]).[5] This office

---

[4] Sadly, the Office of Technology Assessment was abolished in the autumn of 1995 by congressional budget cuts. It will be missed, not only by Congress but by independent researchers. Readers of this book may have noticed the large number of references to OTA studies on arms control and nonproliferation issues.

[5] Much of the following discussion is based on an unpublished briefing (dated March 1993) by Lee Minichiello of Science Applications International Corporation, formerly head of the Strategic Arms Control and Compliance office of Strategic and Space Systems. I want to express my gratitude to Mr. Minichiello for providing a copy of the briefing and for several helpful discussions. Also helpful in writing this section was a briefing I received at the On-Site Inspection Agency in December 1994. Thanks to Lt. Col. Brinn Colenda of OSIA for organizing the visit and

Figure 4.2
Defense Department Treaty Management

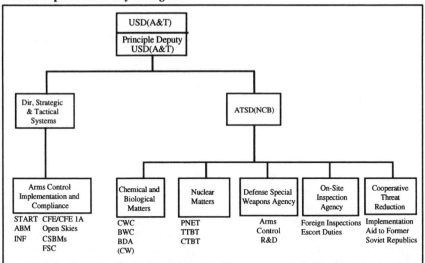

Source: Adapted and updated from Lee Minichiello

creates an interagency working group for each agreement to coordinate DOD implementation activities, and compliance review groups to assess the arms control implications of DOD activities. It also provides technical experts to negotiating delegations and international and interagency meetings dealing with implementation and compliance. Finally, the office directs and oversees research and development in support of implementation and compliance. Just below the level of the Undersecretary and his or her deputy are two offices that have responsibilities for groups of treaties or for specialized tasks (see Figure 4.2) The Office of Strategic and Tactical Systems manages U.S. implementation and compliance for treaties controlling strategic and theater nuclear forces and conventional weapons and forces. The Assistant to the Secretary of Defense for Nuclear and Chemical and Biological Defense Programs (ATSD[NCB]) handles the nuclear testing treaties, the Non-Proliferation Treaty, and the bilateral and international chemical weapons agreements. He or she also supervises the On-Site Inspection Agency and Cooperative Threat Reduction (CTR) Program [12, p. 40]. Funding priorities for CTR are set by an interagency group chaired by the National Security Council [13, p. 6], and the Defense Special Weapons Agency manages the day-to-day supervision of projects in the former Soviet Union [12, p. 40].

When the United States joins the Chemical Weapons Convention and Comprehensive Test Ban, it will create National Authorities to deal with the international implementation organizations associated with the agreements. The CWC National Authority has two components, an interagency policy group

to Director Gregory Govan and Principle Deputy Director Joerg Menzel for their hospitality and cooperation.

chaired by the National Security Council, and an Executive Office located in the Arms Control and Disarmament Agency. The executive office is responsible for liaison with the Organization for the Prevention of Chemical Weapons (OPCW) in the Hague, for data collection and transmission to the OPCW Technical Secretariat, and for administrative support to U.S. implementation activities, which include the destruction operations carried out by the Army (see below) [14, p. 705]. The CTBT National Authority has not been created yet, but it is likely to have a similar structure and functions.

Destroying, Converting, Cascading

Nuclear Weapons

When weapons must be destroyed, it is most efficient to have the service responsible for them do the work. Under SALT and INF the Navy dismantled nuclear missile submarines, the Army destroyed Pershing intermediate range ballistic missiles, and the Air Force took care of strategic bombers and ground-launched cruise missiles. Under START there are no requirements for the United States to destroy any missiles, but a substantial number of launchers, including submarine ballistic missile tubes, ICBM silos, and strategic bombers, will have to be destroyed or converted. The Navy will take care of eliminating submarine launchers, and the Air Force will deal with the missile silos and bombers.

The INF and START treaties contain detailed instructions on how weapons and associated facilities and equipment are to be destroyed and the results either inspected on-site or observed with satellites. For example, U.S. ground-launched cruise missiles from Europe were all destroyed at Davis-Monthan Air Force Base near Tucson, Arizona. After removal of their nuclear warhead, guidance system, and fuel, the wings and stabilizers were cut off and the fuselages were cut in half lengthwise with a large circular power saw, all in the presence of Soviet inspectors. When the U.S. Navy eliminates a Polaris or Poseidon submarine under START, it first removes all of the missiles and leaves the submarine out in the open with all missile-tube hatches up, so that the Russians can photograph it with their satellite cameras. Then, either the entire missile section is removed from the submarine or all the launch tubes and their associated structural components are removed. If the launch tubes are removed, they are sliced into two pieces of roughly equal size and left in the open in the vicinity of the submarine to be observed by Russian satellites. When the elimination is completed, the submarine can be refitted to perform other missions as long as it remains clearly distinguishable from a ballistic missile submarine [15, pp. 32–33].

Nuclear warheads are removed from all missiles and bombers before destruction and can either remain in military custody or be returned to the Department of Energy for storage or dismantlement at the Pantex Plant near Amarillo, Texas [16]. Warhead components are either disposed of or recycled. Tritium gas, used to boost the nuclear reaction in most U.S. weapons, is recycled at the Savannah River Site in South Carolina. Uranium components are returned to the Y-12 plant at Oak Ridge, Tennessee for storage, and plutonium components are stored at Pantex. The question of the ultimate fate of the plutonium from U.S. and Russian nuclear warheads is currently one of the more pressing ones on the arms control agenda. Both the Nunn-Lugar program and the Gore-Chernomyrdin

Commission are working to find effectively verifiable ways of ending the production of weapon-grade plutonium, of managing its safe and secure storage, and ultimately of disposing of it in ways that prevent its recovery for weapons [17].

Conventional Weapons

The United States had much less to do to implement the CFE Treaty than many other parties. In fact, the United States had completed all of its reduction requirements by November 1993, primarily by "cascading" tanks and armored vehicles to its NATO allies. Taking full advantage of this option, the United States transferred 1,993 tanks, 636 armored combat vehicles, and 180 artillery pieces to five NATO allies (Greece, Norway, Portugal, Spain, and Turkey) [18, p. 16]. The only actual destructions were of 639 M-47 tanks, destroyed by the army at a base near Bucino in Italy, and just four M-44 artillery pieces.[6] By the end of the three-year reduction period on November 17, 1995 the United States had reduced its inventories to well below its permitted limits [19].

Chemical Weapons

By far the most daunting implementation challenge facing the United States is the need to destroy more than 30,000 tons of chemical warfare agents and munitions. To accomplish this truly Herculean task the Army plans to build eight incinerators modeled on a demonstration plant on Johnston Island in the Pacific, which has already begun its program of destroying 6.6 percent (about 2,000 tons) of the U.S. stockpile [20]. The remaining inventory of chemical agents declared by the United States is just over 30,000 metric tons distributed over eight sites.[7] The chemicals are contained in rockets, bombs, artillery shells, and a variety of nonweapon metal containers. Their elimination involves considerably more than burning or neutralizing lethal chemical agents. It must also dispose safely of high explosives, rocket propellants, and contaminated metal containers and weapon parts. The Johnston Island facility treats all these components inside a single facility, using remote-controlled mechanical devices to separate each weapon into four separate streams of material, all of which end up being incinerated at high temperatures. Combustion products, consisting mainly of carbon dioxide and water vapor, are released to the atmosphere through filters that remove hazardous compounds. These are dissolved from the filters, solidified as salts, and disposed of in hazardous waste landfills.

The Johnston Island plant experienced a number of problems during its startup. Knowledge gained from solving them has been used to improve the plans for subsequent facilities, and the second one has recently been completed and begun test runs at Tooele Storage Depot, Utah, where 42 percent of the remaining U.S. stockpile is stored. For each of the remaining facilities the army must obtain hazardous waste and air emission permits from the states in which the incinerator is located, and in each of these states powerful opposition has been mounted by environmental groups. Kentucky, Indiana, and Maryland have passed restrictive legislation that would make the approval of incinerators far

---

[6] Thanks to Steven Schieien of the Pentagon's Office of Non-nuclear Arms Control for this information.

[7] This consists of 28,000 agent tons of mustard gas and nerve agents in obsolescent munitions, and 3,200 tons of agents in usable artillery projectiles, spray tanks, and bombs [14, pp. 331–332]. For precise inventories based on declassified army data see *Arms Control Today*, February 1996, p. 34.

more difficult to achieve, and similar legislation is under consideration in other states [21, pp. 29–30]. Concerns about the possibility of harmful releases or catastrophic accidents are legitimate, but it is clearly more dangerous to leave deteriorating chemical weapons sitting where they are. The risks of incineration are considerably lower than the risks of long-term storage [20].

The CW destruction program has been harassed by environmental protests and repeatedly delayed by unforeseen technical and funding problems. For example, in December 1994 the Army confirmed charges by a civilian safety inspector that the Tooele incinerator had experienced some of the same design and operational errors that plagued the Johnston Island plant [22]. According to the Army, the problems could be remedied and would not significantly delay the opening of the Tooele plant. However, by early 1997, almost two years after the scheduled opening date, the Tooele plant was still experiencing serious technical problems, and the future use of incinerators was looking less and less promising [23]. Whatever difficulties the United States is facing pale in comparison with those confronting Russia [24]. Russia's inability to implement the Bilateral Destruction Agreement and its concerns over the costs and domestic politics of chemical weapon disposal are the main reasons for its long delay in ratifying the CWC. Even if both states can at long last bring themselves to ratify the Convention, the most difficult and expensive tasks will have still only begun.

Biological Weapons

The United States undertook unilateral biological disarmament in 1969 when President Nixon renounced the use of biological weapons. The U.S. military was ordered to cease all development work on BW agents and to destroy all existing stockpiles. Political difficulties between the President and Congress led to some delays in implementation of the President's order, but the United States was able to announce on December 16, 1974 that all of its BW agents and toxins had been destroyed except for small laboratory quantities used in research.

Data Exchanges and Notifications

Nothing, with the possible exception of on-site inspections, is more alien to traditional concepts of military secrecy than detailed exchanges of data on weapon inventories or advance notifications of military exercises, weapon movements, or missile test flights. Yet this activity is now a routine part of operations in most European and North American military establishments. It promises to increase even further as the UN Conventional Arms Register expands in membership and the Chemical Weapons Convention and Comprehensive Test Ban enter into force.

Nuclear Weapons

Data on nuclear weapon systems are exchanged under the INF and START treaties via the Nuclear Risk Reduction Center (NRRC) network. The origins of the NRRC lie in the aftermath of the Cuban Missile Crisis, when the "hot line" between Washington and Moscow was created. Its purpose then was to allow communication between national leaderships during a crisis in order to prevent misunderstandings and misperceptions from escalating to nuclear war. The hot line was upgraded several times to include facsimile transmission and other technical improvements and was renamed the NRRC in a 1987 agreement signed only months before the INF Treaty. The original purpose of the NRRC, which used both U.S. and Soviet satellites to transmit facsimile data, was to send notifications of ballistic missile launches and any other communications either party wanted to send "as a display of good will and with a view to building confidence" [25, p. 515]. When the INF Treaty was signed, the NRRC system was designated as the official channel for all data exchanges and notifications required under the treaty [25, p. 530, Article XIII.2]. With the signing of START I in 1991, and its entry into force in 1994, use of the NRRC network was expanded even further. More baseline data, more updates, and many more inspections and other notifications had to be transmitted. Exchanged data also included site plans of bases and photographs of missiles and launchers, for which facsimile capabilities are essential.

The United States installed its NRRC in the State Department, and the Soviet Union placed its station in the Defense Ministry in Moscow. When the Soviet Union fell apart only a few months after the signing of START I, it was necessary to modify the notification arrangements in both INF and START to accommodate the newly independent status of Russia, Ukraine, Belarus, and Kazakhstan, all of which had treaty-limited items on their territories. New terminals were installed in Kiev, Minsk, and Almaty as one of the first projects undertaken by the Nunn-Lugar Program. In the United States each service is responsible for gathering data on its own forces, and the Joint Chiefs of Staff collects and updates U.S. data and provides it to the NRRC.

The CTBT will create an International Monitoring System consisting of four types of sensors deployed at sites all over the world. Data from these sensors will be transmitted to one or more International Data Centers where they will be collected, reduced to some yet to be agreed format, and then transmitted to all states parties for analysis. The data-handling requirements for this system will be substantial. Tens of thousands of events capable of detection by the seismic network alone occur every year, and the analysis of these events will involve the combination of streams of data from dozens of seismographs and seismic detector arrays. How all of this will be done and how the data will be processed and distributed remain to be determined over the next several years by the CTBTO Preparatory Commission meeting in Vienna.

Conventional Weapons

The United States provides conventional weapons data in several venues: to the 29 other parties of the CFE Treaty, to the 51 other members of the Vienna CSBM regime, and to the 19 or more other parties to the Open Skies Treaty (when it enters into force). Many of the parties to these agreements belong to the Packet Switched Data Network coordinated from a center located in the Netherlands. However, a number of parties are not yet connected to the network, so data must be made available in written form. The United States also supplies data on its conventional arms transfers to the United Nations Register of Conventional Arms. ACDA is responsible for communicating data to the UN Office of Disarmament Affairs in New York [26, p. 22]. In the United States the responsibility for collecting and transmitting CFE, CSBM, and Open Skies data and notifications is in the Strategic and Tactical Systems division in the Department of Defense, which uses the computerized Data Management and

Notification System developed by the Defense Special Weapons Agency. The system allows users to generate notifications, pass them up the approval chain, and transmit them to the NRRC for international dissemination [27, p. 28].

Chemical Weapons

All data exchanges under the Wyoming MOU and Bilateral Destruction Agreement are conducted through normal diplomatic channels between the United States and Russia. Data exchanged under these agreements relate primarily to CW stockpiles and production facilities, so the data are gathered and collated by the Army. Other bilateral exchanges take place between groups of experts negotiating the two sides' destruction plans and the design of Russian incinerators [14, p. 695]. When it enters into force, the Chemical Weapons Convention will require an information system capable of storing and processing data on the chemical industries of at least 160 countries. The CWC Preparatory Commission has created a Data System Expert Group, which has been working on an information management system to be installed at the new OPCW offices in the Hague [14, pp. 334–335]. The system has been designed with the help of national data bases supplied by Iran, Russia, Finland, and the United Kingdom, as well as by the United States. In the United States the Executive Office of the National Authority, under ACDA, will be responsible for collating and transmitting data and notifications on the activities of U.S. chemical plants [9, p. 24].

The Commerce Department's Bureau of Export Administration (BXA) has been given the responsibility for gathering data on both scheduled and nonscheduled chemicals from U.S. industry and putting the data into a form suitable for reporting to the U.S. National Authority. The paperwork and data management will be a demanding task. The chemical industry already reports extensively to other government bodies, such as the Environmental Protection Agency, the Occupational Safety and Health Administration, and the Department of Commerce. Existing channels of reporting will be used as much as possible for the CWC, but its requirements are different in important ways from traditional reporting requirements. There are at least 300 facilities in the United States that produce, handle, or store scheduled chemicals and as many as 6,000 that deal with unscheduled, but still reportable, chemicals [28]. BXA received an extra appropriation of $3.4 million to allow it to hire 24 more staff members to deal with this flow of information. The regulations that specify the rights and obligations of industry fill 600 pages and must be reworked to make them more "user-friendly." Even in the United States, which has great administrative and technical advantages over most other countries, it is likely to be several years before the process produces a smooth and reliable flow of data. In other countries, especially in those like Russia with large chemical industries and weak central administrations, it could be significantly longer.

Biological Weapons

Under the Tripartite Agreement the United States, United Kingdom, and Russia have agreed to exchange information on their biological R&D activities, including those with military implications [29]. However, none of the information is made public, and press reports suggest that Russia is not being as forthcoming as it might be [30]. There are no requirements for data exchanges or notifications under the BWC, but a number of proposals are under study by the Ad

Hoc Group designing the new verification regime [31]. A system of notifications does exist under the confidence-building measures created by the Second and Third Review Conferences (see chapter 3). Data gathered by states parties are submitted to the United Nations Department for Disarmament Affairs, but there is no organization specifically designated to receive, collate and disseminate this information to other parties. Signatories to the BWC have not been able to agree on the funding for such an organization [32].

Parties to the BWC are also required to report unusual outbreaks of infectious diseases, and through 1988 the United States had reported a number of them, including, among others, anthrax, dengue fever, eastern and western encephalitis, plague, and Q fever. Such data are routinely collected by the Centers for Disease Control, so there is little extra effort required to supply them to the UN. Significantly more detailed and revealing data exchanges are being contemplated for the future verification regime, but until these become clearly defined it is not possible to predict the demands on the United States for information or how those demands will be met.

Data Management

The vast quantities of data transmitted to the United States under all these agreements are collected and stored by ACDA in the Arms Control Community On-line Repository of Treaty Data (ACCORD) data base [9]. Established in 1993, ACCORD is used to collect data and notifications transmitted over the NRRC and other channels, as well as on-site inspection reports. The system already includes data on INF, CFE, CSBM, START, and the UN Conventional Arms Register. Open Skies, CWC, and presumably CTBT will be added as they enter into force. ACCORD has both classified and unclassified versions for use by agencies with implementation or verification responsibilities. It goes without saying that the data base is also available to the Intelligence Community, primarily the Arms Control Intelligence Staff and Nonproliferation Center, which use it as part of the all-source analysis process and for tasking monitoring assets.

Hosting Inspections

Quotas

There are presently five agreements in force which require the United States to accept on-site inspections (INF, CFE, CSBM, START, and CWC), both on its own territory and on the territory of allies where it maintains bases. Under the INF Treaty inspections were conducted between July 1988 and June 1991 at 21 missile sites and missile-related facilities in the United States, United Kingdom, Germany, Italy, Netherlands, and Belgium [33]. The Soviet Union set up a continuous portal monitoring station at Hercules Plant No. 1 in Magna, Utah, and current plans are for the Russian government to continue to operate that station until May 2001. Russia also conducts 15 short-notice inspections per year at 21 former INF sites.[8] The quota will decrease to ten per year between 1996 and the treaty's expiration in 2001. By June 1, 1995 the INF Treaty had

---

[8] The role of Ukraine and Belarus in the INF inspection process had still not been fully clarified as of this writing.

been in force for seven full years and there had been a total of 569 inspections conducted at United States bases and facilities in Europe and the United States.[9]

When the CFE Treaty entered into force in July 1992, the United States had declared 169 Objects of Verification (OOV), all located at declared sites on the territories of NATO allies. By the end of 1994 more than 100 OOV had been eliminated, leaving just 61 remaining at only 37 declared sites. The total number of passive CFE inspections hosted by the United States as of August 15, 1995 was only 55, which includes both routine and challenge inspections. One reason the number was so small is that the states of the former Warsaw Pact conducted only 50 percent of their allotted number of inspections. In contrast, the NATO states conducted close to their full quotas of inspections of former Warsaw Pact sites, with the United States participating in a large fraction of them [18, p. 4]. CSBM inspections are far less frequent than those for CFE; no state party is required to accept more than three of them per year. Through June 1, 1995 only five had been hosted by the United States.

The START I Treaty entered into force on December 5, 1994, and inspections began in March 1995. The treaty permits 12 kinds of on-site inspections, and the United States will be subjected to 11 of them.[10] Some of these involve yearly quotas while others depend on the schedule of elimination of launchers and closeout of facilities. Baseline data, update data, suspect site, and new facility inspections are lumped together in a single category for which there is a quota of 15 on-site inspections per year for each side. Two other quotas are a maximum of 10 reentry vehicle inspections and three formerly declared facility inspections per year. The total of quota inspections in the United States is therefore 28 per year. Added to this will be inspections associated with conversion or elimination of launchers and closeout of facilities and exhibitions at which the technical characteristics or distinguishing features of individual weapons are verified. This suggests that somewhere between 30 and 40 inspections per year will be conducted on U.S. territory during the lifetime of the START treaty. START II will not change this picture in any significant way, since it mainly just deepens the cuts mandated in START I. The first START inspection on U.S. territory took place on March 6, 1995 at Malmstrom Air Force Base near Great Falls, Montana [34]. In the next four months a total of 37 START inspections and 19 early exhibitions of treaty limited equipment were hosted by the United States.

If and when the Chemical Weapons Convention enters into force, the inspection burden on the United States will increase substantially.[11] Every chemical plant that produces, processes, or consumes more than a threshold quantity of Schedule 2 chemicals is subject to a maximum of two routine inspections per year, and there are between 200 and 300 such plants in the United States [35, p.

---

[9] Personal communication, Joseph P. Harahan, OSIA Historian. The author is grateful to Dr. Harahan for providing updated numbers for all types of inspections conducted by or on the United States through the summer of 1995. Each of the totals given in subsequent paragraphs of this section and in the following section on monitoring has been supplied by Dr. Harahan.

[10] The United States has no deployed mobile ICBMs, so it is not subject to inspections that are permitted after dispersal exercises involving such missiles. Russia has also decided not to exercise its right to conduct CPPM at the Thiokol plant in Promontory, Utah.

[11] The Wyoming MOU had generated five inspections on U.S. territory as of the end of 1994 (see chapter 3), and the Bilateral Destruction Agreement was supposed to have produced many more. But at the end of 1996 the BDA had still not entered into force, and the U.S.-Russian CW inspection process remained stalled.

15]. At least 11,000 other plants produce more than threshold quantities of Schedule 3 chemicals or more than threshold quantities of discrete organic chemicals (see chapter 3 for definitions). These two groups are lumped together in the Convention's Verification Annex, and a quota of 20 inspections per year applies to the entire group. In principle, there could be hundreds of inspections per year at U.S. chemical plants, including an unpredictable but probably relatively small number of challenge inspections.

The real situation will not be as onerous as these numbers suggest. The OPCW will be limited by finances, personnel, and technical capability to a far smaller number of inspections per year. The Technical Secretariat will be responsible for inspecting tens of thousands of facilities all over the world and will not be able to approach the nominal quotas in any single country without incurring charges of unfairness. Inspections of civilian chemical plants will be phased in slowly and will not be up to a steady state until approximately ten years after entry into force. ACDA has estimated that U.S. industry will receive 53 routine inspections per year (40 at Schedule 1 and 2 sites and 13 at Schedule 3 sites), assuming that all Schedule 1 and 2 sites are inspected once in the first three years of the treaty [36, p. 47].

Escort Responsibilities

Inspections of U.S. facilities under all the above agreements follow a similar pattern. The inspecting party notifies the United States of its intention to conduct an inspection and of the time and port of entry at which its team will arrive. The team is met by an American escort team from the On-Site Inspection Agency to whom it announces the specific site it wants to visit. The escorts must then get them there within a fixed time limit—nine hours in INF, START, and CFE and 12 in CWC. U.S. points of entry for INF and START are at Washington's Dulles Airport and Travis Air Force Base near San Francisco. Transportation to the inspection sites is in aircraft supplied and flown by the Air Force Military Airlift Command [33, p. 61]. INF inspection teams can have up to ten members and CFE nine. Baseline, data update, and new facility inspection teams under START can have ten members, and teams for technical and distinguishability exhibitions up to 15. The CWC does not contain any specified limits on inspection teams. Chemical plants vary so widely in size and complexity that it would not make sense to set a specific limit.

Once the team is at the site, a typical inspection will include an initial briefing, the actual inspection, and a period for filling out, signing, and copying reports. Throughout the process the inspection team is accompanied by the escort team. OSIA is responsible for all of the logistical support for visiting inspection teams, and the visitors must be provided at all times with the means to contact their embassy or consulate in the United States or in whatever country the inspection is being conducted. Inspections on U.S. bases in Europe require the cooperation of the government and military of that state, and these arrangements are also the responsibility of OSIA. One of OSIA's deputy directors is a State Department official, primarily because of these requirements for communication with foreign governments. An important part of OSIA's responsibility is the provision of trained linguists for the escort teams as well as for its own inspection teams. In some cases the demand has exceeded OSIA's supply, and independent contractors have been called on to provide extra linguists [37, p. 41].

The Hercules plant at Magna is the only U.S. facility subjected to continuous portal monitoring. A team of 30 Russian monitors is permanently on duty at the only gate in the completely fenced perimeter of the plant. The Russian inspectors live in a specially constructed apartment complex in West Jordan, Utah, about eight miles from the plant. The apartment complex, which includes a clubhouse, spa, swimming pool, and tennis courts, was built in 1989 at a cost of $1.6 million, paid by the Soviet Union [33, pp. 88–90].

Counterintelligence

Last, but far from least, among the tasks associated with hosting inspections is counterintelligence. From the beginning it has been assumed that foreign inspection teams would include agents whose mission was to try to obtain information beyond what is legitimately required to verify the treaty. The importance attached to this problem is perhaps best seen in the leadership of the OSIA, where one of the three deputy directors is provided by the Federal Bureau of Investigation (FBI) and is in charge of counterintelligence operations. Lists of proposed inspectors are vetted by the CIA and FBI, and the United States is free to reject inspectors it doesn't approve of. While inspection teams are on U.S. bases or on U.S. territory they are monitored carefully by the FBI and generally kept well isolated from contacts with anyone besides those directly involved in the inspection process [38, pp. 6–7].

A major aspect of the counterintelligence process is the preparation of sites for inspection. Since most inspections take place on short notice, there is little time for base commanders or plant operators to take precautions to protect secret equipment and activities not covered by the treaty and therefore not legitimately subject to inspection. Much of this preparation must be done before the treaty enters into force, so that when inspections are demanded the facility can be gotten ready quickly. It is assumed that foreign inspection teams will include well-trained intelligence agents, so the preparations can be complex and expensive. Important activities may have to be postponed, transferred, or carried on under cover. Preparations are difficult enough at military bases and at weapons plants operated by government contractors; they could turn out to be even more difficult and inconvenient at private chemical plants and other commercial facilities subject to inspection under the Chemical Weapons Convention.

The counterintelligence task is taken especially seriously at West Jordan and Magna, Utah, where the presence of Russian nationals is the third largest on U.S. territory [37, p. 42]. Thirteen officers were added to the West Jordan police force, and extra FBI agents conduct continuous counterintelligence work. A private contractor has been hired to provide escort services for the Russian inspectors, who must be accompanied everywhere they go. They are allowed limited travel privileges within a 50-kilometer radius, and they often attend public events in the area. Visits to private homes are not permitted, however [33, p. 82].

MONITORING

Monitoring of arms control agreements originated as a pure intelligence activity under the control of intelligence agencies. It has been defined as "the collection, processing, exploitation, analysis, and reporting of information on foreign activities in relation to arms control" [39]. For most of the pre-Gorbachev era the techniques employed were those of the classical intelligence craft, supplemented by the remarkable technical means that emerged during the Cold War. Traditional methods included analysis of military and scientific publications, monitoring of civilian, military, and diplomatic communications, keeping track of the movements and career patterns of military and political leaders, and recruiting agents, defectors, and informers in the target country. The new national technical means (NTM) included satellite imaging in the visible, infrared, and microwave spectral bands, full-spectrum communications and signals monitoring combined with computerized code breaking, networks of seismic, acoustic, and radiation detectors, and a wide variety of other sophisticated sensors and analytical tools for observing the activities of both friends and rivals.

All of these measures are unilateral; they are conducted by a single state, and the information is usually among the state's most sensitive secrets, as are the capabilities and limitations of the techniques themselves. Protecting these "sources and methods" is one of the primary functions of any intelligence community, and the technical capabilities and modes of operation of U.S. sensors are treated with the same sensitivity as the identities of its secret agents and the keys to its secret codes. Information obtained from NTM is often shared with allies, and even with adversaries when it serves a higher political purpose. But the information is usually "sanitized" (much as illegally obtained money is "laundered") to conceal the sources and analytical methods that produced it.

Since the mid-1980s these unilateral methods have been supplemented by a steadily increasing number of "cooperative measures," which in many ways are the direct opposite of traditional intelligence techniques. Cooperative measures include exchanges of data on weapons characteristics, inventories, and deployment patterns; advance notification of and invitations to observe maneuvers and exercises; and on-site inspections of military bases and production or testing facilities. A new word—"transparency"—has been adopted to encompass these new means of exchanging information, and the goal of greater transparency in military affairs has become a major component, if not the very essence, of recent and pending arms control agreements.

The range of monitoring techniques does not form a spectrum so much as a bimodal distribution. The distinction between national technical means and cooperative measures remains distinct and is recognized, either explicitly or implicitly, in all treaties. The information from the two types of sources is collected and handled in different ways and in many cases by different agencies, reflecting the differing objectives of the monitoring effort. Cooperative measures are intended to support arms control agreements, and any intelligence benefit they provide to strategic and tactical missions, while undoubtedly useful, is incidental. On the other hand, the primary mission of NTM is, and always has been, the gathering of strategic and tactical intelligence. Arms control monitoring has been a collateral benefit of this mission, and intelligence support to arms control has been an often awkward "marriage of convenience" into which the Intelligence Community entered with considerable reluctance [40]. The focus of this section is on how the two monitoring efforts—the unilateral/secret and the cooperative/transparent—are organized to inform the arms control verification process.

Policy direction for the overall foreign intelligence effort is provided by the President's National Foreign Intelligence Board (NFIB), which advises the Director of Central Intelligence on the collection, processing, production, review, and coordination of intelligence [3, p. 111]. The responsibilities of the NFIB include reviewing and coordinating national intelligence products and providing operational guidance for intelligence collection systems. Its members include representatives of all agencies with intelligence functions, as well as the directors of the National Reconnaissance Office and National Security Agency (see below) [2, p. 399]. It is at this level that decisions must be made on how the overall intelligence effort is divided among imagery, signals, human, and other forms of acquisition. The NFIB carries out its responsibilities through a number of committees responsible for different types of collection.

National Technical Means

NTM gather information by a process known as "remote sensing," which relies on the ability to detect signals that propagate over long distances. Remote sensing techniques fall into three major categories [41]:

- Imaging sensors use visible light, infrared radiation, and radar waves to form images of the target. These sensors are generally carried on aircraft or satellite platforms that can pass over the target at altitudes ranging from hundreds of meters to hundreds of kilometers.
- Signals and communications sensors detect signals in the radio frequency bands used by radar and most communications systems, such as radio, television, and telephone. Signals sensors are also carried by satellites and aircraft, but they can use fixed and mobile land- and sea-based antennas as well.
- Nuclear explosion detectors exploit a number of forms of radiation, including electromagnetic pulse, visible and ultraviolet light, gamma ray and neutron radiation, and seismic and acoustic waves that travel through the earth, air, or water. Nuclear explosion sensors use a variety of platforms, including satellites, aircraft, land-based seismic networks, and acoustic detectors deployed by the thousands on the ocean floor.

The organization of the U.S. technical intelligence effort reflects this tripartite division of sensors and targets. The acquisition, processing, and analysis of imagery, signals, and nuclear explosion data are conducted by separate agencies with different bureaucratic chains of command and reporting. Since these systems are used for many purposes, including strategic intelligence, threat assessment, and tactical operations, as well as arms control, their tasking must be managed through an interagency process. The bureaucratic structure of this process is thoroughly described by Jeffrey Richelson, on whose work much of this section relies [2]. The application of NTM to arms control is coordinated by the Arms Control Intelligence Staff (ACIS) under the Director of Central Intelligence (DCI). ACIS has several responsibilities relevant to the monitoring of arms control agreements: advising on collection tasking, supporting the treaty inspection process through advising of sites to be inspected, coordinating monitoring and inspection activities, and advising on counterintelligence matters [4]. National technical means are also increasingly employed in support of U.S. nonproliferation efforts. This process is managed by the Nonproliferation Center (NPC), which is also located in the DCI's office. NPC has responsibilities for nonproliferation intelligence similar to those ACIS has for arms control.

Imagery Intelligence

Since the early 1960s most arms control imagery has been obtained from satellites, except for the U-2 and SR-71 aircraft used during the 1950s and 1960s to photograph military installations in the Soviet Union and other countries. It was U-2 aircraft that confirmed the absence of a "missile gap" and discovered Soviet missile installations in Cuba during the Kennedy administration, and SR-71s were able to fly missions over Warsaw Pact territory even after the U-2 became vulnerable to Soviet antiaircraft missiles. However, it is unlikely that this kind of reconnaissance will contribute much to future arms control monitoring, even if a successor aircraft is developed. Satellite capabilities have improved enormously in the past two decades, and they are cheaper and less politically risky to operate than aircraft.

U.S. management of imagery intelligence separates the satellites from the images they produce: satellites are designed, developed, deployed, and operated by one set of organizations, while images are collected, processed, distributed, and interpreted by another. The overall effort is supervised by a committee in the National Imagery and Mapping Agency (NIMA). Below this level there are separate lines of authority for the two different functions. Satellites are managed by the National Reconnaissance Office (NRO), located in the Office of the Secretary of the Air Force in the Department of Defense. The NRO deploys the satellites, turns them on and off, and points them at targets chosen by NIMA in response to priorities set by the National Foreign Intelligence Board [2, p. 29]. The numbers and characteristics of U.S. satellites are classified, but the current constellation is reported to include two advanced optical and infrared imaging satellites, two radar imaging satellites, and a number of ocean surveillance satellites operated by the naval component of NRO [42]. They represent a production capability of several thousand images a day, at least ten times as large as it was when negotiations began on the START Treaty in 1985. Just what fraction of this capability is necessary to monitor arms control agreements is impossible to estimate with any precision, but it is probably quite small. Ten percent of several thousand images per day is several hundred images per day, and this would seem to be more than ample for arms control and nonproliferation monitoring.

The thousands of images generated by the satellite constellation are ordered, collected, and distributed by NIMA, which "addresses the full imagery cycle— tasking, collection, processing, exploitation, production and delivery under all situations from peace through crisis to open conflict" [43, pp. 30–31]. The key word in this list is "tasking," which is the allocation of satellite time to the collection of images. It is in the tasking decisions that priorities are implemented, and it is these decisions that will determine how much satellite time is devoted to arms control monitoring and how much to other tasks.

There has always been competition between the CIA's demand for national or strategic intelligence and the military's demand for tactical and early warning intelligence [2, pp. 473–474]. Arms control and nonproliferation monitoring fall under the former category, and if trends toward greater emphasis on tactical intelligence continue, satellites will spend more of their time photographing tank or missile deployments in potential battle zones like Iraq, Iran, or North Korea and less photographing and missile silos and military deployments in Europe and the former Soviet Union. This will put greater pressure on on-site inspections to monitor compliance with existing treaties. On-site inspections are labor intensive, time consuming, and less flexible than overhead reconnaissance, so if they are not supplemented by sufficient satellite monitoring, some degree of confidence could be lost in the verification process. At the same time, if it is true that arms control and nonproliferation monitoring require only 10 percent or less of existing imaging capability, it would not appear that they pose a serious threat to tactical coverage.

The images collected by NIMA are distributed to a wide variety of agencies for detailed analysis and interpretation. Sophisticated techniques exist for enhancing and interpreting digitized images, and the Intelligence Community and military services will be able to exploit these techniques for their own individual purposes [2, pp. 162–164]. The CIA is responsible for analyzing imagery for arms control, and most of this work is done at the National Photographic Interpretation Center, which employs several thousand photo-interpreters at its facility in the Washington Navy Yard [2, p. 20]. Interpreters are highly skilled at identifying particular types of equipment, deployments, or activities and are responsible for analyzing images to see if they expose anything inconsistent with expectations based on treaty requirements.

Signals Intelligence (SIGINT)

U.S. SIGINT activities are conducted in every environment: from the ocean floor (where telephone cables are tapped by specially equipped submarines), to 22,000 miles out in space (where missile telemetry and radio communications are intercepted by football-field-size antennas), and everywhere in between [2, pp. 171–202]. Receiving antennas are deployed in friendly countries and on ships and submarines all over the world, and SIGINT missions are routinely flown by a variety of specialized aircraft. It was Soviet suspicions that they were seeing such a mission that led them to shoot down an off-course Korean airliner over the Sea of Okhotsk in 1983. The SIGINT space constellation (operated by the National Reconnaissance Office) includes small, low-altitude satellites called "ferrets," satellites in highly elliptical orbits that allow them to spend more time over certain areas of the globe, and geosynchronous satellites that remain permanently stationed 22,000 miles above a chosen location on the equator. Despite their long distance from the Earth's surface these satellites are reported to be able to detect even relatively weak radio signals, such as those used for battlefield communication [42].

Management of the U.S. SIGINT System is the responsibility of the National Security Agency (NSA) based at Fort Meade, Maryland. The agency is estimated to employ about 100,000 people and have an annual budget of $3.5 billion dollars [2, 44]. The NSA (like NIMA for imagery) does not produce finished intelligence but manages the collection and distribution of raw intelligence for a wide variety of consumers with different missions.[12] It has two primary responsibilities: monitoring, collecting, and decrypting foreign signals, and protecting U.S. signals from foreign collection and decryption. Since the latter function has little relevance to arms control, no more will be said about it here.

---

[12] One activity that might be considered SIGINT is the planting of listening devices or telephone taps to monitor conversations or meetings. This is widely practiced but is not managed by NSA. It is handled by the CIA's Directorate of Science and Technology [45, p. 257].

SIGINT is usually broken down into two major subcategories: COMINT is the interception of foreign communications and ELINT is the collection of all other kinds of electronic emissions, such as telemetry, radars, and control systems [2, pp. 171–173]. COMINT is especially important for arms control and nonproliferation, and great effort is expended on listening to, decoding, and analyzing traffic patterns in the military and civilian communications of other states. Because of the tremendous volume of such communications in the modern world, targets must be chosen carefully and sophisticated analytical resources applied to them to obtain a useful product. Just as with imagery, arms control and nonproliferation monitoring have to compete for tasking assignments with the many other intelligence missions NSA performs.

Nuclear Detection

Responsibility for monitoring the production and testing of nuclear weapons lies with the Air Force Technical Applications Center (AFTAC), which employs about 1,200 people and is based at Patrick Air Force Base in Florida. AFTAC operates the U.S. Atomic Energy Detection System, a worldwide system of seismographs, radiation detectors, hydroacoustic monitors, and other sensors that are deployed in more than 35 countries as well as in the oceans, on aircraft, and in space [2, p. 91]. AFTAC operates independently of other Air Force intelligence offices and has traditionally been focused almost entirely on following the development of Soviet nuclear weapons. However, its sensor network covers the entire globe, which enables it to monitor the nuclear activities of all other countries as well. It was an AFTAC satellite that detected what many believe to have been a clandestine nuclear test (often attributed to Israel and/or South Africa) in the South Atlantic Ocean in 1979 [46, pp. 271–283], and it was AFTAC radiation monitors that tracked the fallout from the Chernobyl accident in 1986.

Until the 1980s AFTAC used satellites designed exclusively to detect nuclear explosions in the atmosphere or in space. Since then, nuclear explosion detectors have piggybacked on satellites deployed for other purposes. One set of detectors rides on the Defense Support Program early warning satellites, deployed in geosynchronous orbits to detect the launches of ballistic missiles. The constellation of 24 Global Positioning Satellites (GPS), made famous in the 1991 Gulf War for their role in allowing Allied ground forces and precision guided weapons to navigate with great accuracy, also carries a suite of nuclear explosion detectors. The GPS constellation is designed so that every point on the surface of the earth is in line of sight from at least four satellites at any instant, so worldwide coverage is continuous. Other U.S. satellites, possibly communications or weather satellites, may also carry nuclear detection sensors [2, pp. 221–233].

Underground nuclear tests are monitored by detecting the seismic waves they generate, which propagate through the volume and over the surface of the earth. The AFTAC network of seismographs is distributed throughout the world, with each site having a full range of detection and analytical capabilities [2, pp. 228–229]. There are also many non–AFTAC facilities located at universities and scientific institutes that employ arrays of seismometers capable of detecting and locating underground nuclear explosions in many parts of the world. Still others can detect the very low frequency acoustic waves (infrasound) produced in the atmosphere by nuclear tests, and another group can detect nuclear radiation that may escape from underground tests. Portions of the AFTAC ground-based network will be incorporated into the International Monitoring System created to monitor the Comprehensive Test Ban. Data collected by these stations will no longer be classified but will be shared with all other parties to the treaty once it enters into force.

Data generated by AFTAC is not finished intelligence but must be correlated with other data and analyzed by other agencies. The two most important of these for arms control are the Department of Energy (DOE) and the CIA. From its experience in testing U.S. nuclear weapons DOE has the expertise necessary to interpret the data from AFTAC sources. Its Office of Nonproliferation and National Security manages intelligence activities dealing with nuclear weapons and nuclear proliferation [2, pp. 131–132]. DOE is represented on the National Foreign Intelligence Board by the assistant secretary for defense programs, who is also the senior intelligence officer in the department [3, pp. 136–137].

Human Intelligence (HUMINT)

The revolution in intelligence collection brought about by national technical means has fundamentally altered the monitoring of arms control agreements. The budget of the intelligence community is dominated by the costs of procuring, maintaining, and operating NTM and of processing and analyzing the vast quantities of data they generate. These systems provided the foundation for the first steps in U.S.-Soviet arms control, and they will continue to play a critical role in the monitoring of future treaties. But they can never be the whole story, and traditional forms of intelligence gathering by human beings (aided by still other exotic technologies) continue to be essential to a successful intelligence and monitoring capability.

The primary locus of human intelligence efforts is in the Directorate of Operations of the CIA, which is most famous (or infamous) for its management of covert political and military operations, but which also manages all forms of covert intelligence gathering by human agents, defectors, émigrés, and travelers [2, p. 245]. Virtually every U.S. embassy and consulate includes a CIA station, and CIA efforts to recruit agents and informers in foreign countries are periodically exposed to public view. The case of Aldrich Ames is remarkable for many reasons, but one of the more remarkable was that he ran (and betrayed) more than a dozen agents inside the Soviet Union and later in Russia. Similar operations exist in many countries, both friendly and unfriendly, as evidenced by the expulsion of five U.S. nationals from France in February 1995 for alleged espionage activities [47]. The information provided by such agents, while not usually intended to help verify arms control agreements, provides a valuable complement to and synergism with NTM-based intelligence.

Other agencies besides CIA also conduct HUMINT operations. All the military services assign attachés to U.S. embassies, and the State Department, Department of Energy, and Commerce Department, among others, use human sources to carry out their intelligence missions [2]. Occasionally these efforts are exposed to public view as illustrated by two incidents in the summer of 1995. Two U.S. Air Force officers were caught photographing and videotaping military activities in China, arrested, and then released. A U.S. official acknowledged that the officers were spying, with the offhand comment, "This is what defense attachés do" [48]. In the second incident an Army officer was arrested near the Russian "nuclear city" of Krasnoyarsk-26, one of the many secret cities created by the Soviet Union's nuclear weapon program. He was allegedly caught using "high-precision locating equipment" (presumably a Global Positioning System receiver) and was sent home by Russian authorities [49].

HUMINT has been particularly important in monitoring Russian biological warfare activities. The 1979 anthrax epidemic in Sverdlovsk was exposed by several "eminently credible" witnesses present in the city at the time of the outbreak [50]. This information strengthened U.S. suspicions that a particular military facility in Sverdlovsk was engaged in BW research and production. It was another human source, the émigré scientist Vladimir Pasechnik, who blew the whistle on the St. Petersburg Institute for Ultrapure Biological Preparations, where he had been Director before he defected to Great Britain. Yet another Russian defector told American intelligence that BW development was continuing at the same facility even after President Yeltsin ordered it stopped [14, p. 717].

These incidents highlight an important point about the relative usefulness of NTM and HUMINT. When nuclear weapons and their delivery systems are the target, NTM can provide a great deal of the information necessary to monitor their production, testing, and deployment. HUMINT is more important for detecting incipient nuclear weapons programs, as it did in Iraq when a defecting engineer alerted UNSCOM to the previously unsuspected use of electromagnetic isotope separation techniques for enriching uranium [51]. HUMINT may also have played a role in exposing North Korean efforts to disguise their plutonium separation activity. The International Atomic Energy Agency had become suspicious of North Korean declarations on the basis of measurements on samples of plutonium and waste obtained in an inspection in May 1992. But, according to David Albright, "intelligence agencies provided the IAEA with other information that further increased its suspicions that the North separated significantly more plutonium than it had declared" [52]. It is conceivable that this was NTM information but much more likely that it was HUMINT.

Open Sources

Some of the most important sources of arms control intelligence are not secret at all, but published or broadcast openly. These are called "open sources" by the Intelligence Community, which monitors them for economic, scientific, and diplomatic as well as for military purposes [2, pp. 261–265]. During the Cold War the major focus of the monitoring effort in the CIA and Defense Intelligence Agency (DIA) was Soviet military and technical publications, as well as radio and television broadcasts and the public speeches of prominent political figures. The Foreign Broadcast Information Service (FBIS) is a CIA activity located in the Directorate of Science and Technology. It now routinely monitors about 800 hours of television each week from over 50 countries in 29 languages [2, p. 264].

Open source information is likely to become increasingly important in arms control and nonproliferation monitoring. According to an early Director of Central Intelligence, open source information accounted for 80 percent of the overall intelligence effort in 1948, and it is reasonable to assume that it still makes a major contribution today [2, p. 262]. Open source information can also be useful in building a public case for treaty violations or proliferation threats originally discovered by secret sources and methods [53, p. 48]. With the end of the Cold War, the use of open source material has changed both quantitatively and qualitatively, and the Intelligence Community has responded by reorganizing the effort. The CIA created a new office, called the Community Open-Source Program Office, to supplement its shrinking HUMINT operations [54, pp. 41–42]. Hundreds of thousands of documents, both scientific and otherwise, are stored in CIA and DIA data banks and can be scanned with key word searches to facilitate research on specific topics.

There are other open sources that can be extremely useful to a government official with the right kinds of contacts and inquiring spirit. Frank von Hippel, a long-time public interest scientist and during 1993–1994 an Assistant Director for National Security in the White House Office of Science and Technology Policy, struggled to find solutions to the problem of post-Soviet control over retired nuclear weapons and fissile materials. He found that to answer many of his questions it was necessary "to visit the places of concern and talk with the people who live and work there." According to von Hippel, "the intelligence community is typically the last to be able [to] visit such places and to have open discussions." In his White House experience he had access to most of the classified analyses the intelligence community produced on post-Soviet nuclear affairs, but "I usually found it far more efficient to turn to my public interest and journalist friends for information" [55, p. 8].

With the advent of a more open political process and a relatively free press in Russia, political and environmental activism, government whistle blowing, and investigative journalism will play increasingly important roles. This can provide useful information and context to fill out the picture drawn by secret intelligence. Indeed, such information can in many instances be more credible and reliable than clandestine intelligence, which can be corrupted by planted disinformation or double agents. It remains to be seen, however, whether a U.S. intelligence culture weaned on deep cover and dirty tricks can learn to rely more consistently on what can be seen in broad daylight.

On-site Inspections

From its tentative beginning in 1986, on-site inspection has emerged as a major component of arms control monitoring. The United States demanded on-site inspections in a variety of negotiating forums for most of the Cold War, but in all that time U.S. policymakers had given little thought to how such inspections would be implemented. It was not until two weeks before signing the INF Treaty that the Reagan administration gave the first oral directives to create an On-Site Inspection Agency (OSIA) and not until more than a month after the signing that a formal directive creating the agency was issued [56]. Eleven days after that, on January 26, 1988, OSIA was established as a separate agency in the Department of Defense. Its first Director, General Roland Lajoie, took charge on February 1, and one week later the first 40 personnel reported for duty. Entry into force of the INF Treaty was less than four months away, and preparations had to be made for the intense round of baseline inspections that would follow, as well as for continuous perimeter and portal monitoring operations at Votkinsk and Magna [33, pp. 4, 13].

A few on-site inspections had already taken place before the creation of OSIA. These were conducted under the Stockholm agreement signed on September 19, 1986. The honor of conducting the first arms control inspection belongs to a team of U.S. Army officers led by Colonel Don O. Stovall. His team inspected a Soviet military exercise in Belarus on August 26, 1987 [57]. These inspections continued at relatively low frequency through the unification of Germany and the breakup of the Soviet Union. Their coverage, if not their frequency, was expanded substantially by the Vienna Document of 1992, and they are now just one of the many responsibilities the OSIA has acquired since its creation.

OSIA now conducts inspections under INF, Vienna CSBMs, CFE, START, and the bilateral CW agreements between the United States and Russia. Through the end of June 1995, according to OSIA's historian, it had conducted 764 INF inspections, 462 CFE inspections,[13] 74 START inspections, and 5 Wyoming MOU inspections.[14] In 1993 OSIA took delivery of the first Open Skies aircraft, designated OC-135, and it is ready to begin conducting overflights whenever the treaty enters into force [58]. OSIA's unique experience and expertise have caused it to be assigned other missions less directly related to arms control monitoring. It serves as executive agent for Department of Defense support to UNSCOM operations in Iraq, it assists the State Department in the distribution of food and medical supplies in the former Soviet Union under Project Provide Hope, it assists U.S. forces in Korea to prepare for implementation of the Joint Declaration for the Denuclearization of the Korean Peninsula, and it assists in the delivery of equipment to the four former Soviet republics being aided under the Cooperative Threat Reduction Program [59]. OSIA also provided the linguists needed to conduct the secret negotiations and transfer of nuclear material from Kazakhstan under Project Sapphire (see chapter 3).

At the time of OSIA's creation there was some question about where it should be in the bureaucratic chain of command. Some advocated putting it under the State Department, others argued for the Arms Control and Disarmament Agency, and still others for Defense [60, p. 13]. Theoretically it made the most sense to put OSIA under ACDA: inspection is clearly an arms control implementation function, and one of ACDA's four bureaus is specifically devoted to intelligence and verification. But ACDA is a small agency, and its director at the time did not actively seek the expanded responsibilities OSIA would have represented. In the end it was determined that only the Pentagon had the personnel, technical expertise, and budgetary flexibility to bring the agency up to speed in the short time available [33, 56]. However, ACDA does play a role in overseeing OSIA's operations. It prepares OSIA's personnel for their duties under each new treaty, aids in the development of technologies and inspection techniques, provides experts to participate in practice or actual inspections, offers "lessons learned" from experience in implementing previous agreements, and coordinates with OSIA on logistics [26, p. 54]. The connection between ACDA and OSIA is institutionalized by having the Principle Deputy Director of OSIA be a high-level ACDA official.

---

[13] CFE inspections are sometimes carried out exclusively by American teams and sometimes with American inspectors joining multinational teams. The total of 462 includes both types.

[14] Personal communication, Joseph Harahan, OSIA historian.

OSIA reports to the Assistant to the Secretary of Defense for Atomic Energy. It gets oversight and direction from an Executive Committee made up of the Chairman of the Joint Chiefs of Staff, the Undersecretary of Defense for Policy, and the Under Secretary of Defense for Acquisition and Technology [33, p. 4]. OSIA's director is a high-ranking military officer, and its three deputy directors are appointed from ACDA, State, and the FBI. Military personnel make up the great majority of OSIA's work force, which had grown to over 700 by the beginning of START inspections in the spring of 1995.[15]

OSIA communicates with the Intelligence Community through the Arms Control Intelligence Staff, which uses on-site inspection reports in the verification process and provides instructions and guidance on targets for future inspections. Representatives of OSIA sit on implementation subcommittees for various treaties of the Arms Control Interagency Working Group (see figure 4.1) [18, 37]. OSIA has a NRRC terminal at its Dulles Airport facility, which is connected to the primary node in the State Department and used to receive and send data and notifications. The Agency also administers the Defense Treaty Inspection Readiness Program, an interagency program that helps U.S. facilities and defense contractors prepare for inspections, and which may be expanded to help private industry prepare for overflights and inspections under Open Skies and the Chemical Weapons Convention [61, p. 16].

On-site inspection is exclusively part of the *monitoring* process. In that sense inspectors are functionally indistinguishable from reconnaissance satellites or receiving antennas. Their job is to observe specific treaty-related objects or activities and to record their observations. Inspectors are given explicit instructions about what to look at and measure and are tightly restricted in their activities by their escorts. They have no authority to make judgments about compliance or noncompliance and can at most declare an "ambiguity" if what they see does not appear to be consistent with treaty requirements or declarations. Resolution of ambiguities must be dealt with at higher policy levels as part of the consultation and compliance process.

The presence of an active counterintelligence unit within OSIA clearly suggests that the United States believes that other states will use on-site inspections as a means to gather intelligence. This naturally raises the question of whether some OSIA inspectors may be intelligence agents. This is vigorously denied by OSIA officials, and OSIA is not considered part of the Intelligence Community. Still, it is not difficult to find U.S. officials close to the verification process who are convinced that intelligence agents are routinely placed on OSIA inspection teams. I am in no position to assess the validity of such assertions, but objectively speaking it is difficult to believe that the Intelligence Community would not see attractive opportunities in the access granted American inspectors to military, scientific, and industrial installations in foreign countries. No intelligence agency worthy of the name would want to pass up such an opportunity, and every country hosting on-site inspections assumes that inspection teams include trained agents capable of noticing and appreciating things outside their strictly limited responsibilities under the treaty.

The nature and extent of Intelligence Community involvement in on-site inspection activities cannot be assessed from the outside. Inspectors are certainly

---

[15] Personal communication from OSIA official.

debriefed when they return from inspections, as are many tourists, academics, business people, and other visitors to foreign countries of interest to the Intelligence Community [2]. Such agents would have particular expertise that allowed them to understand more fully and interpret more richly what they are permitted to see during an inspection. Inspections also involve contacts with foreign military, scientific, and administrative personnel, creating the possibility of recruiting agents. Inspectors can be outfitted with sophisticated clandestine sensors or sample-collecting devices that can be left on-site or brought back home to be analyzed. CIA's Office of Technical Services specializes in the development of such devices [2, pp. 265–268]. However, these latter activities could pose serious risks of discovery and exposure, which would be extremely damaging to relations between the parties involved and the treaty regime in general. It seems likely, therefore, that such cloak-and-dagger operations are permitted to intrude into the inspection process only in highly exceptional circumstances.

Analysis and Production

The activities described in earlier sections have involved the collection and processing of information from separate sources. Completion of the monitoring process requires that this information be brought together to provide a full picture of the behavior of other parties. This "all-source analysis" function traditionally belonged almost exclusively to the Intelligence Community, but the advent of on-site inspection has broadened its bureaucratic base somewhat. The interpretation of data from NTM is still primarily the responsibility of Arms Control Intelligence Staff (ACIS) or the Nonproliferation Center (NPC), but OSIA data are also collated by the Arms Control and Disarmament Agency, which provides summaries to other agencies. The goal at this level is to provide a rigorous and objective evaluation of the degree to which other parties are complying with their treaty obligations.

Compared to the massive technical effort exerted in collection and processing, the analysis function involves far fewer people and much less money. One analyst describes it as "a human process, like academic research or high quality journalism," which requires only about one-tenth the resources of the collection effort [62, p. 191]. Even so, ACIS, which once was small enough to be called a "staff" and was confined within the CIA Directorate of Intelligence, has expanded into "a community-wide body several times the original size and directly under the DCI" [63]. ACIS employs approximately 130 personnel, mostly CIA but with representation from several different intelligence agencies. During the negotiating process for a new treaty ACIS advises the National Security Council and the U.S. negotiating delegation on verification questions, and during the implementation process it monitors the compliance of other parties. ACIS produces periodic monitoring reports as well as special reports on specific ambiguities or suspicious activities. It participates in the interagency review of ACDA's annual compliance report, and it provides guidance and advice on inspection priorities to the On-site Inspection Agency and on tasking priorities to the National Security Agency, the National Imagery and Mapping Agency, and the CIA's Directorate of Operations. Its community-wide status gives ACIS access to a wide range of diplomatic, military, and technical data and expertise, and its analysts can focus on the relatively well defined question of whether or not other parties are meeting their formal treaty commitments.

The Nonproliferation Center was created in 1992 and grew rapidly to approximately the same size as ACIS. It is continuing to grow as nonproliferation moves closer to the center of U.S. foreign and military policy. The distinction between the responsibilities of ACIS and NPC is difficult to draw precisely from the outside. It appears that ACIS deals primarily with formal treaties, while NPC is more concerned with states outside of formal treaty regimes. Human intelligence appears to play a more prominent role in NPC's work, while ACIS relies more heavily on NTM. NPC employs a greater percentage of military personnel than ACIS because of the Defense Department's growing interest in counterproliferation.[16]

A major problem to be dealt with in the analytical process is the distribution of intelligence to those with a legitimate "need to know." This is handled through an elaborate system of code words and levels of classification [2, pp. 436–455]. The system is far too complex to describe here except to say that its basic purpose is both positive and negative: to ensure that everyone who needs a piece of information has ready access to it, while at the same time preventing unauthorized persons from obtaining it. That the system too often fails in either or both of these objectives is well known. But given the vast quantities of raw intelligence, the enormous size of the community to which it must be distributed, and the almost infinite variety of questions that a wide range of consumers can legitimately ask of it, it is remarkable that the system works as well as it does.

Once the information is distributed, analysts can use it to generate the final intelligence "product." A wide variety of Intelligence Community members can produce products, and the central problem facing the DCI is to "ensure that departmental intelligence production is consistent with national priorities," that is, to ensure that there is a good match between producers and consumers [2, p. 455]. Here is where technology meets politics and where "monitoring" meets "compliance." It has been one of the persistent problem areas in verification, and I will discuss some of the problems in chapter 6. It will suffice here to note that what looks like a primarily technical process involving satellites, antennas, and seismographs has a political dimension characterized by conflicting values, power relationships, bureaucratic interests, and ideological beliefs. To paraphrase an early theorist of verification, we have reached the boundary where the state of the art meets the art of the state [65].

VERIFICATION AND COMPLIANCE

The day-to-day compliance process is managed by ACDA. Each treaty has an interagency backstopping group that oversees routine implementation responsibilities, and ACDA generally chairs these groups. Important exceptions are the CFE Treaty, CSBM process, and Open Skies Treaty where the lead role in backstopping is taken by the State Department's Bureau of Political–Military

---

[16] As one analyst put it, "If this nation decides to destroy weapons production facilities in another country, intelligence agencies must be prepared . . . to provide detailed maps of where the military must aim to achieve its objectives" [64].

Affairs. A major reason for this is the involvement in these treaties of so many countries and the need for contact with their governments through U.S. embassies [18, p. 27]. Another, more political reason is that these agreements were negotiated at a time when ACDA had been weakened by "migration of ambassadorial-level arms negotiators to the State Department" [66, p. 24]. These and other setbacks encountered by the long-suffering ACDA will be a major focus of chapter 6.

Each treaty has its own consultative commission based in Geneva, Vienna, or the Hague, where implementation and compliance problems are worked out among the parties. ACDA generally provides the lead U.S. representatives to these commissions and coordinates the policymaking process that defines U.S. negotiating positions. Interestingly, ACDA does lead the U.S. delegation to the CFE's Joint Consultative Group (JCG) and the Open Skies Consultative Commission (OSCC) in Vienna. Since 1993, relations between ACDA and State have been greatly improved and the division of leadership between State in Washington and ACDA in Vienna does not appear to create any serious difficulties.[17] Effective backstopping and a smoothly functioning interagency process are essential for a successful compliance process. U.S. delegations to consultative groups must have a clear conduit for reporting back to policymakers and must receive in return prompt instructions on negotiating positions. A backstopping group will have representatives of all concerned agencies, and any instructions sent to the delegation must receive clearance from all of them. This is sometimes a difficult and contentious process, especially when questions of compliance arise.

Section 52 of the Arms Control and Disarmament Act gives ACDA the responsibility to report "on the adherence . . . to obligations undertaken in arms control agreements and on any problems related to compliance by the Soviet Union and other nations with the provisions of bilateral and multilateral arms control agreements" [67, p. 46]. Annual reports focusing on Soviet noncompliance were first demanded by Congress in 1983, in the wake of the discovery of the Krasnoyarsk radar and the Korean airliner incident (see chapter 2). During the Reagan administration these reports were generated by the Arms Control Verification Committee and the National Security Council in a process that involved ACDA only peripherally [6]. With the advent of the Clinton administration and the "revitalization" of ACDA in 1993, the responsibility for an annual report evaluating both compliance and noncompliance of all parties to agreements was given to ACDA. It is produced by the Verification and Compliance Division of ACDA's Intelligence, Verification, and Information Support Bureau, which manages the often controversial interagency process that evaluates the compliance of U.S. treaty partners [9, p. 90]. The annual report, which is usually released sometime in the summer, has both a classified version for Congress and an unclassified version for public release. Since 1995 the unclassified version has been published as part of ACDA's full annual report to Congress. Chapter 7 will take a close look at this report and its contents as part of a more thorough analysis of compliance.

If evidence of violations accumulates, the problem must be dealt with at higher decision-making levels. These are the Arms Control Interagency Working

---

[17] Personal communication from ACDA official.

Group, the National Security Council, and the President. Possible responses include more intense efforts to clarify the situation at consultative group meetings, more focused targeting of intelligence assets to acquire more information, diplomatic or public protests, or, in the most egregious cases, some form of retaliation. Different administrations have had different styles for handling compliance disputes. Generally the proceedings of consultative groups are confidential, so if leaks can be prevented compliance issues can be handled quietly. This is the preferred method if one's primary interest is preserving the treaty and stopping the violation. But leaks often cannot be prevented, and if there is evidence of serious violations, or evidence of violations that some people think are serious, the concerns will generally become public. Many historical examples can be found— from Soviet missile tests to Chinese exports of nuclear technology—of incidents where leaks created difficulties for administrations that would have preferred quiet diplomacy to settle the problem. The one major exception to this rule was the Reagan administration in which officials appeared to revel in accusations of Soviet violations. Accusations were not leaked but trumpeted, and alleged Soviet noncompliance became a cornerstone of the administration's attacks on arms control in general and the Anti-ballistic Missile Treaty in particular. Fortunately, this behavior appears to have been a temporary aberration. Even the second Reagan administration moderated its attacks once genuine arms reductions began to be achieved. Subsequent administrations have returned to the quieter, but infinitely more productive, diplomatic approach to concerns about other states' compliance with agreements [6, 68].

CONCLUSION

Responsibility for effective implementation and verification is spread through all levels of the U.S. government, from the President to the on-site inspector. It is a measure of the importance of this activity to U.S. national security that two new agencies, ACDA and OSIA, have been created to help administer it, and that thousands of government personnel, billions of dollars of taxpayers' money, and some of the finest scientific and engineering talent in the country have been devoted to developing and improving it. This remarkable effort is evidence of a broad consensus that arms control is an integral component of U.S. national security policy. Empirically this suggests that most Americans believe that the benefits of arms control outweigh the costs and risks. But what are those benefits, costs, and risks, and is it possible to make a more analytical and quantitative judgment about their relative weights? This is the question I will turn to next.

REFERENCES

1. *Threat Control through Arms Control,* U.S. Arms Control and Disarmament Agency, July 26, 1996.

2. Jeffrey T. Richelson, *The U.S. Intelligence Community,* 3rd ed. (Boulder, CO: Westview Press, 1995).

3. Mark M. Lowenthal, *U.S. Intelligence: Evolution and Anatomy*, 2nd ed. (Westport, CT, Washington, DC: Praeger, CSIS, 1992).

4. Paula L. Scalingi, "Intelligence Community Cooperation: The Arms Control Model," *International Journal of Intelligence and Counterintelligence*, Winter 1992, pp. 401–410.

5. Jonathan Dean, Multilateral Verification and the Post-Gulf Environment: Learning from the UNSCOM Experience, Centre for International and Strategic Studies, York University, Toronto, 1992.

6. Michael Krepon, U.S. Government Organization for Arms Control Verification and Compliance, *Verification and Compliance: A Problem Solving Approach*, Michael Krepon and Mary Umberger, Eds. (Cambridge, MA: Ballinger, 1988), pp. 282–308.

7. Arms Control: Improved Coordination of Arms Control Research Needed, GAO/NSIAD-92-149, U.S. General Accounting Office, April 1992.

8. *Verification Technologies: Managing Research and Development for Cooperative Arms Control Monitoring Measures*, OTA-ISC-488, U.S. Congress, Office of Technology Assessment, May 1991.

9. *Threat Control through Arms Control*, U.S. Arms Control and Disarmament Agency, July 13, 1995.

10. Public Law 102-228, Chapter 9: Transfer of Certain CFE Treaty Limited Equipment to NATO Members, December 12, 1991.

11. R. Jeffrey Smith, "U.S. Russia Agree to Exchange Nuclear Data," *Washington Post*, December 22, 1994, p. A31.

12. Roland Lajoie, Cooperative Threat Reduction Support to the Destruction of Russia's Chemical Weapons Stockpile, *Chemical Weapons Disarmament in Russia: Problems and Prospects* (Washington, DC: Henry L. Stimson Center, 1995).

13. Weapons of Mass Destruction: Reducing the Threat from the Former Soviet Union, GAP/NSIAD-95-7, U.S. General Accounting Office, October 1994.

14. *Sipri Yearbook 1994* (Oxford: Oxford University Press, 1994).

15. *START Treaty Between the United States of America and the Union of Soviet Socialist Republics on the Reduction and Limitation of Strategic Offensive Arms*, U.S. Arms Control and Disarmament Agency, 1991.

16. *Dismantling the Bomb and Managing the Nuclear Materials*, OTA-O-572, U.S. Congress, Office of Technology Assessment, September 1993.

17. Committee on International Security and Arms Control, National Academy of Sciences, *Management and Disposition of Excess Weapons Plutonium* (Washington, DC: National Academy Press, 1994).

18. Former Warsaw Pact Nations' Treaty Compliance and U.S. Cost Control, GAO/NSIAD-94-33, U.S. General Accounting Office, December 1993.

19. Sarah Walkling, "Final Weapons Reductions under the CFE Treaty," *Arms Control Today*, December 1995/January 1996, pp. 29–30.

20. Carl R. Peterson, "Disposing of Chemical Warfare Agents and Munitions Stockpiles," *Arms Control Today*, June 1994, pp. 8–13.

21. Chemical Weapons and Materiel: Key Factors Affecting Disposal Costs and Schedule, GAO/NSIAD-97-18, U.S. General Accounting Office, February 1997.

22. "Army Confirms CW Destruction Problems," *Arms Control Today*, January/February 1995, p. 27.

23. James Brooke, "Chemical Neutralization Is Gaining in War on Poison Gas," *New York Times*, February 7, 1997.

24. Igor Khripunov, "The Human Element in Russia's Chemical Weapons Disposal Efforts," *Arms Control Today*, July/August 1995, pp. 16–21.

25. Jozef Goldblat, *Arms Control: A Guide to Negotiations and Agreements* (London, International Peace Research Institute Oslo, Sage Publications, 1994).

26. Annual Report to Congress 1993, U.S. Arms Control and Disarmament Agency, March 28, 1994.

27. Program Plan for Research, Development, Test and Evaluation For Arms Control, Fiscal Years 1995–96, U. S. Department of Defense, Office of the Under Secretary of Defense (Acquisition and Technology), May 10, 1995.

28. Lois R. Ember, "Commerce Department Gears Up to Implement Chemical Weapons Treaty," *Chemical and Engineering News,* April 10, 1995, pp. 26–27.

29. Richard Boucher, Joint US/United Kingdom/Russian Statement on Biological Weapons, U.S. Department of State, September 14, 1992.

30. R. Jeffrey Smith, "U.S. Officials Allege That Russians Are Working on Biological Arms," *Washington Post,* April 8, 1994, p. A28.

31. *Arms Control Reporter,* 1994, pp. 701.D.5–15.

32. Alastair Hay and Malcolm Dando, "Warfare: Iron Curtain Goes Up on the Anthrax Offensive," *The Guardian,* November 24, 1994.

33. Joseph P. Harahan, *On-site Inspections Under the INF Treaty* (Washington, DC: On-Site Inspection Agency, 1993).

34. "START I On-Site Inspections Begin on Schedule," *Arms Control Today,* April 1995, p. 22.

35. *The Chemical Weapons Convention: Effects on the U.S. Chemical Industry,* OTA-BP-ISC-106, U.S. Congress, Office of Technology Assessment, August 1993.

36. U.S. Capability to Monitor Compliance with the Chemical Weapons Convention, Senate Select Committee on Intelligence, September 30, 1994.

37. Intermediate-Range Nuclear Forces Treaty Implementation, GAO/NSIAD-91-262, U.S. General Accounting Office, September 1991.

38. Roland Lajoie, "Insights of an On-site Inspector," *Arms Control Today,* November 1988, pp. 3–10.

39. Douglas George, The Estimative Process, *Intelligence and Arms Control,* Thomas J. Hirschfeld, Ed. (Austin, TX: Lyndon B. Johnson School of Public Affairs, 1987), pp. 19–25.

40. Thomas J. Hirschfeld, A Marriage of Convenience, *Intelligence and Arms Control,* Thomas J. Hirschfeld Ed. (Austin, TX: Lyndon B. Johnson School of Public Affairs, 1987), pp. 9–18.

41. Allan S. Krass, *Verification: How Much Is Enough?* (Lexington, MA: Lexington Books, 1985).

42. Dwayne A. Day, "Capturing the High Ground: The U.S. Military in Space 1987–1995," *Countdown,* January/February 1995, pp. 31–41.

43. Annette J. Krygiel, "The Central Imagery Office: Getting the Picture," *Defense 94,* 1994, pp. 30–34.

44. "Intelligence Agencies Seek More Cash, Report Says," *New York Times,* August 29, 1994.

45. Jeffrey T. Richelson, *The U.S. Intelligence Community,* 2nd ed. (Cambridge, MA: Ballinger, 1989).

46. Seymour M. Hersh, *The Samson Option* (New York: Vintage Books, 1993).

47. William Drozdiak, "French Resent U.S. Coups in New Espionage," *Washington Post,* February 26, 1995, p. A1.

48. "China Frees Two U.S. Officers," *Current News,* August 3, 1995, p. 1.

49. "Moscow Tells a U.S. Army Officer to Leave," *New York Times,* August 13, 1995, p. 3.

50. Leslie H. Gelb, "Keeping an Eye on Russia," *New York Times Magazine,* November 29, 1981, p. 31.

51. David Albright and Mark Hibbs, "Iraq's Nuclear Hide-and-Seek," *Bulletin of the Atomic Scientists,* September 1991, pp. 14–23.

52. David Albright, "North Korean Plutonium Production," *Science & Global Security,* No. 1, 1994, pp. 63–85.

53. *Export Controls and Nonproliferation Policy*, OTA-ISS-596, U.S. Congress, Office of Technology Assessment, May 1994.

54. Intelligence Authorization Act for Fiscal Year 1995, House Select Committee on Intelligence, June 9, 1994.

55. Frank von Hippel, Working in the White House On Nuclear Nonproliferation and Arms Control: A Personal Report, Federation of American Scientists Public Interest Report, March/April 1995.

56. George L. Rueckert, Managing On-Site Inspections: Initial Experience and Future Challenges, *Verification: The Key to Arms Control in the 1990s*, John G. Tower, James Brown, and William K. Cheek, Eds. (Washington, DC: Brassey's [US], 1992), pp. 154–172.

57. Don O. Stovall, The Stockholm Accord: On-Site Inspections in Eastern and Western Europe, *Arms Control Verification and the New Role of On-Site Inspection: Challenges, Issues and Realities*, Lewis A. Dunn and Amy E. Gordon, Eds. (Lexington, MA: Lexington Books, 1990), pp. 15–38.

58. "OC-135B Ready for Open Skies Flights," *Aviation Week & Space Technology*, July 5, 1993, p. 21.

59. Fact Sheet, On-Site Inspection Agency, February 1994.

60. Michael Krepon and Sidney N. Graybeal, "How to Streamline the Arms Control Bureaucracy," *Arms Control Today*, November 1988, pp. 11–14.

61. Intelligence and Security Implications of the Treaty on Open Skies, Senate Select Committee on Intelligence, May 19, 1993.

62. Michael Herman, Intelligence and Arms Control Verification, *Verification Report 1991*, J. B. Poole, Ed. (London, New York: VERTIC, Apex Press, 1991), pp. 187–196.

63. Paula L. Scalingi, "U.S. Intelligence in an Age of Uncertainty: Refocusing to Meet the Challenge," *The Washington Quarterly*, Winter 1992, pp. 147–156.

64. Loch K. Johnson, "Strategic Intelligence and Weapons Proliferation," *The Monitor, Center for International Trade and Security, University of Georgia*, Spring 1995, p. 5.

65. Amrom H. Katz, Verification and SALT: The State of the Art and the Art of the State, Heritage Foundation, Washington, DC, 1979.

66. Michael Krepon, Amy E. Smithson, and James A. Schear, The U.S. Arms Control and Disarmament Agency: Restructuring for the Post-Cold War Era, The Henry L. Stimson Center, 1992.

67. Sherman M. Funk, New Purposes and Priorities for Arms Control, U.S. Arms Control and Disarmament Agency, December 14, 1992.

68. Allan Krass and Catherine Girrier, *Disproportionate Response: American Policy and Alleged Soviet Treaty Violations* (Cambridge, MA: Union of Concerned Scientists, 1987).

5

COSTS, RISKS, AND BENEFITS

During the Nixon, Ford, and Carter administrations verification was supposed to be "adequate." The Reagan administration decided that wasn't good enough and tried to make verification "effective." Now, with the Soviet Union gone and the threat it posed largely evaporated, a new standard is emerging. Verification must now be "cost-effective," with a steadily increasing emphasis on the first syllable. During the height of the Cold War few people thought much about the cost of implementing or verifying arms control agreements between the super-powers while each side was spending hundreds of billions of dollars every year on military preparations. Even though the satellites, seismographs, and antennas used to monitor the Soviets were certainly expensive, their primary missions were threat assessment, order of battle surveillance, and strategic warning, all seen as essential to deterrence and military readiness. As far as arms control monitoring was concerned, they were considered a "free good" [1, p. III–23], and it would not have occurred to anyone that the costs of using them in this way were even remotely comparable with the benefits of controlling the arms race and enhancing crisis stability.

The world has changed, and so have the questions being asked about arms control. As perceptions of imminent threat have decreased, awareness of cost has increased, and this book is being written at a moment when the two curves appear to be crossing. A few examples will illustrate the point. One analysis of the Comprehensive Test Ban (CTB) negotiations noted

CTB negotiators are increasingly sensitive to the cost of implementation. While most would agree that multilateral verification, non-discriminatory decision making, and prompt, non-confrontational inspections are desirable, there is a limit to what they are willing to pay for what might come to be seen as too much of a good thing. [2]

A second example of cost consciousness can be found in the instructions to the verification experts group evaluating transparency measures for the

Biological Weapons Convention. One of the explicit criteria against which possible BW verification measures must be measured is their "financial implications" [3]. This concern for costs in the BWC derives from the realization that the Chemical Weapons Convention will impose significant financial burdens on both governments and private industry, burdens that were not given much weight in the early negotiations, when the primary goal was ridding the world of chemical weapons. There are still few who would question the value of the goal, but many more are beginning to realize just how expensive it will be to achieve. Future financial problems of the Organization for the Prevention of Chemical Weapons (OPCW) may be foreshadowed by those currently experienced by the International Atomic Energy Agency (IAEA). IAEA safeguards funding has been essentially level since 1984, even though the number of facilities and the amount of fissile material requiring safeguards have steadily increased [4].

Within the U.S. government, implementation and verification costs are now serious political issues. A study by the General Accounting Office (GAO) of the Conventional Forces in Europe (CFE) Treaty suggested that the Pentagon had been a bit overzealous in destroying equipment and participating in inspections, and a bit extravagant in using military instead of commercial aircraft to deliver inspection teams to their points of entry. According to GAO, the latter practice alone added about $3 million to the cost of implementing CFE [5, pp. 28–29]. It is not necessary to argue the merits of this criticism here, only to notice that no one would have quibbled about $3 million in 1988 when Europe was armed to the teeth with vast arsenals of conventional and nuclear weapons and when on-site inspection was seen as a dramatic and highly reassuring breakthrough in arms control monitoring. Another example involves an important innovation of the Intermediate Nuclear Forces (INF) Treaty: continuous perimeter portal monitoring. It has fallen from favor in subsequent agreements as its relatively high cost-to-benefit ratio has become more apparent [6, pp. 56–57].

These examples will suffice to make the point that a consciousness of the financial costs of arms control is beginning to assert itself in both domestic and international politics. The traditional criteria of "adequacy" or "effectiveness" for monitoring were difficult enough to define precisely based on an assessment of the "military significance" of potential violations. Now the criterion of military significance is being replaced by the even more subtle concept of "cost-effectiveness." This was emphasized by the Arms Control and Disarmament Agency's Inspector General in a 1995 report. He concluded in no uncertain terms:

The United States will not be able to meet the funding obligations implicit in all arms control agreements currently contemplated. It will be difficult to fully fund U.S. participation in even those agreements to which the United States is already a party. All such agreements should be subjected to a rigorous cost-benefit analysis of the contribution each makes to vital U.S. interests. It is no longer sufficient to argue that international commitments require these budget outlays. Increasingly—as Congressional limitations on funding for UN assessments underscore—trade-offs will have to be made within budget categories. Budgetary constraints, including the political momentum to achieve a balanced budget early in the next century, require persuasive evidence that expenditures to implement current and proposed international understandings serve priority U.S. interests. [7, p. 38]

It is worth noting that the United States is a *rich* country compared to many of its arms control partners. The financial costs of arms control are felt even more strongly by developing countries and by the financially strapped newly independent states of the former Soviet Union.[1]

It is difficult to argue with the principle underlying the Inspector General's warning. Cost-effectiveness is as necessary and legitimate a criterion to apply to arms control as to any other activity. At the same time, it will become clear as this chapter unfolds that the amounts being spent on arms control are dwarfed by the funds appropriated for sophisticated weapon systems for which little or no national security justification can be found. Just one example will illustrate the point. Many in Congress seem more than willing to abandon the ABM Treaty, which is quite inexpensive to implement and verify, in order to permit deployment of a nationwide ballistic missile defense, which would not only cost many tens of billions in its own right, but which would probably sacrifice much of the substantial savings anticipated under the START I and II treaties and their successors. Common sense would suggest that Congress apply the same rigorous standards of cost-effectiveness to military expenditures as it would like to see applied to arms control implementation.

Not all of the costs of arms control, in some cases not even the most important ones, are financial. There are also risks of undetected cheating, risks of loss of military or commercial secrets, and risks of complacency or false assumptions of security. These must be added to the financial costs to produce a fair assessment of the value of any agreement. For example, the United States benefits from on-site inspections because of the opportunity to examine the military activities and equipment of potential adversaries. Those potential adversaries also benefit from their inspections of U.S. bases and facilities, which poses some risk to U.S. security. Unfortunately, comparison of these benefits and risks defies quantitative analysis. The Office of Technology Assessment (OTA) found it "difficult to get net assessments of the gains and losses of sensitive information that come with on-site inspections" [8, p. 8]. OTA speculated, "Somewhere in the government, there may be rigorous, all-source analysis comparing the values of the potential gains and losses." But it is highly unlikely that such analyses exist, since the risks and benefits they would compare are both unquantifiable and incommensurate.

No purely quantitative cost-benefit analysis of arms control is possible. Even in purely quantitative terms most costs can be estimated to within 10 or 20 percent at best and others only to an order of magnitude. Benefits and risks are inevitably qualitative and often depend on the analyst's values and basic assumptions. The best that can be done in this chapter is to summarize the available information on costs and define the essential categories that determine risks and benefits. Some judgments are relatively easy to make, but others are far more difficult and must ultimately be made by the political process. Examples of both will be encountered in the following analysis.

---

[1] One example is Belarus, which was not only saddled with major CFE elimination obligations because of all the Soviet equipment left on its territory, but has also been faced for more than a decade with the enormous expense of cleaning up after the Chernobyl accident and caring for its victims. The latter activity alone is reported to require 12 percent of the Belarussian national budget (*Baltimore Sun*, September 29, 1995).

GENERIC COSTS

Figure 5.1 illustrates the evolution of costs for a generic arms control agreement.[2] Most of the money is spent during the period between signature and a few years after entry into force (EIF), precisely the period we are interested in here. The curves for costs and manpower requirements are qualitatively correct for the nuclear and conventional treaties, but a bit misleading for the bilateral and international chemical weapons agreements, for which high implementation costs will persist much longer after EIF. Another variation on the generic picture may be introduced by U.S.-Russian negotiations to clarify the distinction between theater and strategic ballistic missile defenses. If this distinction is made more precise, it could increase the costs of verification, and this could cause the curve to begin to rise again in the long-term compliance phase of the ABM Treaty. Figure 5.1 shows several treaties in the medium- to long-term compliance phase: ABM, INF, CFE/CSBM, and START I. BDA, CWC, Open Skies, START II, and CTBT remain in limbo between signature and EIF. However, a significant fraction of the total costs of a treaty is spent in this period, so there should be enough data on these ten agreements to make reasonably reliable cost estimates. Several such estimates have already been made, and this chapter will rely heavily on them.

NATIONAL TECHNICAL MEANS

It has never been possible to obtain reliable estimates of NTM costs attributable to arms control. The Intelligence Community has been steadfast in its unwillingness to make such estimates, or, if they have been made, to share them with other agencies, even in classified form [6, p. 43]. The ostensible rationale is the protection of sources and methods, and while there is some basis for this argument, it is unclear why aggregate estimates cannot be released without compromising sensitive information. During the Cold War the "free good" assumption for the contribution of NTM to arms control was probably an acceptable first approximation. But U.S. arms control and nonproliferation commitments have increased substantially in the past several years, suggesting that monitoring for these purposes now accounts for a significantly larger portion of the activities of U.S. NTM. Testifying in support of START II ratification, the CIA's Deputy Director for Intelligence pointed out, "The Intelligence Community has reduced its resources devoted to Russian military developments across the board. . . . But, in reality, there are now no fewer questions being put to us by the Executive Branch and Congress on strategic military-related issues—from the location and status of Russian nuclear warheads, to the production and potential proliferation of all kinds of weapons and missiles, to command and control of the strategic forces, to monitoring strategic arms control agreements" [9, p. 9].

---

[2] Figure 5.1 is adapted from one provided by Lee Minichiello of Science Applications International Corporation. The author thanks Mr. Minichiello for his permission to update and use the figure.

Figure 5.1
Generic Cost Curve

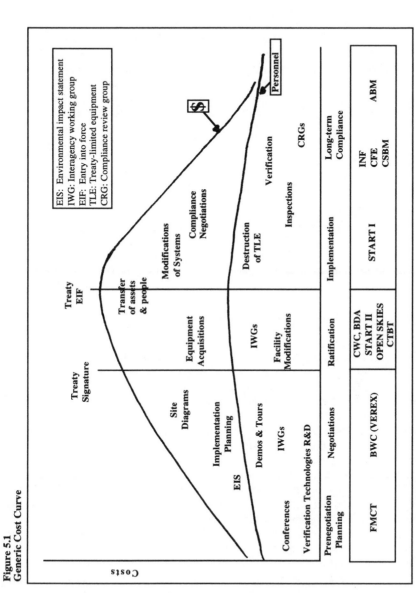

Source: Adapted and updated from Lee Minichiello, with permission.

The National Reconnaissance Office (NRO) accounts for a sizable fraction of the approximately $28 billion U.S. intelligence budget [10, p. 12]. The Reagan administration launched a major effort to modernize and expand U.S. satellite capabilities, and NRO's budget has remained at an estimated $7.0 billion per year [11]. A large imaging or signals satellite costs at least a billion dollars,[3] and the U.S. aerospace industry has been producing them at a steady rate since the mid-1980s. The imagery and signals obtained by NRO satellites are processed and distributed by the National Imagery and Mapping Agency (NIMA) and National Security Agency (NSA) (see chapter 4). NIMA's predecessor, the Central Imagery Office (CIO) had a budget request for FY 1995 of $123 million, but the Defense Department is anticipating a substantial increase in this appropriation over the next few years. Planning for the 1996–2001 period shows an average yearly budget for CIO (now absorbed into NIMA) of $300 million [12]. NSA's budget is estimated to be about $3.5 billion [10, p. 27].

In chapter 4 I estimated that arms control monitoring accounts for at most 10 percent of the overall intelligence gathering effort. This suggests that a rough upper limit for NTM costs would be 10 percent of the total budgets of NRO, CIO, and NSA. This comes to just about $1 billion in very round numbers. As we will see shortly, this is roughly comparable to the total annual cost of cooperative measures. If more treaties enter into force with more extensive cooperative monitoring regimes, the relative contribution of NTM may decrease. It is difficult to estimate the tradeoffs at the margin between NTM and cooperative measures. They have generally been seen as complementary rather than substitutable, and this still appears to be the appropriate way to think about them.

RESEARCH AND DEVELOPMENT COSTS

A major portion of the expenditures in the preratification phase of any agreement are on research and development, which are almost always necessary for both implementation and verification. For example, in preparation for START the Defense Department planned to spend $62 million over a three-year period developing an environmentally acceptable technique for destroying solid fuel rocket motors [13, p. 35]. As it turned out, the United States was not required to destroy missiles under START, but the study was still necessary in view of Congress' order to the Air Force to make sure that the environment was not harmed by the destruction of obsolete missiles. Other examples of preratification R&D can be found in the development and testing of Open Skies sensors, in the practice on-site inspections carried out in preparation for START and CWC, and in the very expensive effort to develop a safe and environmentally sound method of disposing of chemical weapons.

The money spent on verification R&D is significant, and the large portion of it devoted to developing NTM is secret. However, it is reasonable to assume that a substantial fraction of the budgets of CIA, NSA, and NRO, probably totaling several billion dollars per year, is spent to develop new satellites, aircraft, sensors, communications, cryptology, and information systems. A relatively new area, measurement and signatures intelligence (MASINT), which develops new

---

[3] The Hubble Space Telescope, which cost approximately $2 billion, is similar in many ways to the KH-11.

methods of detecting and identifying substances, devices, facilities, or activities related to weapon proliferation or ballistic missile defenses, has also grown in recent years [10, pp. 233–234]. Most R&D money is paid to private contractors, but a significant amount is spent in the national laboratories, which do R&D on both NTM and cooperative measures.

Spending on R&D for cooperative verification is more open and therefore more accessible to analysis and oversight. There are four main agencies involved in this activity (see chapter 4): the Defense Special Weapons Agency (DSWA), the Advanced Research Projects Agency (ARPA), the Department of Energy's Office of Arms Control, and the Arms Control and Disarmament Agency (ACDA). Figure 5.2 shows funding histories for these agencies during the FY 1986–1994 period. Total R&D spending rose from $83 million in FY 1986 to a peak of $260 million in FY 1991. It then declined to about $220 million in FY 1994 where it has leveled off. The rapid rise in DSWA's funding was associated with the newly created On-Site Inspection Agency, which began operation in mid-1988 and grew rapidly as it acquired more responsibilities. DOE's verification budget requests for the three years from FY 1989 to FY 1991 were all increased 10 percent or more by Congress, which felt that verification R&D was inadequately funded [13, p. 15]. In FY 1992 DOE expanded its program and increased its budget request, which has remained at historically high levels ever since.

IMPLEMENTATION AND INSPECTION COSTS

With this introduction we can now examine the costs, risks, and benefits of individual agreements, first those that have a solid record of implementation and then those either just ratified or still awaiting EIF. I will start with the INF Treaty and not examine earlier ones such as the Limited Nuclear Test Ban, the Strategic Arms Limitation Treaties (SALT I and II), or the ABM Treaty. As already noted in chapter 2, none of these involved any actual implementation, and all have been monitored entirely with NTM, for which costs are notoriously difficult to estimate. The SALT agreements have been superseded by START, but the LTBT and ABM agreements are still in force and still being closely monitored. Indeed, many of the systems used to monitor the LTBT will be adapted to help monitor the Comprehensive Test Ban when it enters into force.

INF Treaty

The INF Treaty provided the first hard data on the costs of implementation and verification, and the results were encouraging. In the three years from June 1, 1988 to May 31, 1991 the U.S. Army and Air Force destroyed a total of 403 Pershing ballistic missiles and 443 ground-launched cruise missiles at a total cost of $128 million [6, p. 45]. The great majority of this amount (84 percent) was spent on destroying the Pershings, and much of the cost was incurred because all of the missile stages were flown back to the United States from their West German bases for destruction. Only the Pershing launchers were eliminated on West German territory [14, pp. 100–101]. As has been the case in every treaty so far, the USSR had far more missiles to eliminate (1,846 vs. 846) and far more infrastructure and supporting equipment to destroy as well.

Figure 5.2
Verification Research Funding

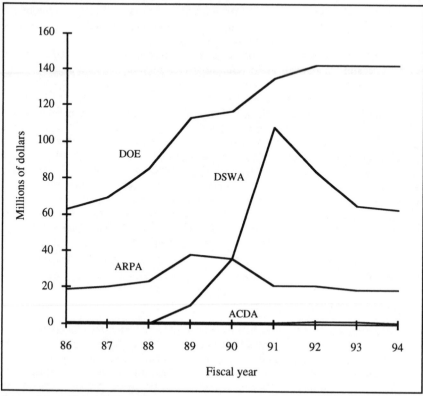

Source: Adapted from ref. 13, p. 16.

Nevertheless, the Soviets were able to meet these requirements on time and with no external aid.

Monitoring the INF Treaty has proven to be less expensive than anticipated, although there are hidden costs that make the savings less impressive than they appear at first glance. In 1990 the Congressional Budget Office estimated that quota inspections at Warsaw Pact bases would cost $1–2 million per year, giving an estimate of $10–20 million for the 1991–2001 period [15, p. 18]. Only one year later the GAO estimated $7.5 million for the same inspections over the same period, an average of $60,000 per inspection [6, p. 48]. These are the costs of *conducting* inspections, but experience has shown that it is generally more expensive to host an inspection than to conduct one.[4] Considerable effort and expense are necessary to prepare a base or facility for an on-site inspection in order to protect classified or proprietary information from foreign inspectors.

An even bigger difference can be found in the estimates of continuous perimeter-portal monitoring costs at Magna and Votkinsk. The CBO estimated an annual cost to the United States of $30–50 million at the two sites, but GAO

---

[4] Personal communication, Lee Minichiello.

estimated an average cost of only $12.4 million per year in constant 1989 dollars. Still, $12.4 million per year is about ten times what it costs to conduct the full quota of on-site inspections in that year, and it is not obvious that the added benefits justify the greater cost.[5] The total cost of monitoring the INF treaty for its 13-year lifetime computed from 1990 CBO estimates is in the range $641–1,216 million [15, p. 18]. A subsequent analysis by the Institute for Defense Analysis (IDA), based on two more years of implementation experience projected only $490 million for the total monitoring costs [1, p. III-26]. It is clear in retrospect that for INF the early estimates were far too high.

The implementation and inspection costs considered in these estimates are only those directly attributable to the Army, Air Force, and OSIA. They do not include a variety of hidden costs which for various reasons are difficult to estimate or to obtain. For example, the salaries of military personnel serving with the OSIA are not counted. The GAO identifies several other hidden costs, which include FBI counterintelligence activities, preparation costs for Soviet inspections at overseas bases, temporary duty personnel from other agencies that accompany on-site inspections, personnel costs for the interagency committees and consultative bodies that analyze compliance and engage in negotiations, State Department support for OSIA in foreign countries, and others. The lack of detailed accounting for many of these costs is not surprising; they are often difficult to apportion accurately to different agreements, and in some cases it would not be worth the extra effort and cost to keep track of them. Such hidden costs are an unavoidable aspect of the implementation of any arms control agreement. They constitute a kind of "overhead" that will typically add a few percent to estimates of explicit costs.

Are these costs reasonable compared with the benefits of the INF Treaty? The answer seems clearly to be yes, with the possible exception of the continuous monitoring at Magna and Votkinsk. Not only has the precedent of intrusive on-site inspection been established, but several classes of nuclear-armed missiles have been completely eliminated, including two of the most modern and threatening: the Soviet SS-20 and the U.S. Pershing II. Even in strictly financial terms, the costs of destroying these missiles and verifying the treaty were less than the lifetime operational costs of the weapons had they remained deployed. This was the conclusion reached by the CBO, which advised the Senate Foreign Relations Committee in 1988, "Savings totaling as much as $1.1 billion would accrue each year from lower force levels including fewer military and civilian personnel and other lower operating costs" [16, p. 178]. CBO's estimate was challenged by Senator Jesse Helms, who asked the General Accounting Office for a second opinion. GAO did estimate smaller savings, but they were still substantial. According to GAO, the treaty would save $219 million and $240 million in FY 1988 and 1989, respectively, and savings on the Pershing II program between April 1988 and September 1995 would total about $1.2 billion. Another GAO study identified 16,701 personnel, including 15,559 military and 1,142 civilians, who could be reassigned or retired as a result of the treaty [17]. Both CBO and GAO concluded that the treaty represents a net financial savings when costs avoided are balanced against the costs of implementation and verification.

---

[5] CPPM has been substantially downgraded in START, largely because of its poor benefit-cost ratio. See below and chapter 3.

Intangible political benefits from the INF Treaty are much more important than the relatively small financial benefits. The on-site inspections in the treaty represented a historic increase in transparency and have served as models for inspections under all subsequent treaties. The contacts they have established between Russian and American military and civilian personnel and organizations have been a major factor in removing long-held Cold War assumptions and fears. While these political benefits are unquestionable, the contribution of on-site inspections to reducing the risk of clandestine cheating is harder to estimate. By targeting the most likely facilities and bases where clandestine production, testing, or deployment might be carried out, inspections make cheating more difficult, risky, and expensive, thereby reducing the risk of cheating below what it would be without inspections. At the same time, it was evident in the context of U.S.-Soviet relations in the late 1980s that neither side had a military incentive to cheat, and both sides had strong political incentives to make the treaty work.

It has always been clear that "inspections are likely to be most useful precisely when they are least needed—when parties to an agreement have a strong desire to cooperate"[6] [18, p. 26]. Their greatest benefit derives not from their ability to detect or deter cheating, but from the political message they convey that the parties do in fact have a "strong desire to cooperate." Willingness to agree to intrusive inspections has continued to carry this message to the present day, just as an unwillingness to accept inspections conveys the opposite message. South Africa, by renouncing nuclear weapons and opening all of its former weapons plants to IAEA inspections, provides an excellent example of the former. Iraq and North Korea are good examples of the latter because of their many efforts to delay, evade, or mislead inspectors from UNSCOM or IAEA.

Strategic Arms Reduction Treaties

START I and II build directly on many of the precedents set by the INF Treaty but extend them over a wider scope as well as into qualitatively new areas. There are more kinds of missiles and aircraft to be monitored, more bases and facilities to be inspected, and more technical information to be collected and analyzed. The result is a treaty that is considerably more expensive to implement and verify than INF but that also accomplishes a great deal more in the way of nuclear arms reductions and transparency. START entered into force in December 1994 and began its baseline inspections in March 1995. However, as noted in chapter 2, both the United States and Russia had begun their implementation activities well in advance, and by the time of entry into force the United States had already dismantled 41 ICBM silos, 15 ballistic missile submarines, and 230 strategic bombers [19]. (Unfortunately, no cost figures are available for this activity.)

The CBO estimated START implementation costs in 1990, and as with INF, the estimates appear to have been too high. At that time the prospects were for considerably more equipment to be eliminated, continuous portal monitoring to

---

[6] This suggests that most of the benefits (political if not intelligence) from OSI under INF may have already been achieved, which raises the question of whether it is cost-effective to carry out all of the remaining short-notice inspections through 2001.

be conducted at four or five sites in each country instead of the one finally agreed on, and a considerably larger list of prospects for challenge inspections, or what the START Treaty calls "special access visits."[7] CBO's estimate for full implementation included one-time costs of $410–1,830 million and annual costs of $100–390 million [15, p. 29]. Of the one-time costs, $260–1,090 million were for elimination of U.S. equipment and the rest for one-time monitoring procedures, such as baseline inspections and setting up portal monitoring stations. Two years later, when the treaty was submitted to the Senate for ratification, the Foreign Relations Committee (SFRC) estimated $200–1,000 million for one-time expenses and total inspection costs over the 15-year life of the treaty of $1,250–2,050 million [20, p. 159]. A third study, by the Institute for Defense Analysis (IDA), made at about the same time as the SFRC estimate, looked only at verification costs. It projected a total of $760 million over the life of the treaty, significantly less than the SFRC's estimate [1, p. III-26]. Comparing the three studies' amortized annual cost of implementing START I, we find: CBO (1990) $127–512 M; SFRC (1992) $100–200 M; and IDA (1992) $51 M (verification only). Allowing for the cost-saving modifications made in the treaty between 1990 and 1992, and allowing a small adjustment for the tendency to overestimate verification costs, I will use values of $200–$1000 M for one-time costs and $50–$100 M per year for recurring costs.[8]

These are the costs to the United States of carrying out its own obligations under START. But the United States is also providing considerable aid to the four former Soviet republics through the Cooperative Threat Reduction (Nunn-Lugar) Program. In the first three years of its existence the program received annual appropriations of $400 million, and a sizable fraction of this has been directed toward START implementation. Through the end of September 1996 the total amount obligated to strategic nuclear weapons elimination in Russia, Ukraine, Belarus, and Kazakhstan was $354.3 million [21]. Another $237 million was still in the pipeline going through the long bureaucratic process required to obligate the funds to actual projects. The total of $591 million over six years gives an average of just under $100 million per year contributed by the United States to START implementation in the former Soviet Union. This is about the same as the U.S.'s own annual implementation costs, so if Nunn-Lugar support continues at the same level throughout the life of the treaty it will roughly double the cost to the United States of START implementation.

For this money the United States will achieve a reduction of about 75 percent in the former Soviet strategic nuclear weapon force from nearly 12,000 to 3,500 [22]. The United States will also save a lot of money that in the absence of a treaty would have to be spent to maintain, operate, and modernize U.S.

---

[7] Cost played an important role in getting the United States to settle for fewer CPPM sites and for special access visits instead of genuine challenge inspections. Special access visits are less intrusive, allow more time for preparation by the challenged party, and can be refused if the challenged party can find an alternative way of satisfying the concerns of the challenging party [1]. With respect to CPPM, the number of proposed sites dropped from five in the initial U.S. draft to only one in the final treaty. Even that one was ultimately given up by both sides, primarily because of excessive costs.

[8] Some original investment costs may be recovered through conversions of ICBMs to commercial space-launch vehicles, and there may be other opportunities for such recoveries as well. In its implementation of the INF Treaty, the Air Force was able to recover and adapt to other uses over $500 million worth of equipment and more than $40 million in previously approved construction funding due to project cancellations [16, pp. 360–361].

strategic nuclear forces. The CBO estimates an overall saving of $46 billion in the first five years of the treaty and as much as $130 billion through 2010. This averages out to savings of $9 billion a year for 15 years, which is at least 20 times the cost of implementing the treaty for the same period, depending on what is assumed for the amount of Nunn-Lugar aid required [20].

The risks associated with START are that the Russians will cheat, or that Russian intelligence will benefit in unforeseen ways from on-site inspections at U.S. bases and facilities. The risks of cheating were evaluated at the time of ratification by the Senate Intelligence Committee, which expressed some concern about covert production of launchers and undeclared mobile missiles, counting warheads, and monitoring bombers and cruise missiles. In each case, however, the Joint Chiefs of Staff assessment was that the likelihood of a militarily significant violation was acceptably small [20, pp. 191–205].   Careful preparations would be necessary for special access visits (see above) at U.S. facilities, but the Committee was satisfied that the administration shared its concern for this problem and would fund appropriate security and counterintelligence measures. Presumably, these costs, which can be substantial, are already included in the CBO and SFRC estimates.

In summary, while the costs of implementing and verifying START are substantial, the risks of Russian cheating and espionage are manageable, and the benefits in the form of reduced Russian nuclear capability, reduced U.S. expenditures on strategic weapon modernization, and increased transparency are considerably greater. START appears to be an excellent bargain for the United States from both the security and economic points of view.

CFE Treaty and CSBM Agreements

The CFE Treaty entered into force in the summer of 1992. Unlike INF, which appeared suddenly with no attempts to estimate the costs of its implementation ahead of time, CFE was anticipated well in advance. Therefore, it is possible to compare *a priori* cost estimates with actual expenditures. Nearly two years before EIF, the CBO estimated one-time costs associated with CFE implementation at between $105 and $780 million, and annual costs in the range $25–100 million [15, p. 32]. Amortizing the one-time costs over the first ten years of the treaty gave an average annual cost of $35–178 million for U.S. implementation. The large range of these estimates reflected uncertainty at the time about how much would have to be spent to close or reconfigure U.S. bases in Europe and how much of those costs should be attributed to the CFE Treaty. Other uncertainties included whether there would be an aerial reconnaissance arrangement added to the treaty and how much it would cost to prepare U.S. bases for inspections. CBO's estimates were updated in March 1991 for the use of the Senate Foreign Relations Committee in its ratification hearings, and on the basis of these estimates (which were slightly higher than the earlier ones but had at least as wide a range of uncertainty) the Committee estimated an average annual cost of $50 million, close to the lower end of the CBO range [23, p. 51].

In 1993 the GAO evaluated implementation through the end of the first one-year reduction period and found actual expenditures of $60.2 million in FY 1992 and $38.5 million in FY 1993 [5]. GAO projected costs of $36.2 million for FY 1994. These numbers included all the money spent on destruction of U.S.

equipment, which was completed by November 1993. For inspections and escort duties alone GAO estimated $10.4 million in FY 1994. However, an OSIA summary dated January 1995 gives a figure of $8.6 million for OSIA's CFE expenses in FY 1994.[9] Since OSIA has other responsibilities besides conducting and escorting inspections, its figure of only $8.6 million suggests that actual monitoring costs for FY 1994 were well under the GAO projection.

CFE inspections have proven to be "surprisingly inexpensive" for the United States, although not necessarily for other parties [1, p. III-30]. There are several reasons for this. One is the limited geographical area of the treaty (Atlantic to Urals), which means that only U.S. bases in Europe are inspected, and no inspections are conducted on U.S. territory. Second, the treaty limits annual inspection quotas to only a small fraction of objects of verification, and, third, the U.S. quota is only a fraction of the full NATO quota. The United States has saved even more money by joining with NATO allies to form joint inspection teams. Finally, CFE inspections are "low-tech" operations that do not require highly skilled or specialized inspectors. All U.S. inspectors are military personnel, and their salaries are not even counted as inspection costs. The rationale for this is that if they weren't doing CFE inspections they would be doing something else for the military. It would be more consistent, however, to count their salaries as a hidden or overhead cost of implementing the treaty.

The GAO has suggested some ways in which OSIA could save money on CFE inspections. These include not carrying out the full quota of allowed inspections and using commercial flights instead of military aircraft for transportation to ports of entry and inspection sites [5, pp. 28–29]. So far U.S. policy has been to rigorously adhere to the letter of the treaty in carrying out inspection activities, so these savings opportunities have not been exploited. Even if they were, the savings would be small, at most a few million dollars per year.

Cost estimates for the Stockholm-Vienna CSBMs do not seem to exist, but they are definitely much smaller than those for CFE. There are many fewer CSBM inspections, and most of the monitoring activity involves observation of military activities, attendance at conferences and seminars, and other relatively low cost activities. No expensive equipment or specially trained personnel are required, and there is far less traveling involved than under CFE.

As in the case of INF, the benefit-cost ratio for CFE and CSBMs is clearly favorable, especially for the United States. One measure of the benefits is financial, a savings of $10–14 *billion* per year resulting from the substantial reduction of U.S. troop deployments in Europe [23, p. 51]. It would be an exaggeration to attribute all of this to the CFE Treaty, since the relaxation of tensions in Europe and the removal of the Soviet invasion threat would have allowed the United States to reduce its deployments anyway. Still, even if only a fraction of these billions are attributed to the treaty, when they are added to the benefits of increased transparency and reduced threat of invasion, the benefits greatly exceed the relatively modest price of $134 million estimated by the GAO for the entire first three years of CFE [5, p. 26]. The verification regime appears to be working well, and most members have been able to demonstrate their compliance to the satisfaction of all other parties. There are a few compliance questions of

---

[9] Thanks to Brinn Colenda of OSIA for providing this figure as well as other useful information on OSIA's role in implementation and inspection.

varying levels of seriousness (see chapter 7), but they involve substantive and open disagreements about treaty requirements or financial or political difficulties, not attempts to evade limits by clandestine means.

Nuclear Testing Treaties

The Threshold Test Ban Treaty (TTBT) entered into force in December 1990, so it has a record, however brief, of implementation and verification. The TTBT was ratified by the U.S. more than 16 years after it was signed, and only after an on-site yield measuring technique had been added to the verification protocol. In this technique a satellite hole is drilled next to the emplacement hole for the nuclear device, and electrical signals are transmitted through a coaxial cable run down the satellite shaft.[10] The energy released by the explosion is estimated from the speed of the shock wave as it crushes the cable [24].

Most professional seismologists argued that the new procedure was unnecessary. Seismic monitoring of Soviet testing over a period of 20 years had produced ample evidence of Soviet compliance with the TTBT as negotiated in 1974 [24, p. 126]. But the Reagan administration insisted that the new technique was necessary to make the TTBT "effectively" verifiable, and for reasons of its own, Gorbachev's government went along. A Joint Verification Experiment was conducted at the Nevada and Semipalatinsk test sites in 1988 in which the on-site method was compared with remote seismic measurements of two explosions of known yield. The results were never released by the U.S. government, but leaks to the media suggested that the comparison was inconclusive. Nevertheless the on-site procedure was incorporated into the TTBT and plans were made to use it to monitor all U.S. and Soviet underground tests with yields greater than 50 kilotons. This would have required the continuous presence at the test site of personnel from the monitoring country for "perhaps 10 weeks or so before as well as during each test" [24, p. 137]. If Russia conducted five or six high-yield tests per year, the presence of U.S. personnel would have to be essentially continuous. They would need equipment for drilling the satellite hole and operating the electronics and diagnostic instruments. A large shipment of such equipment was flown to the Soviet test site in C-5A transports for the joint experiment, and more would have been required to sustain an ongoing on-site monitoring capability.

Surprisingly, no one thought to ask at the TTBT ratification hearings how much this would cost. Nor does the Senate Foreign Relations Committee's report on the TTBT mention implementation costs, as it has done in all its reports on other treaties since that time [25, 26]. The only estimate available for the cost of monitoring Russian testing under the TTBT was done by the CBO in 1990 [15, pp. 34–37]. CBO estimated one-time costs of $85–200 million and annual costs of $50–100 million depending on how many tests Russia conducted at yields of 50 kilotons or greater. The cost range quoted assumed a range of from two to six such tests per year.

What would have been the benefits of such an operation? Even if the technique had fully lived up to its promoters' hopes the United States would have

---

[10] The technique is called "continuous reflectometry for radius versus time experiments" or CORRTEX.

improved its estimates of Soviet test yields by about 20 percent. Unless one wants to place a value on scientific precision for its own sake, it is difficult to understand what would have been gained by this improved accuracy at yields that were already at 150 kilotons. Nor is the technique of any use in monitoring a comprehensive test ban. It can be used only if the test is announced in advance and has a relatively large yield. Verification of a CTB requires the ability to detect and identify small clandestine explosions with no advance warning. For this the world possesses an excellent seismic network, of which a substantial portion has been created by the United States. The U.S. nuclear explosion monitoring network costs between $10 and $100 million per year and provides a reliable means of detecting, and in many cases identifying, nuclear explosions down to yields of 1 kiloton or lower [25, p. 74].

The story of the TTBT is a textbook example of verification overkill, an arrangement in which the costs clearly outweighed the benefits, however the latter are defined. It was, in the words of one critic, "a monument to the incredible lengths to which the United States is prepared to go to achieve technical solutions to unimportant or even non-existent problems" [27]. Fortunately the problem evaporated when nuclear testing moratoria were declared and the Comprehensive Test Ban Treaty (CTBT) was signed.

The CTBT bans all nuclear tests and all other nuclear explosions. It was opened for signature in September 1996 and by the end of the year had been signed by more than 130 countries. In all likelihood this achievement has put an end to nuclear explosive testing, even by countries that have no present intention of adhering to the treaty. The broad endorsement of the treaty implicit in so many early signatures has significantly raised the political costs to be paid by any state that violates the norm it establishes.

Entry into force is another matter all together. The CTBT cannot enter into force until 44 specifically named states ratify it, and two of these 44 are India and Pakistan, neither of whom can even bring themselves to sign it. Ratification may face significant obstacles in other countries as well, including the United States. Several influential senators have expressed skepticism about the benefits of the treaty to U.S. national security, and convincing two-thirds of a conservative-dominated Senate that the CTBT's benefits exceed its costs may prove to be more difficult than anticipated when the Clinton administration decided to make the concessions required to obtain broad international support for the treaty.

With entry into force several years in the future even under the most optimistic scenarios, it is too early to make precise cost projections. The most important costs of implementing the CTBT will be those associated with operating the International Monitoring System. Plausible estimates for these costs are $100 million for startup and $60–80 million per year for the indefinite future [28, p. 706]. The United States will most likely contribute its usual 25 percent, although it may get some credit for contributing components of its national monitoring system to the international system. This money will create and operate a worldwide network of four kinds of monitoring sensors: seismic, infrasound, hydroacoustic, and radionuclide—all connected by electronic communication links to one or more international data centers, where the data from hundreds of sensors will be collected and processed for distribution to the states parties. There are also on-site inspection provisions, although the high cost of such inspections and the difficult approval procedure prescribed by the treaty is likely to make them relatively infrequent. Finally, there are provisions for confi-dence-building measures that could include data exchanges, notifications, and possibly invitations for observers at large chemical explosions connected with mining or construction activity.[11]

If all of this were to cost the United States just $25 million up front and $15–20 million per year, it would not add greatly to the sum of other arms con-trol obligations the United States has already accepted. And the benefits would be substantial. The development of new weapon designs by the nuclear weapon states would be made more difficult if not impossible, and the development of sophisticated thermonuclear weapons by threshold and nonnuclear weapon states effectively prevented. A CTBT would also fulfill the political commitment made by the nuclear weapon states at the 1995 NPT Review and Extension Conference and realize a hope that can be traced all the way back to 1949, when U.S. scientists proposed that a test ban be negotiated with the Soviet Union to head off development of the hydrogen bomb [29, p. 401]. The realization of this hope by putting an end to all nuclear explosions, something the nonnuclear states have been demanding almost as long as nuclear weapons have existed, would be well worth several times the projected costs of the international monitoring effort.

However, this will be only a small fraction of the full cost of a test ban to the United States, which has determined that it must make provisions to main-tain the safety and reliability of its stockpile of nuclear weapons for the indefi-nite future in the absence of nuclear testing. The Clinton administration has es-tablished a Stockpile Stewardship and Management Program designed to "ensur[e] the safety, security, and reliability of the U.S. nuclear weapon stock-pile . . . for the foreseeable future" [30, p. iii]. The costs of this program dwarf the cost of monitoring a test ban. They include the construction of several new facilities for simulating different aspects of fission and fusion explosions, for producing tritium (an isotope of hydrogen used to enhance the efficiency of nuclear weapons), and for maintaining a cadre of weapon scientists capable of dealing with problems of aging or deterioration that may appear in the stockpile. The program is also mandated to preserve the capability to resume testing at any time in the future if the President determines that vital national security interests require it.

The Department of Energy estimates that the Stewardship Program will cost $3.6–4.0 billion per year to operate, at least 50 times the cost of monitoring a CTBT. It is not clear what fraction of this amount to attribute to the CTBT, since many of the stewardship and maintenance activities would continue even if testing were to continue. But some facilities, such as the National Ignition Facility (NIF), are justified almost entirely on the basis of their ability to com-pensate for the absence of an active testing program. The facility will in fact have little relevance to maintenance problems that are likely to arise in the weapon stockpile. Nevertheless, the Energy Department has sold the facility to Congress and to the administration almost entirely on the basis of its necessity for a test ban, and it is highly unlikely that it would be funded without this ratio-nale [31]. The NIF alone will cost at least $1.1 billion to build and approxi-mately $115 million per year to operate, more than any savings the United States

---

[11] A complete text of the CTBT can be found in *Arms Control Today*, August 1996, pp. 19–30 or on the World Wide Web site of the Arms Control and Disarmament Agency (see bibliography).

will realize by not conducting the five or so tests per year it claims it would need to maintain the stockpile if testing were permitted.[12]

If one accepts the argument that an expensive stockpile stewardship program is essential to U.S. acceptance of a test ban,[13] one is forced to the conclusion that a test ban is no bargain in purely economic terms. The benefits must be counted in the less tangible realm of a CTB's contribution to nuclear nonproliferation, especially its political role in maintaining the legitimacy of the NPT in the eyes of the states not permitted to have any nuclear weapons, safe and reliable or otherwise. Unfortunately, even this contribution is somewhat diluted by perceptions among many states that the U.S. Stockpile Stewardship Program, along with similar programs now being created by France and other nuclear weapon states, are really just nuclear testing by other means. References by the Departments of Energy and Defense to the "enduring nuclear stockpile," which must be maintained for the "foreseeable future" [30, p. 2], do not inspire confidence that the United States is serious about another important commitment it made at the NPT renewal and extension conference—a commitment to ultimate nuclear disarmament. If the credibility of this commitment is undermined, the benefits of a CTBT may be considerably less than hoped for, and the costs may begin to appear disproportionately large.

Non-Proliferation Treaty

The Non-Proliferation Treaty (NPT) has had 25 years of experience with on-site inspections under the IAEA Safeguards system, a record unapproached by any other agreement. At the beginning of the Review and Extension Conference in April 1995 there were 172 signatories to the NPT, and 102 of them had signed safeguards agreements with the IAEA [4, p. 41; 32]. At the end of 1994 the Agency was safeguarding 170 nuclear power reactors, 158 research reactors, 196 other facilities (including conversion, fabrication, enrichment, reprocessing, and storage facilities), and 334 locations outside of safeguarded facilities. The number of facilities under safeguards has increased steadily at a rate of approximately ten per year, with South Africa, Brazil, and Argentina providing much of the increase during the early 1990s [4, p. 29; 33, p. 29]. Ukraine's decision to join the NPT in December 1994 will add another 16 power reactors to IAEA's burden. Many of them are similar to the Chernobyl reactor, a proliferation-prone design that requires more intensive inspections [33].

The total amount of plutonium under safeguards has also continued to grow. Nearly 500 metric tons of plutonium (both in spent fuel and reprocessed) was under IAEA safeguards at the end of 1994, and the amount has been increasing at a rate of at least 50 metric tons per year in recent years [4, p. 40]. IAEA does all of this on an annual safeguards budget of about $70 million, of which the

---

[12] Total lifetime costs for the NIF are estimated at over $4.5 billion for 30 years. See FY 1996 DOE Congressional Budget Request, Vol. 1, Project Data Sheets, Weapons Activities, p. 332.

[13] For some critical views of the Stockpile Stewardship Program see: Frank von Hippel and Suzanne Jones, "Take a Hard Look at Subcritical Tests," *Bulletin of the Atomic Scientists*, November/December 1996, pp. 44–47; Richard L. Garwin, "Stewardship: Don't Claim Too Much or Too Little," *Bulletin of the Atomic Scientists*, May/June 1997, pp. 21–24; and Ray E. Kidder, "Problems with Stockpile Stewardship," *Nature*, April 17, 1997, pp. 645–647.

United States contributes about 25 percent, or $18 million.[14] Despite the continuing increase in safeguards requirements this budget has remained virtually constant (adjusted for inflation) since 1984 [4, p. 39]. As a result, the annual number of person-days of inspection has fallen nearly 14 percent from a high of 11,000 in 1990 to about 9,500 in 1994. Also down is the percentage of facilities at which IAEA has been able to achieve its full safeguarding objectives. This had dropped from 83 percent in 1990 to 68 percent in 1994. This is clear evidence of a "deepening financial crisis" faced by the IAEA, a crisis that appears to have no resolution in sight [33, pp. 30–31]. IAEA points to economies of scale that allow it to supervise larger facilities and greater quantities of material for the same total cost [4, p. 21]. But the declines in inspector-days and achieved goals suggest that the quality of safeguards protection is deteriorating despite what may well be significant improvements in efficiency.

On the whole the NPT experience has been positive, and in the vast majority of cases the IAEA has been able credibly to certify that states have not diverted safeguarded nuclear materials from peaceful to military uses. The IAEA safeguards regime has made it much more difficult, expensive, and politically risky for new states to acquire nuclear weapons. In addition, export controls, which require full-scope safeguards in states receiving nuclear technology even if they are not parties to the NPT, have inhibited proliferators by forcing them to rely more heavily on indigenous technology and expertise. The result seems clearly to have been worth the effort and expense of the safeguards program. Certainly from the U.S. point of view the benefits have amply justified an expenditure of less than $20 million per year.

Despite their generally positive record some disturbing developments in the past several years have begun to raise questions about the effectiveness of IAEA safeguards as they are presently constituted. Iraq was a party to the NPT, its nuclear facilities were routinely visited by inspectors, and it was routinely given a clean bill of health. Yet for more than ten years Iraq was building and operating a massive clandestine nuclear weapons program that completely escaped detection by the IAEA. There were suspicions that something was going on, and the United States devoted some intelligence efforts to try to learn more about what Iraq was doing. But everyone was surprised at the nature and extent of the Iraqi program when it was exposed in the wake of the Gulf War [34, 35, 36, 37].

North Korea provides another uncomfortable example. It signed the NPT in 1985 but took seven more years to reach a safeguards agreement with the IAEA which would allow inspections to begin [38]. When IAEA analysis of plutonium samples taken in the first inspections suggested discrepancies in North Korea's declarations, North Korea refused to allow further inspections that might have resolved the discrepancies and threatened to withdraw from the NPT. An agreement reached with the intervention of the United States has smoothed over some of the difficulties, but the on-site inspections of two waste sites demanded by the IAEA have been delayed for at least five years [39, 40]. These inspections would not incur great costs, but the benefits in clarifying the nuclear status of North Korea would be substantial.

---

[14] Safeguards account for only about one-third of the IAEA's total regular budget, so the full U.S. contribution to IAEA is close to $50 million per year.

Meanwhile, the IAEA spends the great majority of its time and budget inspecting states about which virtually no one harbors suspicions of cheating. Because safeguards monitoring is politically neutral and focused on fissile materials, most of IAEA's inspections and surveillance are concentrated where the largest amounts of plutonium and enriched uranium are produced and used [41, p. 4]. This means that 60 percent of IAEA's safeguards budget is spent in Germany and Japan alone. Another 10 percent is spent in Canada, 8 to 10 percent in the nuclear-weapon states, and a "sizable share" in Belgium, Sweden, Spain, the Czech Republic, and Slovakia [33]. Altogether, at least 85 percent of all safeguards funds are spent on countries that pose no proliferation threat.

Most people would happily trade ten years of routine monitoring of Canada's nuclear fuel inventories for just one day at the two North Korean waste sites, but the prospects for shifting resources to states of more serious proliferation concern do not seem promising [33]. As an international organization the IAEA cannot overtly discriminate between states in the application of safeguards [41]. As far as the IAEA is concerned, the threat of diversion associated with any state is proportional to the amount of nuclear material in that state. Any formula that included political factors in weighing diversion risks would almost certainly be unacceptable to nonnuclear weapon states parties.

The experiences of Iraq and North Korea have led the IAEA to propose an expansion of its safeguards procedures. Called Program 93+2,[15] the initiative involves broader access to information about states' nuclear programs, including expanded declarations of nuclear activities, environmental sampling during on-site inspections, and increased physical access to declared facilities and to locations requested by the agency where that access can help clarify questions of compliance [42]. Some of the measures proposed by the IAEA could be added without additional legal authority, and the Agency began using these so-called "Part I measures" in 1996. Part II measures will require expanded legal authority, and this must be granted by the Governing Board made up of a broad spectrum of states parties, some of whom are not enthusiastic about giving the IAEA even more power than it already has to request information and inspect their facilities. A major criterion for acceptance of 93+2 measures is that they "reduce implementation costs while maintaining or improving safeguards effectiveness," but states like Germany and Japan have so far remained unconvinced that what they see as a disproportionate burden of costs will in fact be reduced.

Another effort to improve the system has been a more forceful effort to employ "special inspections" based on evidence supplied to the IAEA by member states. IAEA Director Hans Blix proposed such an arrangement in 1991, but little progress has been made in implementing it since then [43]. North Korea was an important test case, and the failure of the IAEA to gain access to the sites it wanted to inspect shows how difficult it will be to conduct special inspections at the times and places where they are most needed.

All of this adds up to an ambiguous cost-benefit analysis for NPT safeguards. So far they have not been overly expensive, but they are now unquestionably underfunded and will require both structural changes and substantial increases in national contributions to avoid further degradation of their effective-

---

[15] The new program was begun in 1993 and was to have been completed in 1995. It didn't make the deadline but the name has stuck anyway.

ness and credibility.[16] They have succeeded in monitoring the vast majority of nuclear activities and fissile materials in the world, but the things they have missed have been enough to damage their credibility with political leaders and opinion makers in many countries. Nevertheless, a substantial majority of states endorsed an indefinite extension of the NPT in April 1995, and this would appear to express an overall sense of confidence in the treaty and, by implication, in the safeguards regime that supports it [44].

Open Skies Treaty

The Open Skies Treaty had still not entered into force at the end of 1996. Of the 27 signatories, five, including Russia, Belarus, Ukraine, Georgia, and Kyrgyzstan, had not ratified it, and there was no information available about when they intended to do so. Nevertheless, the United States has gone ahead with preparations, and enough has been done to be able to make reasonably accurate projections of the costs of implementation if the treaty ever does enter into force. Since Open Skies is not arms control, there are no weapons or bases to be eliminated. The entire cost will be for monitoring, and the unique feature of this treaty is that the monitoring need not be connected with the verification of any specific agreement. It is a pure confidence-building measure intended to provide all parties with opportunities to observe anything about their neighbors that can be seen from an aircraft equipped with modern imaging sensors, albeit with some relatively tight restrictions on their capabilities. There are even mechanisms in the treaty for recovering some of the costs, since the data from any Open Skies flight can be purchased by any other state party.

The treaty was signed in Helsinki in March 1992, and even before ratification the Defense Department began allocating funds in preparation for EIF. A total of $93.7 million was appropriated in FY 1992 and 1993, mostly to be spent on modifying the three WC-135 aircraft that will be used in U.S. observation flights [45, p. 19]. The first modified aircraft, now redesignated OC-135B, was delivered to the On-Site Inspection Agency at the end of June 1993 [46]. It is equipped with four optical cameras but no infrared or radar equipment. The treaty requires these sensors to be phased in three years after EIF. Two other WC-135s are being modified to include the full suite of permitted sensors and are scheduled to be delivered to OSIA by the time they are needed. Any new kinds of sensors, such as radiation or chemical detectors, that could add to the cost of implementation must be agreed to by all states parties in the Open Skies Consultative Commission.

Long-term costs of Open Skies will depend on how many flights are conducted. The initial U.S. quotas allow for 31 active and 31 passive flights in the first year after EIF [45, p. 4]. The limit will rise to 42 per year once the treaty achieves its steady state, but it is unlikely that the full quota will be used. From the beginning of on-site inspection it had been U.S. policy to exploit all monitor-

---

[16] There are additional "hidden costs" to safeguards that result from the traditional insistence by developing states that any increases in the safeguards budget be matched by increases in voluntary contributions of technical aid from states with developed nuclear industries. In the past this has effectively doubled the marginal cost of improving or expanding safeguards.

ing opportunities to the fullest extent allowed by each treaty.[17] However, in the case of Open Skies the costs of such thoroughness may not be justified by the benefits. The Senate Intelligence Committee pointed out that under present plans all resources needed to analyze Open Skies imagery will come from existing budgets and personnel and will therefore compete with other Defense Department priorities. The committee noted, "Executive branch managers recognize the distinct possibility that the costs of Open Skies exploitation will exceed the expected value of the data" [45, pp. 11–12]. It seems unlikely, therefore, that the United States will conduct or receive its full quota of overflights. One projection by the Department of Defense assumes that the United States will conduct and receive just 15 flights per year for the first three years and 22 per year thereafter, only about half of what is permitted [47, pp. 26–27].

The cost of a U.S. Open Skies flight over another state (an "active" flight) has been estimated to be $100–150 thousand for operation of the aircraft alone. For flights by other states over the United States ("passive" flights), most of the cost is borne by the inspecting party, but there will be an estimated $25,000 per flight in nonreimbursable costs to the United States. These include ground support and security for the foreign aircraft, support of an OSIA escort team, and monitoring the processing of data obtained by the flight. If the United States were to use its full quota of passive and active flights (31 per year for the first three years and 42 per year thereafter), and average costs are $125,000 per active flight and $25,000 per passive flight, the total cost of operating the aircraft would be $4.65 million per year in the first three years, rising to $6.3 million per year thereafter. Using the Defense Department projections, the corresponding numbers are $2.25 million and $3.3 million. The latter figure is about 40 percent of OSIA's projected annual budget for Open Skies in 2001 ($8.5 million).[18] Other expenses besides those directly attributable to overflights include management, data processing, maintenance, counterintelligence, assistance to foreign countries, and participation in the Open Skies Consultative Commission. Early expectations were that the Department of Defense would spend $20–40 million per year in the period FY 1994–1997 to implement the treaty, but these figures probably included money spent on modifying the two remaining WC-135s [48, p. 142]. A reasonable estimate of the annual implementation costs would be $10–15 million over the long term, depending on how many flights the United States chooses to conduct.

The benefits of Open Skies for the United States go well beyond the intelligence value of the imagery itself and involve both diplomatic and national security benefits. Open Skies imagery will add only marginally to what the United States can already obtain from satellite sensors, but for states without such assets it represents an unprecedented opportunity to observe their neighbors and possible adversaries. The benefits to the United States from this added transparency cannot be quantified but would appear as increased stability and security in Europe, and increased acceptance of the legitimacy of intrusive confidence

---

[17] In its assessment of CFE Treaty implementation the General Accounting Office called attention to the expectation that all U.S. agencies "aggressively implement the treaty" and "take maximum advantage of U.S. inspection rights" [5, pp. 27–29]. OSIA officials have confirmed in personal communications to the author that this policy still applies to INF, START, and other treaties as well as to CFE.

[18] OSIA briefing chart, 25 January 1995.

building measures. If Open Skies could be extended to unstable areas like the Middle East or South Asia, the benefits would be even greater. Unfortunately, the prospects for such extensions appear dim as this is written. Still, the existence of an Open Skies regime and the experience gained from it could provide incentives for new states to join.

From the point of view of U.S. national security, the Senate Armed Services Committee was able to see a wide range of benefits. The treaty will open all areas of states parties, including areas formerly restricted for national security reasons,[19] to aerial observation and will establish a new framework for contacts, cooperation and consultation among participating states [48, p. 141]. Open Skies flights can be used to orient START and CFE inspectors at inspection sites and to help in selecting sites to be inspected. With or without additional radiation or chemical sensors, it could be useful in monitoring the Comprehensive Test Ban and the Chemical and Biological Weapons Conventions.

There are some risks associated with Open Skies. Allowing foreign aircraft to overfly military or industrial facilities will require precautions to ensure that sensitive information is not revealed, adding an unpredictable increment to the cost of implementation. There is also a risk that data from overflights will fall into the hands of nonparticipating states or even terrorist groups. The treaty requires that the data from all flights, while available to all states parties, "shall be used exclusively for the attainment of the purposes of this Treaty" [48, p. 143]. But there remains a small risk that data will be stolen by or leaked to unauthorized groups and be used for hostile or criminal purposes. Finally, there are safety concerns associated with the use of aircraft in a foreign country. An accident in which foreign inspectors are killed or injured during an inspection could create an awkward diplomatic incident. The coordination of Open Skies flights with normal commercial and military traffic will be an important part of implementing the treaty successfully.

On balance, the Open Skies Treaty appears to be worth its costs and risks, at least from the perspective of the United States. Annual costs will be much less than those of any other agreement, and risks will be relatively easy to manage. The benefits of Open Skies to the United States, while largely indirect, will derive from increased transparency and military stability in conflict-prone regions of the world. The value of establishing a precedent of full use of active quotas and the wide distribution of the data they generate could turn out to be well worth a few million dollars per year in added costs. Unfortunately, it has become increasingly clear that many Russians assess the treaty far more negatively. Excessive costs have been repeatedly mentioned, along with what some Russians perceive as an inequality in the allocation of passive and active overflights, as reasons for the Duma's reluctance to ratify the treaty.

Chemical Weapons Agreements

There are two major chemical weapons treaties to which the United States is party: the Bilateral Destruction and Non-production Agreement (BDA) and the international Chemical Weapons Convention (CWC). The costs to be incurred

---

[19] Of particular interest to the United States is the portion of Russia east of the Ural Mountains, which is not available for inspections under CFE or the Vienna CSBMs.

under the BDA include the destruction of national stockpiles of CW agents and weapons and the elimination or conversion to peaceful activities of the facilities at which they are manufactured, stored, and deployed. They also include bilateral monitoring of the destruction and nonproduction of these agents in Russia and the United States for the indefinite future. Expenses under the CWC will be associated almost entirely with monitoring the chemical industries of all states parties, which will be done by the international Organization for the Prevention of Chemical Weapons (OPCW), supported by contributions from states parties in roughly the same proportion as their contributions to United Nations operations. The United States will therefore contribute about 25 percent of the OPCW's operating budget.

All analysts agree that these treaties will be expensive to implement and verify. The initial estimate of the cost of destroying the full U.S. stockpile of chemical weapons and agents was $1.7 billion in 1985 [49, p. 15]. By 1996 it had passed $12 billion[20] as technical problems and environmental, health, and safety concerns forced costly delays and modifications in the destruction process (see figure 5.3) [51]. But only a fraction of these costs should be attributed to the BDA and CWC. The vast majority of U.S. chemical weapons were already obsolete and in some cases dangerously unstable, and Congress had ordered their destruction long before either agreement was signed.[21] The avoidance of future investments in modern binary chemical weapons can legitimately be counted as a benefit of the CWC, since the U.S. promise not to use chemical weapons in warfare and to eliminate its entire stockpile is contingent on theConvention entering into force.[22] Just how large this saving will be is impossible to estimate, especially since U.S. spending on *defensive* CW preparations will continue at a relatively high level even after the Convention is ratified. According to Joint Chiefs Chairman John Shalikashvili, "The Defense Department . . . is committed to maintaining a robust Chemical Biological Defense program . . . to protect U.S. forces under all possible conditions of deployment" [54].

---

[20] The $12 billion estimate applies only to the actual U.S. stockpile. There are also thousands of tons of old chemical weapons and agents buried in many locations around the United States. The Army estimates that it will cost $17.7 billion to clean up these sites [50]. This expense is not attributable to the CWC because the Convention specifically exempts chemical munitions buried on a party's own territory before January 1, 1977 or dumped at sea before January 1, 1985 (Article IV.17). For a more recent survey of the problems facing the U.S. CW cleanup effort see Chemical Weapons and Materiel: Key Factors Affecting Disposal Costs and Schedule, GAO/NSIAD-97-18, U.S. General Accounting Office, February 1997.

[21] The congressional action, taken in 1985 at the height of an intense debate over the future of chemical weapons, did not represent a renunciation of CW, as President Bush's did six years later. The Congress mandated the destruction of the stockpile of obsolete and dangerous *unitary* chemical weapons. However, many members of Congress, as well as the Reagan administration, still had high hopes for the deployment of *binary* chemical weapons, which were supposed to be safer and more militarily effective than the old unitary weapons.

[22] The United States formally agreed to eliminate "the preponderance of [its] chemical weapons stockpile" when it signed the BDA in June 1990 [52, p. 24]. President Bush's announcement renouncing the use of CW under any circumstances was made in May 1991 and was intended to move CWC negotiations forward in the Conference on Disarmament in Geneva [53]. However, Bush's renunciation of CW use will become effective only after the CWC enters into force. So, until the U.S. ratifies the CWC it is not legally committed either to complete chemical disarmament or to its promise never to use chemical weapons in warfare.

Figure 5.3
Projected Costs of U.S. CW Destruction

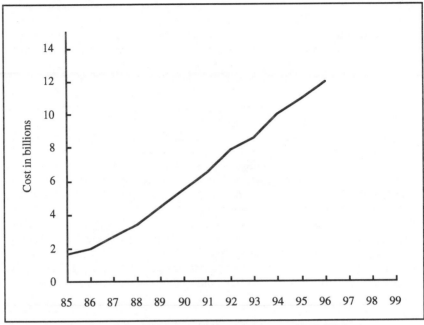

Sources: Sipri Yearbook 1995, Table 10.1 and *Washington Post*, January 23, 1996.

The costs of verification are not much easier to predict than the costs of implementation. There have been trial inspections under the Wyoming Memorandum of Understanding and in preparation for the CWC. The former have focused on weapons facilities and their results remain classified. The latter, called National Trial Inspections, have focused on chemical industrial sites, have been carried out in many signatory states, and have been used by the Conference on Disarmament and the OPCW Preparatory Commission to design the CWC inspection regime. By mid-1993 there had been more than 200 trial inspections in many countries, and a U.S. contractor had developed a computerized data base to organize the information generated by them [55, pp. 28–29]. Estimates of the cost of inspections of commercial facilities are derived from this experience, but substantial uncertainties will remain until implementation begins. The cost of an inspection will depend on its type (baseline, routine, or challenge), the size and nature of the facility being inspected, and the degree to which the inspection requires major preparations or interferes with normal production activities. OTA estimates range from a low of $10,000 to a high of $500,000 per inspection. This large range of uncertainty makes reliable estimates of overall costs difficult, but an order of magnitude estimate suggests that the cost to U.S. chemical facilities of CWC inspections might be about $5 million per year.[23]

There will also be costs of data collection and reporting for which each facility will be responsible under the Convention. OTA did not provide quantitative estimates of these costs but did note that efforts are being made to reduce paperwork to a minimum by having all reports done on simplified standard forms. Companies would "simply check off boxes and fill in blanks" [55, p. 24]. Given the already substantial reporting costs that U.S. chemical facilities incur under environmental, health, safety, and export control regulations, the marginal costs of CWC reporting do not appear to be unreasonable.[24] A possible exception would be the costs to small firms of on-site inspections. Since these are likely to be relatively rare, it should be possible for the industry to spread the costs, possibly by creating an on-site inspection insurance fund.

The U.S. taxpayer will also contribute to implementing chemical disarmament. To administer the CWC the OPCW is expected to need $150–250 million per year, which means that the U.S. contribution will be in the range of $40–60 million [58, p. 50]. For the BDA, the Nunn-Lugar program has already committed $55 million to help Russia design a CW destruction facility, but this is only a drop in the bucket. The Russian stockpile is at least 33 percent larger than the U.S. stockpile and will cost a comparable amount to eliminate. There was a time when Soviet authorities could simply have ordered the destruction of CW agents wherever and however they chose. But those days are long gone in Russia, and from now on, "human factors—including health concerns, environmental impact, worker's compensation, insurance programs and guarantees, safety and public opinion in the local communities—will play a key role in shaping Russia's chemical demilitarization efforts" [59, p. 21]. These are precisely the factors that continue to drive up the cost of U.S. disposal efforts. Inspections under the BDA will also be expensive. OSIA anticipates that CW inspections will account for more than half of its projected $150 million budget in 2001.[25] If this happens, chemical weapons inspections in Russia and the United States will cost more than inspections for all other treaties combined.

There are two available estimates of the full cost of implementing the BDA (exclusive of weapons destruction), one by the CBO in 1990 just after the agreement was signed [15, pp. 37–40], and the other by the GAO in March 1994 [60, pp. 32–34]. CBO estimated one-time costs of $45–220 million and average annual costs of $15–70 million. These numbers give an average annual cost of $19.5–92 million. GAO used actual expenditures between FY 1989 and FY 1993 in its estimate. A total of $165 million was spent during this period, about 60 percent of it for research and development and 35 percent for compliance and verification activities. Projected expenditures for the next six fiscal years (1994-1999) total $716 million ($120 million per year average), which includes some

---

[23] This is obtained by assuming an average cost per inspection of $100,000 and 50 inspections per year in the years immediately after EIF [56, p. 47]. Note also that some inspections each year may be conducted at government-owned facilities in which case the costs would not be borne by industry.
[24] The Chemical Manufactures Association estimates that compliance with U.S. environmental regulations alone already costs the chemical industry nearly $5 billion per year [55, p. 20]. This can be placed in perspective by noting that in 1991 the U.S. chemical industry had total sales of $380 billion and employed 846,000 people with a payroll of $31 billion [57].
[25] OSIA briefing chart, January 25, 1995. OSIA has only minor responsibilities under the CWC, so the cost estimates are almost entirely attributable to the bilateral agreement.

money for the OPCW PrepCom and Nunn-Lugar aid already committed by FY 1994. However, GAO's estimate of $20 million for the U.S. contribution to the OPCW appears too low by a factor of two or three. Implementing and verifying the BDA and CWC will therefore cost the U.S. at least $100 million per year, and possibly as much as $150 million per year.[26] This adds 10 to 15 percent to the $1 billion per year required to eliminate the U.S. stockpile by 2005 and still doesn't include any future aid to Russia's CW destruction program.

By any measure, then, eliminating chemical weapons under a verified international convention will be very expensive. Will the benefits justify the costs? There can be no definitive, much less quantitative, answer to this question. Kathleen Bailey, who opposes ratification of the CWC, explains her position succinctly: "Although these moneys would not be too much to pay for effective verification, they are excessive for marginal verification" [61, p. 54]. However, the Chairman of the Joint Chiefs of Staff, testifying in support of ratification, did not feel that CWC verification was "marginal." He stated that while verification is "less than perfect, the verification regime allows for intrusive inspection while protecting national security concerns . . . [and] reduces the probability of U.S. forces encountering chemical warfare in regional conflicts" [54]. He concluded, "The Convention's advantages outweigh its shortcomings."

Jessica Eve Stern, another supporter of ratification, acknowledges the high cost of implementation, but concludes that "few opponents of the CWC are likely to consider [the elimination of Russia's stockpile] a bad bargain" [58, p. 50]. She recommends that verification costs be kept down by reducing the number of routine inspections and emphasizing challenge inspections [58, p. 39]. This would avoid the IAEA's practice of spending most of its safeguards budget on countries of little or no proliferation concern, but it could conflict with the principle of nondiscrimination fundamental to international disarmament conventions. Stern concludes that "despite its imperfections, the CWC is a better deterrent to chemical warfare than the status quo" [58, p. 32]. This conclusion avoids the more difficult question raised by Bailey, i.e., whether it is a sufficiently better deterrent to warrant the high costs. According to Stern:

The CWC is an historic achievement in that it bans outright a particularly abhorrent class of weapons. It contains unprecedentedly intrusive verification measures. And it is the first disarmament treaty to contain provisions that explicitly call for a collective response to violations. [58, p. 52]

While Bailey would probably agree that the verification measures are "unprecedentedly intrusive,"[27] she nevertheless concludes that the CWC is "only minimally verifiable" and "not . . . worth the cost" [61, pp. 52, 58].

A quantitative cost-benefit calculation cannot settle this argument. At its roots it has much more to do with political assumptions about the value of international regimes and arms control than it does with estimates of financial costs. The CWC is expensive in absolute terms, but the costs are relatively small compared to those required to modernize, maintain, or even eliminate existing U.S.

---

[26] CW inspections appear to be an exception to the rule that actual costs are less than early projection. In this case the CBO estimates made in 1990 appear to have been too low.

[27] In fact, this feature of the treaty forms the basis of another conservative argument against its ratification [62].

and Russian stockpiles. If the major powers have decided that chemical disarmament is in their interests, an international regime of verification adds only marginally to expenses they would have to incur in any event. Meanwhile it adds significantly, if not absolutely, to their confidence that disarmament is really taking place, while complicating, but not necessarily preventing, clandestine violations. It also creates a regime that establishes and to some degree enforces an international norm against the manufacture and use of these weapons. In the current state of international politics the institutionalization of such norms appears to have positive value.[28] States that do not join the convention or that try to cheat on it risk ostracism and sanctions that would be harder to impose in the absence of a formal convention. The inefficiency of subjecting the most highly industrialized states to most of the routine inspections appears to be an unavoidable consequence of this kind of treaty. It is unquestionably burdensome, but it does contribute to the legitimacy of the regime and adds to both the pressures and incentives for smaller states to join it.

There are some risks associated with a CWC. Some states may simply refuse to join and will have to be deterred or prevented from acquiring chemical weapons by traditional diplomatic, economic, or military measures, or simply be allowed to have them. Experience with the nuclear NPT should allow no illusions about this risk. The Convention may create a false sense of security, causing some states to reduce traditional intelligence activities and to ignore defensive preparations that hedge against violations. Finally, the inspection regime may lead to an increase in industrial espionage and even to a higher risk of proliferation as more inspectors get to see the insides of advanced chemical plants and take this knowledge back to their home countries.

All of these risks are real, and the drafters of the Convention were clearly aware of them. The risk of loss of proprietary information has been reduced by the use of "managed access" restrictions for challenge inspections [55, pp. 43–59]. The tension in this situation is quite obvious: to do their jobs well inspectors should be highly skilled, knowledgeable, observant, and persistent. At the same time it is precisely these qualities that could enable them to discover information that would compromise industrial secrets. The chemical industry is worried about this aspect of the convention, and programs have been instituted by ACDA, OSIA, and the Department of Commerce to teach operators of U.S. chemical plants how to prepare for inspections and guard against loss of proprietary information.

In conclusion, the CWC is a close call. In order to support its ratification one must believe that the benefits of establishing an international regime banning chemical weapons are worth an annual cost to the United States of $100–150 million, as well as both political and commercial risks. The CWC will improve transparency and reduce some military risks, but it will not make the world safe from chemical weapons. One need go no further than the sarin attack on the Tokyo subway in March 1995 to find evidence for this unhappy reality. There is nothing in an international convention that can prevent such incidents, although a regime that rigorously monitored the production and transfer of key

---

[28] According to Antonia and Abram Chayes, "Unlike deterrence, which relies on strategic interactions between opposed states, the key to reassurance is a reliable normative and institutional structure" [63, p. 65].

precursor chemicals might make it somewhat more difficult. At the same time there are clear positive benefits associated with increased transparency and widely accepted norms of behavior, enforced by systematic inspections and continued national vigilance. There would also be a substantial political cost associated with a U.S. decision to refuse to join an international agreement it had done so much for so long to try to achieve.

Biological Weapons Agreements

There are currently no implementation or verification costs associated with the BWC, aside from the minor costs of reporting U.S. activities under the 1986 and 1991 confidence-building measures. One could try to attach a cost to the UN Special Commission's efforts to find and destroy Iraq's BW capabilities, but this is a very small and in many ways unique operation that would provide little insight into the costs of an international BW verification regime. Reciprocal inspections (official U.S. jargon refers to them as "visits") have taken place among the United States, United Kingdom, and Russia, but data on them are inaccessible because of secrecy. One positive aspect of biological weapons is that they are a lot easier and cheaper to destroy than chemical weapons or nuclear materials. The quantities involved are typically several orders of magnitude smaller than for chemical weapons, and since most BW agents are living organisms, they die out relatively quickly unless sophisticated measures are taken to preserve them. Even then they can only survive for several months[29] [64, p. 93].

If international verification were added to the BWC, costs could increase dramatically. As noted in chapter 3, even such common commercial facilities as breweries or yogurt plants could be used to produce BW agents. A verification regime that could subject all such facilities to even a small risk of on-site inspection would be even more expensive than the CWC and still not particularly reassuring to people concerned about BW proliferation. These issues have already been addressed briefly in chapter 3, so I will take them no further here. It will be sufficient to note that the instructions given to the VEREX group clearly require that the "financial implications" of proposed verification measures must be considered along with their technical effectiveness.[30] The financial criterion will be one of the most important in the evaluation by the United States of whatever proposals are made by the Expert Group. In view of its already heavy financial commitment to arms control implementation and its often articulated skepticism of the possibility of meaningful verification of the BWC, the United States will be a hard sell on an international BW verification regime.

SUMMARY AND OBSERVATIONS

Is arms control worth the cost of implementation? If we focus on those treaties that have already been implemented the overall evaluation is positive,

---

[29] One exception is anthrax, which forms spores that can live in a dormant state for decades. Anthrax stockpiles would have to be destroyed by incineration or by some kind of chemical treatment, but the cost would be trivial compared with CW disposal.

[30] See the Summary of VEREX Evaluations of Potential Verification Measures, BWC/CONF.III/VEREX/8, Attachment to the Summary Report, reprinted in the *Arms Control Reporter*, 1994, 701.D.5–15.

but there is at least one clear exception and another for which questions can legitimately be raised. INF, START, and CFE are clearly worth their costs of implementation and verification, the Threshold Test Ban clearly was not, and IAEA safeguards are a close call. This is not to suggest that the NPT itself is of dubious value; it obviously is not. The treaty continues to serve the interests of the vast majority of its signatories, and it creates a desirable international norm that complicates and stigmatizes attempts to evade it. Still, it is legitimate to ask whether the safeguards system that has grown up under the NPT is the most cost-effective way to achieve the treaty's objectives. Similar questions arise in the international treaties controlling chemical and biological weapons and the one proposed to cut off production of fissile materials for weapons. The requirement that international treaties be politically neutral inevitably requires that large sums be spent monitoring large and industrially advanced parties. The benefits of this arrangement derive less from the deterrence or detection of violations than from the political legitimacy given to surveillance of states more likely to be tempted to acquire prohibited weapons.

There are three general observations that can be made on the basis of the experience so far. The first is that the cost of implementation is a strong function of the nature of the weapons controlled by the treaty. Solid fuel rocket engines, like those in intermediate- and long-range ballistic missiles, are a lot more expensive to eliminate (assuming reasonable attention to environmental protection and health and safety of workers) than tanks or artillery pieces. It is also much more expensive to prepare a strategic missile base or production facility for inspection than a tank regiment or helicopter base. The second is that on-site inspection has consistently proven to be cheaper than anticipated. A typical INF inspection costs at most a few tens of thousands of dollars, and a CFE inspection considerably less. The cost of inspection, like the cost of implementation, depends on the complexity of the target and the technical sophistication required of inspectors. A nuclear weapon or ballistic missile engineer costs more than an artillery or tank officer, so personnel costs can vary widely for different kinds of inspections. Finally, continuous monitoring is more expensive than periodic inspections, and in most cases does not appear to be worth the additional costs. The virtual abandonment of continuous portal monitoring in START suggests that the benefit-cost ratio is much less favorable than many people thought it would be in the 1980s.

The cost estimates made in this chapter are summarized in table 5.1. While the results for individual treaties have uncertainties of as much as 50 percent, the overall totals probably give a reasonable picture of the costs of implementing and verifying agreements already in force or on the visible horizon. Comparison with the original Congressional Budget Office study shows that the numbers in the table tend to be at the low end of CBO's range of uncertainty [15]. This supports the observation made at the beginning of the chapter that arms control has turned out to be less expensive to implement than anticipated. The tendency to overestimate costs in the early stages of negotiations was primarily a result of assuming that verification would be more comprehensive and intrusive than it turned out to be. In practice, mostly as a result of increasing awareness of costs, inspection and other monitoring provisions have been scaled back to levels below what many believed would be necessary a decade ago. There is little or no evidence that this more cost conscious approach to verification has weakened any of the treaties or led to increased incidence of noncompliance.

A few general comments can be made on the basis of table 5.1. First, it is striking how high the costs of chemical disarmament are compared to all other treaties. If CW destruction were included in the total it would dominate all other estimates combined. These costs are real, but only a small fraction of them at most can be attributed to implementing the Chemical Weapons Convention. The stockpiles of aging and unstable chemical weapons in the United States and Russia must be eliminated with or without a treaty because they pose a growing danger of gradual or catastrophic release of hazardous agents into the environment. The high cost of their elimination is more appropriately attributed to the unwise and short-sighted decisions made by both superpowers to produce them in the first place.

Second, it is remarkable that Nunn-Lugar aid to the former Soviet Republics accounts for almost half of the annual U.S. expenditure on arms control implementation. In effect, the United States is spending just about as much to disarm the former Soviet Union as it is to disarm itself. But while the costs are approximately the same, the benefits are very different. Nunn-Lugar funds provide benefits in the form of enhanced U.S. security and increased Russian transparency. This represents a recognition by the Congress and the administration that the Cooperative Threat Reduction Program is probably the most cost-effective investment the United States can make in its national security at this point in history. The real questions about CTR are not whether the United States can afford it, but whether the Russians will continue to cooperate with it and whether a politically conservative and budget conscious Congress will continue to support it.

One final observation. The overall cost of implementing all of the agreements considered in this study is just under one billion dollars per year, even including a generous subsidy for implementation in the former Soviet Union. This means that total arms control implementation costs would have to nearly triple before they would equal just 1 percent of the U.S. military budget of $260 billion. The international norms and military transparency created by the interaction of these regimes shows promise of creating a fundamentally different environment for international relations, and I will examine the arguments for and against this point of view in chapter 7. But, even if one believes that arms control contributes only marginally and temporarily to national security, it is difficult to argue that the treaties negotiated so far are not worth the expense of implementing them.

CONCLUSION

In ACDA's 1994 Report to Congress the Director's Overview begins with the observation, "Arms control is threat control. It is national defense by cheaper means. If viewed as a 'weapon' for removing threats, arms control is staggeringly cost effective" [65, p. 1]. The Director illustrates his point with the START Treaty, and most would agree that this example comes closest to deserving the hyperbolic adverb "staggeringly." The Director does not mention the Threshold Test Ban, which could just as well be labeled "staggeringly cost-

Table 5.1
U.S. Arms Control and Nonproliferation Costs (millions of dollars)

TREATY	ONE-TIME COSTS	ANNUAL COSTS
R&D	—	220[a]
INF	130	20
START	200–1000	50-100
Nunn-Lugar	—	400
TTBT[b]	(85–200)	(50–100)
CTBT	25	15–20
NPT/IAEA	—	20
CFE	27	35
CSBM	small	small
Open Skies	100	3–5
BDA/CWC	(12,000)[c]	100–150
BWC	small	small
TOTAL[d]	480–1,280	860–970

[a] Does not include R&D on national technical means.
[b] Russian and U.S. nuclear testing is currently suspended and unlikely to resume in the foreseeable future. So there are no implementation costs for the TTBT except for a small standby appropriation for the On-Site Inspection Agency.
[c] The $12 billion estimate for chemical weapons elimination is tentative, and no attempt has been made to estimate the fraction of it to be attributed to the agreements.
[d] Totals do not include costs of NTM , CW elimination, or TTBT monitoring.

ineffective," or the Chemical Weapons Convention, which falls well short of deserving any hyperbole at all. In short, it is not particularly illuminating, and could even be misleading, to make judgments about the overall costs and benefits of generic arms control.

There can be no question that cost-effectiveness has become a key criterion in arms control, but as this study has demonstrated, this criterion is going to be difficult to apply in practice. Not only are financial costs difficult to estimate in advance, but issues of benefit and risk will never be quantifiable in any meaningful or useful way. The criterion continues to beg the question of what "effective" actually means in each new treaty. This question was difficult enough to answer when military and political risk were the major factors in assessing it. When cost is added to the equation, the proper balance becomes even more difficult to find.

Judgments of cost-effectiveness will inevitably be political and subjective and will have to be made in the negotiating process. This suggests that an integral part of the backstopping of any U.S. delegation should be a capability to estimate the costs of verification and implementation proposals as they arise in negotiations. Just as military and intelligence representatives have traditionally advised delegations on the security risks and benefits of particular provisions, economic and technical advisors should be available to provide estimates of costs. The more timely and credible these estimates are, the more useful they will be in negotiations, not only in informing U.S. positions but in providing solid arguments to challenge those made by states who use exaggerated cost projections to oppose provisions they do not like for other reasons. Credible cost projections will also be crucial in gaining support for ratification of treaties in the Senate, where traditional opponents of arms control are beginning to discover the opportunities for delay and obstruction inherent in raising questions about costs.

In conclusion, it is worth repeating the ACDA Inspector General's warning quoted at the beginning of the chapter. "Budgetary constraints . . . require persuasive evidence that expenditures to implement current and proposed international understandings serve priority U.S. interests." The Clinton administration has so far found the evidence persuasive, as have all previous administrations, both Democratic and Republican, dating back to Eisenhower. The total cost of implementing and verifying all of the treaties so far in force and under negotiation is still only a tiny fraction of the money spent by the United States on its military forces. In order to prevent erosion of treaties in force and to allow further progress in arms control, especially nuclear arms control, the case will have to be made that expenditures on arms control can still increase security far more cost-effectively than equivalent or even much greater expenditures on military hardware. Senators Nunn and Lugar made that case well in selling the Cooperative Threat Reduction Program, and ACDA Director Holum makes it well when he points out that Russian ICBM silos, which were once targeted by U.S. nuclear warheads, are now being destroyed under START, "with far higher confidence, without fear of bloody retaliation, and at cost three orders of magnitude lower" [65].

The case for international verification of the Chemical and Biological Weapons Conventions is not quite so easy to make, as we have seen. It must be made by showing that these regimes will significantly increase the difficulty for states to acquire and use chemical and biological weapons, and that the institutions and norms the conventions establish will be capable of isolating and stigmatizing violators to a degree that makes it highly desirable for all states to be members in good standing. Such a regime already exists in the NPT and the IAEA safeguards system that supports it. One of the most important steps the world community could take to demonstrate its belief in the cost-effectiveness of such regimes would be to increase the IAEA safeguards budget, which has been level for more than a decade despite rapidly increasing demands for coverage.

The most important conclusion of this study is that while arms control is not cheap, neither is it all that expensive. Costs have risen rapidly because so many treaties have entered into force in such a short time, and the great majority of costs of each treaty must be paid during the early implementation years. Awareness of cost has risen even faster than the costs themselves, largely because the old perceptions of threat that made rigorous verification seem so important have been replaced by a more diffuse perception of threat and a concern with weapons far less easy to identify than the ones that dominated negotiations during the Cold War. These new concerns will not be easy to assuage, but an international regime that prohibited weapons of mass destruction, put stronger limits on the deployment and transfer of advanced conventional weapons, and created effective institutions to monitor the entire regime would go a long way toward achieving that goal. The benefits of such a regime would be worth many times the amount so far spent on arms control.

REFERENCES

1. Jeffrey H. Grotte and Julia L. Klare, Balancing Cost and Effectiveness in Arms Control Monitoring, Institute for Defense Analysis, September 1992.

2. Patricia M. Lewis, Organizing for Effective Implementation, *SIPRI Research Report No. 8, Implementing the Comprehensive Test Ban: New Aspects of Definition, Organization and Verification*, Eric Arnett, Ed. (Oxford: Oxford University Press, 1994), pp. 86–102.

3. *Arms Control Reporter*, 1994, pp. 701.D.5–15.

4. Activities of the International Atomic Energy Agency Relevant to Article III of the Treaty on the Non-proliferation of Nuclear Weapons, International Atomic Energy Agency, February 1, 1995.

5. Former Warsaw Pact Nations' Treaty Compliance and U.S. Cost Control, U.S. General Accounting Office, December 1993.

6. Intermediate-Range Nuclear Forces Treaty Implementation, U.S. General Accounting Office, September 1991.

7. Report of Inspection, U.S. Arms Control and Disarmament Agency, Office of Inspector General, August 1995.

8. *Verification Technologies: Managing Research and Development for Cooperative Arms Control Monitoring Measures*, OTA-ISC-488, U.S. Congress, Office of Technology Assessment, May 1991.

9. Douglas MacEachan, Statement for the Record on the START II Treaty, Senate Foreign Relations Committee, February 28, 1995 (Washington, DC: CIA Office of Public Affairs).

10. Jeffrey T. Richelson, *The U.S. Intelligence Community*, 3rd ed. (Boulder, CO: Westview Press, 1995).

11. Walter Pincus, "Spy Agency Hoards Secret $1 Billion," *Washington Post*, September 24, 1995, p. A1.

12. "Intelligence Agencies Seek More Cash, Report Says," *New York Times*, August 29, 1994.

13. Arms Control: Improved Coordination of Arms Control Research Needed, GAO/NSIAD-92-149, U.S. General Accounting Office, April 1992.

14. Joseph P. Harahan, *On-Site Inspections under the INF Treaty* (Washington, DC: On-Site Inspection Agency, 1993).

15. U.S. Costs of Verification and Compliance Under Pending Arms Treaties, U.S. Congress, Congressional Budget Office, September 1990.

16. The INF Treaty, Senate Foreign Relations Committee, April 14, 1988.

17. INF Treaty: Army and Air Force Personnel Reductions, GAO/NSIAD-89-173FS, U.S. General Accounting Office, June 1989.

18. Sidney Graybeal and Michael Krepon, "The Limitations of On-site Inspection," *Bulletin of the Atomic Scientists*, December 1987, pp. 22–26.

19. "U.S.-Russian Strategic Weapons Dismantlements," *Arms Control Today*, May 1995, p. 32.

20. The START Treaty, Senate Foreign Relations Committee, September 18, 1992.

21. "U.S. Security Assistance to the Former Soviet Union," *Arms Control Today*, September 1996, pp. 25–26.

22. Robert S. Norris and William M. Arkin, "Estimated Russian (CIS) Nuclear Stockpile, September 1994," *Bulletin of the Atomic Scientists*, September/October 1994, p. 61

23. The CFE Treaty, Senate Foreign Relations Committee, November 19, 1991.

24. *Seismic Verification of Nuclear Testing Treaties*, OTA-ISC-361, U.S. Congress, Office of Technology Assessment, May 1988.

25. Threshold Test Ban Treaty and Peaceful Nuclear Explosions Treaty, Hearings before the Senate Foreign Relations Committee, January 13, 15, 1987.

26. Threshold Test Ban and Peaceful Nuclear Explosions Treaties, Senate Foreign Relations Committee, September 14, 1990.

27. Spurgeon M. Keeny, Jr., "Notes from Underground," *Arms Control Today*, June 1988, p. 2.

28. *Sipri Yearbook 1995* (London: Oxford University Press, 1995).

29. Richard Rhodes, *Dark Sun: The Making of the Hydrogen Bomb* (New York: Simon & Schuster, 1995).

30. The Stockpile Stewardship and Management Program, U.S. Department of Energy, May 1995.

31. Hugh Gusterson, "Nif-ty Exercise Machine," *Bulletin of the Atomic Scientists*, September/October 1995, pp. 22–26.

32. "Factfile: Affiliations and Nuclear Activities of 172 NPT Parties," *Arms Control Today*, March 1995, pp. 33–36.

33. David Fischer, Innovations in IAEA Safeguards to Meet the Challenge of the 1990s, *A New Nuclear Triad: The Non-proliferation of Nuclear Weapons, International Verification and the International Atomic Energy Agency* (Southampton: Mountbatten Centre for International Studies, 1992), pp. 27-43.

34. Anthony Fainberg, Strengthening IAEA Safeguards: Lessons from Iraq, Center for International Security and Arms Control, Stanford University, April 1993.

35. David Albright and Mark Hibbs, "Iraq and the Bomb: Were They Even Close?" *Bulletin of the Atomic Scientists*, March 1991, pp. 16–25.

36. David Albright and Mark Hibbs, "Hyping the Real Iraqi Bomb," *Bulletin of the Atomic Scientists*, March 1991, pp. 26–28.

37. David Albright and Mark Hibbs, "Iraq's Nuclear Hide-and-Seek," *Bulletin of the Atomic Scientists*, September 1991, pp. 14–23.

38. David Albright, "How Much Plutonium Does North Korea Have?" *Bulletin of the Atomic Scientists*, September/October 1994, pp. 46–53.

39. "Agreed Framework between the United States of America and the Democratic People's Republic of Korea," *Arms Control Today*, December 1994, p. 19.

40. Jon B. Wolfsthal, "U.S., Pyongyang Reach Accord on North's Nuclear Program," *Arms Control Today*, November 1994, pp. 25, 32.

41. Lawrence Scheinman, "Lessons from Post-war Iraq for the International Full-Scope Safeguards Regime," *Arms Control Today*, April 1993, pp. 3–6.

42. Richard Hooper, "Strengthening IAEA Safeguards in an Era of Nuclear Cooperation," *Arms Control Today*, November 1995, pp. 14–18.

43. "IAEA Director Hans Blix: Keeping an Eye on a Nuclear World," *Arms Control Today*, November 1991, pp. 3–6.

44. Lewis A. Dunn, "High Noon for the NPT," *Arms Control Today*, July/August 1995, pp. 3–9.

45. Intelligence and Security Implications of the Treaty on Open Skies, Senate Select Committee on Intelligence, May 19, 1993.

46. "OC-135B Ready for Open Skies Flights," *Aviation Week & Space Technology*, July 5, 1993, p. 21.

47. Program Plan for Research, Development, Test and Evaluation For Arms Control, Fiscal Years 1995–1996, U. S. Department of Defense, Office of the Under Secretary of Defense (Acquisition and Technology), May 10, 1995.

48. Treaty on Open Skies, Senate Foreign Relations Committee, August 2, 1993.

49. Chemical Weapons Destruction: Issues Affecting Program Cost, Schedule, and Performance, U.S. General Accounting Office, January 1993.

50. Michael Renner, Budgeting for Disarmament: The Costs of War and Peace, Worldwatch Institute, 1994.

51. "U.S. Army Details Extent and Content of Chemical Arsenal," *Washington Post*, January 23, 1996, p. A12.

52. "Joint Statements, Chemical Accord, and Summary of Testing Protocols," *Arms Control Today*, June 1990, pp. 22–27.

53. Statement by President Bush on Chemical Weapons Initiative, White House Press Secretary, May 13, 1991.

54. John Shalikashvili, Chemical Weapons Convention Ratification, Testimony before the Senate Armed Services Committee, August 11,1994.

55. *The Chemical Weapons Convention: Effects on the U.S. Chemical Industry*, OTA-BP-ISC-106, U.S. Congress, Office of Technology Assessment, August 1993.

56. U.S. Capability to Monitor Compliance with the Chemical Weapons Convention, Senate Select Committee on Intelligence, September 30, 1994.

57. Elizabeth A. Palmer, "For Businesses, a High Price for Chemical Weapons Ban," *Congressional Quarterly Weekly Report*, September 17, 1994, pp. 2584-2587.

58. Jessica Eve Stern, "Co-operative Security and the CWC: A Comparison of the Chemical and Nuclear Weapons Non-proliferation Regimes," *Contemporary Security Policy*, December 1994, pp. 30–57.

59. Igor Khripunov, "The Human Element in Russia's Chemical Weapons Disposal Efforts," *Arms Control Today*, July/August 1995, pp. 16–21.

60. Status of U.S.-Russian Agreements and the Chemical Weapons Convention, GAO/NSIAD-94-136, U.S. General Accounting Office, March 1994.

61. Kathleen C. Bailey, Why the Chemical Weapons Convention Should Not Be Ratified, *Ratifying the Chemical Weapons Convention*, Brad Roberts, Ed. (Washington, DC: Center for Strategic and International Studies, 1994), pp. 52–59.

62. Frank J. Gaffney, Jr., "A Noxious Treaty on Chemical Weapons, "*Wall Street Journal*, September 29, 1994.

63. Antonia Handler Chayes and Abram Chayes, Regime Architecture: Elements and Principles, *Global Engagement: Cooperation and Security in the 21st Century*, Janne E. Nolan, Ed. (Washington, DC: Brookings, 1994), pp. 65–130.

64. *Technologies Underlying Weapons of Mass Destruction*, OTA-BP-ISC-115, U.S. Congress, Office of Technology Assessment, December 1993.

65. *Threat Control through Arms Control*, U.S. Arms Control and Disarmament Agency, July 13, 1995.

6

PERSISTENT PROBLEMS

The next two chapters deal with the problems of arms control, but before plunging into them it is worth emphasizing how remarkably well the process has worked overall. Agreements that would have been unachievable only a decade ago have been signed, ratified, and implemented with unprecedented speed and effectiveness and in many cases surprisingly low cost. The U.S. national security bureaucracy has responded to new demands with considerable flexibility, efficiency, and interagency cooperation; the research community has identified and developed needed technologies, sometimes on very short notice; the parties to agreements have in the vast majority of cases lived up to their commitments and participated constructively in the implementation process; and the United States and Russia, once the most implacable of adversaries, have reached a level of cooperation and transparency in their military relationship that no one could have imagined, much less predicted, during the Cold War. Most of the material in the preceding three chapters supports these general conclusions, so no further argument or evidence is necessary here.

Despite this undeniable record of success, each of the four areas mentioned—bureaucracy, technology, compliance, and U.S.-Russian transparency—has experienced problems. This revelation will surprise no one; a process that combines so many aspects of politics, technology, and national security policy can hardly be expected to be free of difficulty. The problems are both short-term and long-term. Short-term problems come up every day in arms control: ambiguities are discovered in on-site inspections, errors are made in data exchanges, interagency disputes hold up advice to consultative delegations, deadlines for notifications are not met, destruction of equipment does not conform to specifications, and so on *ad infinitum*. As irritating and time-consuming as such problems may be, they are almost always amenable to short-term political and/or technical solutions and will not be analyzed here. Long-term or persistent problems are another matter. They arise out of structural flaws, fundamental conflicts of interest, or uncontrollable historical forces. In general they cannot be solved; instead they must be managed and lived with. These are the problems that will concern us in this and the next chapter. This chapter will focus on bureaucratic problems; compliance and transparency issues will be addressed in chapter 7.

The organization of arms control and nonproliferation in the United States has had both successes and failures. On one hand there is the remarkable success of the On-Site Inspection Agency. It was created almost as an afterthought in the excitement accompanying the signing of the INF Treaty. Since then it has grown rapidly, taken on an increasing variety of missions, and has impressed almost everyone with its effectiveness. In contrast, the Arms Control and Disarmament Agency (ACDA) has lived from the moment of its creation under the threat of dissolution, absorption, or impotence. Despite repeated attempts to reform or "revitalize" it, ACDA's problems persist because of its small size, its awkward position in the arms control bureaucracy, and the chronic inability or unwillingness of many conservative political leaders to see international arms control as a legitimate and necessary component of national security.

Another long-term bureaucratic problem concerns the proper role of the Intelligence Community in arms control. The relationship between the intelligence and policy communities has never been smooth, but the end of the Cold War focus on the Soviet Union and the increased priority of nonproliferation and counterproliferation intelligence have made a difficult relationship even more complex. The essence of the problem has been compared to a clash of cultures [1]. Intelligence is supposed to be objective and free of political influence; its goal is to inform policy, not make policy. Not surprisingly this ideal is rarely, if ever, achieved in practice. The more important the issue, the more likely it will be that political considerations will influence both the collecting and analysis of intelligence. Influence flows in the other direction as well. Ideally national security priorities should dictate the targets and analytical focus of intelligence. In reality these are often influenced by the bureaucratic interests and ideological beliefs of intelligence agencies and personnel. There are few areas in which effective communication between the policymaking and intelligence communities are more important than in arms control and few in which they have been more difficult to manage.

A third problem, which is also primarily organizational, is managing the research and development of new technology for implementing and verifying arms control. The United States currently spends over $200 million per year on publicly acknowledged R&D for verification and implementation, not including classified work on national technical means (see chapter 5). A number of studies have suggested that not all of this money is being spent wisely and that communication among the scientists who develop these systems, the diplomats who incorporate them into treaties, and the inspectors and analysts who use them in the field is not as effective as it might be. Devices or techniques that are elegant and effective in the lab may prove overdesigned, inappropriate, or politically unacceptable in the field. Verification schemes that fit certain diplomatic or national security objectives may be scientifically or technically unfeasible or too expensive and sophisticated to be practical. Requirements and capabilities must somehow be brought into correspondence in a cost-effective way. It's a difficult problem, and the absence of any quick solution to it qualifies it for further consideration in this chapter.

THE TRIALS OF ACDA

No other activity of modern governments so thoroughly integrates the diplomatic, military, and technical/scientific dimensions of national policy as arms control. The uniqueness and importance of this integration was recognized in 1961, when the Arms Control and Disarmament Agency was created by a collaboration between the Kennedy administration and Congress [2]. Thirty-six years later the United States remains the only state to have created an agency devoted entirely to arms control and nonproliferation [3, p. 31]. This says a great deal about the leadership the United States has exercised in making arms control legitimate and effective, and about the awkward relationship between arms control and the diplomatic and military aspects of national security policy.

I have already quoted Paul Warnke's characterization of arms control as an "unnatural act" (see chapter 2). Warnke's comment was not meant to be derogatory; he was a strong advocate of arms control from the beginning and was by most accounts one of the most effective of ACDA's Directors [4, pp. 222–232; 5, p. 21]. But he was also one of the most controversial, ultimately resigning his directorship in the hope that by removing himself as the lightning rod for conservative criticism he would improve the prospects for SALT II ratification [6]. Warnke's experience epitomizes ACDA's dilemma. The agency's sole mission is arms control (which in its broad sense includes nonproliferation), a process for which liberals sometimes hold out excessively high hopes and about which conservatives sometimes harbor excessive fears and suspicions. There is a symmetry between these contrasting attitudes toward arms control and corresponding attitudes toward military power. For the latter it is conservatives whose hopes are often excessive, and liberals who are fearful and suspicious. For much of ACDA's history, arms control and military power have been viewed by too many of both persuasions as contradictory approaches to national security, and this tension has been at the root of much of ACDA's trouble.

In fact, arms control and military preparation are complementary to each other, a complementarity reflected in the analogous positions occupied by ACDA and the Joint Chiefs of Staff in Executive Branch policymaking.

By statute, the JCS Chairman is the principal military advisor on military affairs to the President, the National Security Council, and the Secretary of Defense. Also by statute, the ACDA Director is the principal advisor to the Secretary of State, the National Security Council, and the President on arms control. [7]

This structure puts war and peace, force and diplomacy, Defense and State in a nicely symmetrical arrangement. Arms control is theoretically and structurally on the same footing as military power.

That was the hope of ACDA's founders, but it has proven to be unachievable in practice. War and peace do not have the same cachet in Washington, or in other great power capitals: "The real players in this game are people with guns, and ACDA has no guns"[1] [5, p. 46]. It is difficult to imagine a set of circumstances in which ACDA's Director could wield the kind of influence over

---

[1] A variation on the same theme is ACDA historian Duncan Clarke's observation that "The Navy will be influential even if it has a mediocre Chief of Naval Operations and its airmen feud with the submariners. But ACDA cannot afford such luxury" [4, p. 210].

major national security decisions that, for example, JCS Chairman Colin Powell did in the period preceding and following the Gulf War.[2] The Pentagon's budget begins to become controversial at around \$230 billion, while, as we saw in chapter 5, arms control implementation is already becoming controversial at under \$1 billion.[3] This provides a rough measure of both the perceived relative utilities of the two approaches to national security and the bureaucratic power of the constituencies promoting the two approaches. Arms control is new to the game of international politics, and by its very nature it cannot generate the public passions and financial incentives that military preparations can. Arms control and military preparations are complementary in a well-formulated national security policy, but they are also sometimes substitutable at the margin. It is in judgments about the relative marginal utility of arms control and military measures that liberals and conservatives most often disagree. The analysis of chapter 5 makes clear that arms control proponents are still a long way from winning the argument.

In its original conception ACDA was to provide the President with technically competent advice that represented the interests of arms control and was independent of, and yet responsive to, the State and Defense Departments and the Atomic Energy Commission (now the Department of Energy). At the same time, as the result of a compromise between the Senate and House, ACDA was given a special relationship to the Secretary of State (see above) [5, pp. 2–3]. According to Duncan Clarke, "ACDA is neither a bureau of the State Department nor wholly independent. It is quasi-independent" [4, p. 209]. This awkward arrangement has often made it difficult for the agency to provide a truly independent voice for arms control. Depending on the ideology and/or management style of the administration in power, ACDA found itself subordinated either to State or to Defense. In the period of détente it appeared as a creature of the State Department and generated hostility in the Pentagon. During the Reagan administration the relationship was reversed for a while, and many saw ACDA as an arm of the Pentagon dominated by anti–arms control hawks, especially in its approach to verification and compliance. Twice in its history the agency has suffered politically inspired purges, and these have had a serious impact on its morale and ability to recruit and retain high-quality personnel [5].

With the end of the Cold War and the achievement of much of the traditional U.S.-Soviet and NATO-Warsaw Pact arms control agendas, questions were raised about the continued need for an independent ACDA. In 1992 ACDA's Inspector General (IG) led a review of the agency's role and narrowed a long list of possible alternative structures down to two: fold ACDA into the State Department or retain a "reshaped and rejuvenated" ACDA as an independent agency. The IG

---

[2] For an excellent account of Powell's role in formulating and promoting U.S. post–Cold War military policy see Michael Klare, *Rogue States and Nuclear Outlaws* (New York: Hill & Wang, 1995). Powell had all the access he needed to the President to argue for his policy recommendations. On the other hand, "No ACDA director has ever enjoyed direct access to the Oval Office that would fully correspond with his statutory role as the president's principal advisor on arms control and disarmament" [5, p. 23].

[3] The Office of Technology Assessment noticed the same disproportion in the context of research and development: "There is a marked contrast between the many millions of dollars spent each year on the analysis of new weapons systems . . . and the relative absence of comparable contracted, or external, analysis of arms control monitoring regimes" [8, p. 8].

recommended that ACDA remain independent (or quasi-independent) and that it be given a more focused mission and enhanced budgetary support:

It remains important to have a specialized, technically competent arms control institution. We felt that a separate agency is the better solution to retaining continuity, enhancing technical expertise, fostering innovation and providing a needed independent perspective on arms control issues. [9, p. 4]

The report also pointed out that ACDA was uniquely well suited to contribute to both nonproliferation and arms control policymaking, and that its independent status "enabled it to force discussion of issues on which other agencies held opposing views" [9, p. 5].

Another argument in the IG's report deserves special attention. The absorption of ACDA's technical experts into the State Department would require "major changes . . . within the State Department's personnel system, a system which is one of the most resistant to change ever devised by man or woman. . . . The unhappy truth is that the Department of State is not a congenial home for scientists and technical specialists, [who] feel strongly and bitterly that they are considered as second-class citizens . . . and frequently subordinated to Foreign Service officers with vastly inferior backgrounds in the specialties and disciplines involved" [9, pp. 5–6]. A similar conclusion was reached by the Henry L. Stimson Center, which feared that "high-level arms control experts would find their jobs taken by rotating, advancement-seeking Foreign Service Officers . . . with little background in the field" [5, p. 43]. The integration of scientific and technical expertise into the policymaking process was one of the original inspirations behind the creation of ACDA, and arms control has been one of the most effective avenues for scientists and engineers to participate in and influence public policymaking. There is no question that this avenue would be severely restricted if an attempt were made to graft the arms control function onto the diplomatic culture of the State Department.

Congress responded positively to the Inspector General's recommendations, and in 1994 ACDA's mandate was renewed and its budget slightly increased with little dissent. ACDA undertook an internal reorganization, removing some areas of overlap with other agencies and reflecting its new priorities and responsibilities in the post–Cold War era. The IG had listed four priority arms control tasks for the 1990s [10, pp. 11-12]:

- Eliminating the overarmament of the Cold War, primarily that of the former Soviet Union
- Fostering nonproliferation of weapons of mass destruction
- Contributing arms control techniques to the settlement of regional disputes
- Establishing global norms for the control of arms

ACDA's four bureaus correspond roughly to these four priorities [11, pp. 85–95]. Strategic and Eurasian Affairs (SEA) focuses on nuclear arms control and the former Soviet Union, including the ABM and START treaties and the Cooperative Threat Reduction Program. Nonproliferation and Regional Arms Control (NP) combines the second and third priorities by working with the IAEA and several suppliers groups to control proliferation of nuclear, chemical, and biological weapons and aid regional agreements like the growing number of nuclear weapon free zones. Multilateral Affairs (MA) contributes to the establishment of global norms by focusing on the Chemical and Biological Warfare Conventions, the European Security Regime, nuclear testing policy, and the many multilateral treaties to which the United States is party, such as the Antarctic, Seabed, and Environmental Modification Treaties. Intelligence, Verification, and Information Support (IVI) carries out ACDA's responsibilities for analyzing the compliance of other states and informing the policy community and public of the status of implementation and compliance.[4]

Two key elements of ACDA's work are to represent the arms control and nonproliferation position on interagency policymaking groups and to backstop U.S. delegations to international negotiating and implementation forums (see chapter 4). At the highest level an ACDA official sits on the Arms Control Interagency Working Group, and ACDA is represented on a variety of panels at lower levels in the bureaucracy. It also chairs many of the interagency panels that supervise individual agreements and provides guidance and expert staff to the On-Site Inspection agency and the Arms Control Intelligence Staff in their monitoring work. Overseas, ACDA leads the U.S. delegation to the Conference on Disarmament in Geneva and to most of the consultative bodies associated with arms control agreements. In its backstopping role ACDA prepares analyses and instructions for these delegations and is the channel through which they can communicate with decision makers in Washington. ACDA has primary responsibility for U.S. contacts with the International Atomic Energy Agency and will be the Executive Agent for the U.S. National Authority under the Chemical Weapons Convention.

Simply to list these functions is to appreciate how awkward and difficult it would be for the State Department to assume responsibility for them. The Inspector General thought that the choice between ACDA's continued independence and absorption into State was a "close call," but its report consists primarily of strong arguments for independence and provides few countervailing arguments to suggest why the call is close [10, p. iii]. The Stimson Center presented the arguments for absorption into State more fully, but also came down strongly in favor of keeping ACDA as independent as possible and "rejuvenat[ing it] with a clear and practical mandate to energize U.S. Government policy in dealing with . . . nonproliferation, regional arms control, export controls, and treaty implementation" [5, pp. 59–60].

The argument that absorbing ACDA into State will improve efficiency and save money finds no support in either study. ACDA is a surprisingly small agency in view of its broad responsibilities. Its staff numbers about 250, and its annual budget is only about $40 million. If it were absorbed into State, there

---

[4] The IG Report had recommended reducing the number of ACDA bureaus from four to three by combining MA and IVI into a single "arms control services" bureau [10, p. 29]. The rationale was that "since virtually all agreements are now becoming multilateral, there is no longer any meaningful rationale for a separate bureau responsible for multilateral affairs as such." But multilateral agreements like the Chemical and Biological Weapons Conventions and the pending comprehensive test ban and fissile material cutoff are different in important ways from bilateral agreements with Russia or with groups of former Soviet republics. It is true that multilateral agreements are emerging as the preferred type, but the bilateral agreements (some of which themselves have become multilateral) remain distinct and important. For these reasons ACDA chose to retain its four-bureau structure.

would be some reduction in overhead in areas of duplication (e.g., computer support, public affairs, legal counsel), but most of ACDA's current work would still have to be done. It would most likely be divided among several agencies, creating problems of communication and coordination and conceivably even increasing the overall cost of administration [12]. The Stimson report specifies seven major changes that would have to be made in current agency missions if ACDA's functions were absorbed and recommends several procedures that would be necessary to ensure that arms control and nonproliferation policy would not suffer from the loss of its focus in an independent agency [5, pp. 78–83].

ACDA's smallness can be used to support arguments either for or against its absorption into the much larger State Department [10, p. ii]. If it remains independent, "a small agency such as ACDA can too easily be swept aside in policy considerations." If it were absorbed into State there would be "the possibility that the arms control aspect of an issue might be overwhelmed by other considerations." The premise of both arguments is that arms control concerns are both important and unique, but that they have a tendency to be subordinated in the policymaking process because their constituency is so small. This is the crux of the problem. It derives from the disparity discussed at the beginning of this section between the political and economic clout of arms control versus military power. The problem is not that arms control is unimportant or that it does not warrant an independent voice within the bureaucracy. The problem is that an important job has been given to a small agency.[5] It goes against every rule of bureaucratic politics to expect a small budget to influence or control large budgets. Whether ACDA remains independent or is absorbed into State, arms control will remain marginalized until its priority relative to military power is reflected in the scope of its mission, its annual appropriation, and its bureaucratic status.

If arms control and nonproliferation are as important as the past three administrations have said they are, then ACDA should by rights be a much larger agency. From this point of view ACDA would have been the appropriate place to put the On-Site Inspection Agency,[6] and ACDA should also have greater management responsibility over the Cooperative Threat Reduction program, nonproliferation export control policy, arms control implementation, intelligence tasking, and research and development. Such changes would make ACDA a more powerful agency with a more impressive budget, and they would be appropriate given the increased role of arms control in U.S. national security policy.[7] At the same time, they would challenge traditional roles, missions, and budgets in the Defense Department, Energy Department, and Intelligence Community. Only the most determined and coordinated presidential and congressional commitment to ACDA's empowerment could overcome the bureaucratic opposition such a challenge would engender.

---

[5] It is important to recognize that State, Defense, and Energy also have important arms control and nonproliferation responsibilities, and that all three agencies dwarf ACDA in personnel, budgets, and, in some cases, technical expertise.

[6] According to the Stimson Center, "many saw OSIA's placement as a clear encroachment on ACDA's statutory turf by the Pentagon, and it raised the question once again of why ACDA was needed" [5, p. 26].

[7] A proposal similar to this was one of the options considered by the Office of Technology Assessment in 1991 for improving management of verification R&D (see below) [8, pp. 15–16].

The essence of ACDA's value in its current form is in its understanding of the interaction between the technical and diplomatic aspects of arms control, its independence of either the purely diplomatic or purely military point of view, and its ability to bring that independence to bear at key decision points in the bureaucracy. Its independence is simultaneously ACDA's greatest strength and greatest weakness. The agency has always had the potential to provide an alternative point of view if the President wants to hear one. ACDA's effectiveness as an independent advocate is ultimately dependent on a strong presidential commitment to arms control and effective channels of communication between ACDA's Director and the President. ACDA's subordination and impotence in the past can be traced to a lack of one or both of these requirements, and its periods of influence and success coincide quite clearly with periods of maximum presidential involvement [4].

As this is written, ACDA's future as an independent agency remains in jeopardy. The "rejuvenation" or "revitalization" so eagerly hoped for and overwhelmingly approved by both houses of Congress in 1992 has not been allowed to take place. Rather than increasing ACDA's size and influence, influential Republican legislators in both houses of Congress favor abolishing it and transferring most of its personnel and mission to the State Department. Even if this effort is unsuccessful, Congress has the power to starve ACDA of funding and hold up appointments to high-level administrative positions. Perhaps most important, presidential involvement in arms control was not a high priority in the first Clinton administration, and questions remain as this is written about the priority it will be given in Clinton's second term.

Whatever happens to ACDA, arms control is unlikely to regain the prominence it enjoyed during the Cold War. New agreements will be achieved at a much slower rate than they were in the 1986–1991 period, and considerable political commitment will be required even to preserve and strengthen the regimes that already exist. The latter mission depends critically on the effective coordination of a wide variety of agencies, and that coordination requires leadership by a competent and respected office with strong presidential support. That leadership and support cannot come from a weakened and marginalized ACDA. Just where it will come from remains the most important question facing U.S. arms control and nonproliferation policy in the 1990s and beyond.

A CHANGING INTELLIGENCE MISSION

Throughout the Cold War the Intelligence Community played a central role in arms control. During negotiations it provided the diplomats with estimates of the monitorability of prospective treaty provisions, and after a treaty entered into force it operated the technical and human systems that did the monitoring.[8] The vast majority of U.S. intelligence activity (65 to 70 percent by one estimate [13]) was directed at the "Soviet target," and the monitoring systems were designed almost entirely with that target in mind.[9] Now the Cold War is over, and

---

[8] For a brief, but informative, description of the role of intelligence in Cold War arms control see Douglas George, The Estimative Process, in *Intelligence and Arms Control*, Thomas J. Hirschfeld (ed.) (Austin, TX: Lyndon B. Johnson School of Public Affairs, 1987).

[9] The phrase "Soviet target" is from Jeffrey Richelson, *American Espionage and the Soviet Target* (New York: Morrow, 1987). Other references on the same topic are Lawrence Freedman, *US*

the resources devoted to Russia have dropped to about 15 percent of the entire intelligence effort [13]. The Intelligence Community is confronted with a major reorientation of its mission, substantial cuts in personnel, and, at best, level funding. In early 1995 there had already been a 12 percent reduction in personnel [14], and a total reduction of 23 percent was anticipated by the end of the decade [15]. The number of deployed satellites was to be cut nearly in half, and even deeper cuts were anticipated in satellite ground stations. Also underway was a "radical restructuring" of signals and human intelligence activities [15].

At least three different groups were doing major studies of the Intelligence Community in 1996, suggesting that the perception of trouble was widespread in the government. One was a blue-ribbon panel led by the chair of the President's Foreign Intelligence Advisory Board (called the Aspin Panel after its first chairman, the late Secretary of Defense Les Aspin), another was a group from the House Permanent Select Committee on Intelligence called the Intelligence Community in the 21st Century (IC-21) Study, and a third represented the so-called National Performance Review. Each group examined different aspects of the IC, from missions and functions to costs and efficiency [16]. In remarks made soon after his appointment as Director of Central Intelligence, John Deutch promised a major reorganization "down to the bare bones" [17] that would make the CIA more effective and accountable.

All of this cutting, trimming, and restructuring comes at a time when CIA morale is near an all-time low. The Aldrich Ames and Harold Nicholson betrayals, the murder in Guatemala—possibly by a CIA asset—of a U.S. citizen and the husband of another, and accusations (whether just or unjust) of failure to predict or correctly assess such monumental events as the Soviet Union's collapse and the Iraqi nuclear weapon program have put the Agency on the defensive. A number of reports have suggested that the CIA is losing influence in the national security bureaucracy and being increasingly overshadowed by Department of Defense intelligence [18]. Other analysts have singled out the human intelligence activities of the Directorate of Operations for scathing criticism. According to former Deputy Director Bobby Ray Inman, "Most if not all human agents [of the CIA] over 20 years were double agents" [19].

It is unclear how much these developments have affected the work and influence of the Arms Control Intelligence Staff (ACIS) or the Nonproliferation Center (NPC). ACIS went through a period of substantial growth after the INF Treaty was ratified, and it seems to have survived the budget and personnel cuts relatively intact. NPC did not even exist before the Gulf War, and one of the primary factors motivating its creation was to remedy the gaps that had permitted the full extent of Iraq's nuclear weapon program to escape detection by U.S. intelligence [13]. ACIS was taken as the model for NPC, adding further to the general perception that ACIS has been a success [20]. NPC already employs a large number of civilian and military personnel from the Defense Department, so it would not seem to be as vulnerable to erosion from turf struggles with the Pentagon as other CIA offices. At the same time, the strong Pentagon influence on NPC could lead to an increasing emphasis on counterproliferation (military) relative to nonproliferation (diplomatic) intelligence production.

Intelligence and the Soviet Strategic Threat, 2nd ed. (Princeton, NJ: Princeton University Press, 1986) and John Prados, *The Soviet Estimate* (New York: Dial Press, 1982).

In summary, then, the scandals and alleged failures of the Intelligence Community do not appear to have affected the arms control and nonproliferation functions in any serious way. Nevertheless, there are a number of long-term problems in the interaction between intelligence and arms control monitoring that arise from the political nature of arms control and the bureaucratic structure of the Intelligence Community. One set of problems is internal to the intelligence community and concerns the inefficiencies and blindness created by compartmentalization, bureaucratic rivalry, or duplication of effort. The other set arises from the interaction between the producers and consumers of intelligence and the potential for politicization of the intelligence product.

Internal Problems: Competition versus Synergy

The essence of arms control and nonproliferation monitoring is the bringing together of information from a wide variety of sources to form an accurate picture of the military and industrial activities of other states. A word often used both inside and outside the Intelligence Community to describe the process is "synergy," defined as "the interaction of discrete agencies or agents such that the total effect is greater than the sum of the individual effects."[10] Synergy is supposed to make arms control verification both more effective and less expensive by combining information from on-site inspections, data exchanges, notifications, national intelligence operations (including national technical means, human intelligence, and open source analysis), and confidence-building measures.

If synergy is to occur, the verification process must be set up to maximize interactions among many sources of information. However, because key elements of the process employ sensitive sources and methods and are conducted by agencies jealous of their budgets and "equities," it is difficult in practice to achieve the optimum level of interaction [8, p. 8]. Traditionally, and often for very good reasons, the intelligence process is compartmentalized. This helps protect sources and methods, but, according to former Deputy DCI Bobby Ray Inman, "it automatically limits the number of people who can offer thoughtful judgments either about arms control proposals or about verification risks" [24, p. 47]. It also places strict limits on the use of information gathered by technical or human means in the international compliance process. According to one knowledgeable source, considerable progress has been made in downgrading classifications and sanitizing sensitive-source information since Inman spoke in 1987.[11] Still, the basic dilemma remains: sensitive sources and methods must be protected, yet as arms control becomes more multifaceted and international, and as nonproliferation becomes one of the highest national priorities, the need for sharing information, both internally within the U.S. government and externally in the international community, continues to increase.

The roles of ACIS and NPC at the apex of the monitoring process were described in chapter 4. ACIS seems well placed to exploit the synergies that exist among different sources of intelligence. Satellite surveillance of chemical plants or missile bases can be used to trigger on-site inspections or Open Skies over-

---

[10] Webster's *Ninth New Collegiate Dictionary*. The most thorough analysis of the role of synergy in verification was done in 1993 for the Canadian Department of External Affairs as part of a three-part study of arms control verification in the post–Cold War world [21, 22, 23].

[11] Personal communication from Richard Gronet.

flights. Data exchanges and notifications can be used to program satellite cameras or communications monitoring.[12] It is not as simple as it looks, however. There are many other demands on U.S. national technical means, and many agencies must compete for limited time on satellites or computers. A major factor in the competition is the increasing demand for tactical military intelligence by theater commanders. One of the alleged failures of the intelligence process during the Gulf War was the inability of the Intelligence Community to get satellite photographs and other information into the hands of field commanders in a useful and timely form for bomb damage assessment [25, pp. 232–236]. This was true even though the United States had more satellites in orbit at that time than it has ever had before or since [26, pp. 122–125]. The problem was therefore not one of quantity, but one of appropriate choice of targets, proper photographic resolution, and timely distribution.[13] This experience led to an increased emphasis on adapting satellite imaging assets to the needs of tactical commanders and was one of the major factors used to justify creating the National Imagery and Mapping Agency (see chapter 4) [16]. According to a former Central Imagery Office director, "The key missing ingredient in today's imagery environment is responsiveness to the access and dissemination needs of DOD and civilian operational components. This is especially critical in support to war fighters during crisis and combat operations" [27, p. 32].

It is hard to estimate how much this new priority for tactical military intelligence will compete with the requirements of ACIS and NPC for access to satellite imagery and other intelligence assets. A major portion of arms control monitoring now involves comparing on-site inspections with formal data exchanges and notifications. NTM and HUMINT are less important than they were in monitoring Russian nuclear weapons before INF and START, and conventional forces before CFE. Still, they are an essential complement to cooperative monitoring, and there are more treaties about to enter into force. According to a former staff member of the House Intelligence Committee, "Monitoring the new conventional and strategic nuclear arms control treaties will be a major drain on [intelligence] community resources" [28, p. 153].

ACDA Director John Holum made a similar observation in congressional testimony in June 1994. He emphasized that "arms control implementation is becoming a *mammoth* mission,"[14] and that to do its job of verifying compliance ACDA must "depend heavily on physical and analytical capabilities controlled by other agencies" [29, pp. 27–28]. He gives the example of the Cobra Dane radar located in the Aleutian Islands, which played a key role in monitoring Soviet missile flight tests during the Cold War and made possible the inclusion of limitations on throwweight and other design features in the SALT and START treaties. The Intelligence Community, faced with declining budgets and a greatly reduced Soviet/Russian threat, wanted to stop operating the radar, but

---

[12] See Patricia Bliss McFate, Sidney N. Graybeal, George Lindsey, and D. Marc Kilgour, Constraining Proliferation: The Contribution of Verification Synergies, Nonproliferation, Arms Control and Disarmament Division, Department of External Affairs, Ottawa, March 1993, p. 3 for a comprehensive table of interactions among verification methods.

[13] According to Rick Atkinson, "By war's end, there were two hundred tons of intelligence 'product'—including countless sheaves of satellite and U-2 photos—in Saudi Arabia. The Americans commandeered Saudi bread trucks to haul the stuff around" [25, p. 233].

[14] Emphasis in original.

ACDA wanted to continue to use it to monitor the treaty. Holum provided a happy ending to this particular story, noting that ACDA was able to work with DOD and CIA to keep the radar operating.[15] But he went on to say that the incident revealed a "long-term systemic danger to the arms control implementation and verification mission . . . we are piling up arms control implementation and verification requirements," but "deep [budget] cuts are expected from agencies like Defense, Energy, and Intelligence," and that "these agencies quite reasonably will apply their own standards of cost-effectiveness to their budgets, balancing defense or intelligence requirements against arms control verification. You can see the tension," said Holum, "already it has occupied a considerable amount of my time . . . In the months ahead it could well become a preoccupation."

Although arms control and nonproliferation appear to be converging, they also remain quite distinct in several ways. NPC's mission is both different from and complementary to that of ACIS. Where ACIS monitors formal treaties and relies to a considerable degree on information openly gathered and voluntarily provided, NPC relies much more on clandestinely gathered information and covert operations. The targets of ACIS monitoring are states parties to arms control agreements, while NPC's targets tend to be those states who do not choose to join such agreements.[16] ACIS is aided in its mission by transparency while NPC must overcome opacity. However, there are also significant areas where ACIS and NPC could compete for Intelligence Community resources.

We saw in chapter 4 how important human intelligence was in exposing Russian biological weapons activities or the Iraqi nuclear and biological weapon programs. It will also be important in monitoring the Chemical Weapons Convention. Joining the CWC will not guarantee that a state has given up its chemical weapons program, and although the Convention contains provisions for international challenge inspections, the United States will have to acquire intelligence outside of these formal procedures if it is to know which facilities to challenge. A similar situation exists with nuclear weapons. Iraq, Iran, and North Korea are all parties to the NPT, but all were suspected, and Iraq was proven, to be developing nuclear weapons in violation of their commitments. The NPT allows for "special" inspections, and an effort was made by the IAEA to conduct one in North Korea in 1994. U.S. intelligence was instrumental in providing the evidence required for the IAEA to demand an inspection. The effort in North Korea failed, but there are likely to be other attempts in other countries in the future. An active intelligence effort by the United States and other states seems essential to supplement the normal IAEA safeguards monitoring [30].

Just how ACIS and NPC will interact to exploit synergetic opportunities, or how they might compete for turf and interfere with each other, cannot be pre-

---

[15] The ending was happy for ACDA, whose concern is rigorous verification of Russian commitments under START. But this begs the question of whether the radar is truly cost-effective as a monitoring device in the post–Cold War political climate. It seemed much more important in the 1970s and 1980s to monitor the throwweight of new Soviet missiles than it does in the 1990s. START limits throwweight, and rigorous verification of START in principle requires careful monitoring of missile payloads. But the Cobra Dane radar is an expensive installation, and its other major function—early warning of Soviet missile attacks—is no longer needed. It is therefore not obvious that ACDA was right to save the radar.

[16] This distinction is a bit neater than reality. ACIS has other responsibilities that involve the full range of intelligence targets, and NPC works with the International Atomic Energy Agency to help monitor the Nonproliferation Treaty. (Personal communication from Dick Gronet.)

dicted from the outside. Nevertheless, both possibilities exist, and careful attention will have to be paid to the interaction of these two agencies. This seems particularly true in the case of Russia, where arms control and nonproliferation concerns exist in close proximity to each other. The tasking of human and technical assets, the use of signals intelligence and open source information, and the monitoring of commercial and scientific transactions could have significant overlaps for ACIS and NPC. Such overlaps can create synergism or bureaucratic conflict, or possibly both at the same time. One useful innovation has been the creation of a National Human Intelligence Tasking Center at CIA [31, p. 12]. This is supposed to centralize the tasking of HUMINT operations in much the same way that NIMA and NSA manage the acquisition of overhead imagery and signals intelligence. Much duplication of effort and bureaucratic friction can be eliminated by such mechanisms.

In 1994 the House Intelligence Committee pointed out that ACIS and NPC were about the same size, had major similarities in their missions, and a potential for "significant synergies, and perhaps some economies, to be achieved from a closer working relationship" [32, pp. 35–36]. The Committee recommended that the Director of Central Intelligence look into merging ACIS and NPC into a single unit. According to CIA officials, the merger idea was studied but was decided against, in large part because certain consumers, in particular the National Security Council, preferred to keep them separate.[17] The NSC is organized into separate arms control and nonproliferation working groups (see chapter 4), and these may find it easier to deal with an Intelligence Community divided along similar lines. The key to successful exploitation of synergies is, as the House panel noted, a close working relationship and sharing of information and assets between the two groups. There is no reason in principle why such a relationship requires a merger, and there are no publicly available studies of the costs and benefits of such a merger. Still, whenever two groups have significantly overlapping areas of responsibility there is a potential for turf battles and bureaucratic backstabbing. Close congressional oversight will continue to be required to minimize this potential.

External Problems: Producers versus Consumers

In chapter 4 I introduced the distinction between monitoring and verification. This separation, which is essentially the same as the more general distinction between intelligence and policymaking, is reflected in the structure of the U.S. arms control bureaucracy. Monitoring is the responsibility of the Intelligence Community, and verification is the province of decision makers who must take responsibility for compliance judgments and their consequences. The distinction between the two functions emerged clearly during the bitter debates over Soviet compliance during the 1970s and 1980s. During the SALT process, according to Michael Krepon, "The intelligence community took pains to separate its monitoring judgments from the verification pronouncements of policy-makers" [33]. This reflected an understanding that the process of gathering and analyzing information should be as objective and free of political influence as possible. However, while "the intelligence community tends to see itself, correctly or not,

---

[17] Personal communication, CIA official.

as a value-free service agency, . . . at its upper levels the line begins to blur" [1]. It is at these upper levels, where the Director of Central Intelligence interacts with the National Security Council and the Oval Office, that politics and objective analysis are most difficult to separate.

Influence flows in both directions at these levels. According to Henry Kissinger, "What political leaders decide, intelligence services tend to seek to justify. In the real world, intelligence assessments more often follow than guide policy decisions" [34]. But influence does work the other way as well, if only because an intelligence expert almost always knows more about a particular issue than a high-level decision maker does. According to one former official, "The intelligence community retains an expertise . . . that should not be ignored out of some overly fastidious concern about the line between policy and intelligence" [35].   A former staff member of the House Intelligence Committee has tried to make explicit where the boundary between politics and objective analysis can be, and often is, crossed. In an analysis of ACIS she emphasizes,

Selection of policy options on such functional issues [as arms control] is heavily dependent on intelligence support. In policy deliberations, the [intelligence] community is represented on interagency committees at all levels, and must speak with a single voice to avoid confusing the policymaker and to maximize the community's influence . . . policymakers want a focal point through which to request intelligence analyses and other information. [20]

It is at this focal point, which in the U.S. government is at the National Security Council staff or the congressional oversight committees, that politics and intelligence often interact. Intelligence is supposed to inform policy, but just as with Newton's Third Law, for every action there is a reaction. The bureaucratic and political interests of the intelligence community can influence negotiating positions and compliance judgments, just as political judgments and ideological biases can influence the kinds of evidence that are collected and how it is analyzed and presented. The boundary between monitoring and verification, just like the boundary between intelligence and policymaking, will never be as clear as purists would like it to be.

Mark Lowenthal has provided one of the more colorful descriptions of the relationship between producers and consumers of intelligence. In his view, "the consumer-producer relationship resembles that of two closely related tribes that believe, mistakenly, that they speak the same language and work in the same manner for agreed outcomes" [1]. In fact, the interests of the two tribes often conflict, and Lowenthal draws on examples from the arms control process to illustrate the conflict. One example is the demand by policymakers for "visibly intrusive monitoring methods" (e.g., on-site inspections), which may contribute only marginally to verification but which can pose serious counterintelligence problems for the Intelligence Community (IC).[18] Another is the increasing need to share intelligence with states or with international bodies to aid nonproliferation efforts. The Clinton administration greatly expanded U.S. intelligence cooperation with other states, and the IC was ordered to share information with

---

[18] However, as already discussed in chapter 4, on-site inspections can provide valuable collection opportunities at facilities not accessible by other means. The balance between costs and benefits could go either way, depending on the nature and frequency of inspections.

the United Nations Special Commission on Iraq (UNSCOM) and with other states attempting to control sensitive exports or arms trafficking [13]. Occasionally, secret intelligence is even made public in order to justify policy initiatives (e.g., noncompliance accusations) or to build international support for nonproliferation or counterproliferation policies (e.g., sanctions or military action against proliferators).

The Intelligence Community does not like to share information with foreign or international agencies. When intelligence is shared, every effort is made to conceal crucial details of the sources and methods by which it was obtained. Often, this dilutes its impact and makes it less persuasive than it might be. For example, the United States may have learned about a clandestine uranium enrichment plant from informers and then gathered supporting evidence in the form of decrypted signals interceptions, overhead imagery, and water and air samples collected by military attachés or agents posing as tourists. Under the Nonproliferation Treaty the IAEA would be entitled to request a special inspection (assuming that the target state was an NPT party), but the United States would have to present enough evidence to the IAEA to convince it that an inspection was warranted. Very little of the evidence just described could be shared in its original form without compromising important sources and methods. What appeared to the U.S. Intelligence Community as a nearly airtight case might appear quite weak to the IAEA. To deal with this problem the NPC has emphasized the acquisition of "actionable" intelligence, which can be safely shared in cooperative nonproliferation efforts [36, p. 48].

There are also problems between producers and consumers within the U.S. government. Producers are jealous of their professional integrity, and consumers prefer good news over bad news. Consumers who don't get answers they like can "shoot the messenger," challenge the data, or simply ignore the message [1, p. 160]. Analysts who don't get political results they like can compromise their objectivity by oversimplifying or exaggerating their data or analyses, or they can leak information to journalists or members of Congress. All of these things have precedents in arms control. President Carter was not happy with the bad news of an apparent Israeli–South African nuclear test in 1979, and his administration devoted considerable effort to discrediting the evidence. President Ford "shot the messenger" with his notorious Team B exercise in 1976. This was an experiment in "competitive threat assessment" inspired by "conservative cold warriors determined to bury détente and the SALT process" [37]. Team B was made up entirely of "hard-liners" who were determined to present a more alarming picture of Soviet military capabilities and intentions than had the CIA.[19] They began to leak to the press almost immediately after their first meetings, and the leaks accelerated after Ford lost the election to Carter [37]. The messenger was badly wounded—CIA credibility and internal morale were significantly damaged by the incident.

With the fall of the Soviet Union and the dissipation of much of the fear, suspicion, and ideological passion that characterized the 1970s and 1980s, the relationship between policymakers and the Intelligence Community has become

---

[19] The most authentic and controversial exposition of Team B's analysis was given by its chairman Richard Pipes in "Why the Soviet Union Thinks It Could Fight and Win a Nuclear War," *Commentary*, July 1977, pp. 21–34.

less emotionally charged. But difficulties persist, especially as evidence of proliferation activities by China and Russia create difficult and embarrassing problems for policymakers interested in good political relations and improved trade balances. Bad news is difficult to keep secret, and leaks are a traditional outlet for pent-up frustrations in the Intelligence Community. In a series of articles in the spring and summer of 1995 the Washington Post cited IC sources in exposés of Chinese nuclear cooperation with Pakistan [38], Russian missile technology sales to Brazil [39], Chinese missile-related exports to Iran [40], and Chinese ballistic missile shipments to Pakistan [41]. Intelligence producers feel they have solid evidence for these transfers, all of which would require political and economic sanctions against the offending countries or an openly declared presidential waiver under U.S. law. But sanctions are often inconvenient, and waivers are sometimes embarrassing. The Clinton administration finally did waive sanctions for the Russia-Brazil transaction in June 1995 [42], but continued to insist that the evidence against China was inconclusive, a position that made some members of the Intelligence Community "unhappy in the extreme" [41].

If the ideal separation between intelligence and policy existed, there would be no reason for the IC to feel unhappy. If they have done their job by gathering and analyzing the evidence competently, it is none of their business how policymakers weigh that information in making political decisions. But intelligence analysts have both political views and professional pride, and both may be offended when their work is ignored or overridden. In the Chinese missile case, for example, the IC claims that evidence from satellite photos, intercepted communications, and human intelligence all supports their conclusion that Chinese-made missiles have been in Pakistan since November 1992. The missiles are being stored outdoors in their original shipping crates at Sargodha Air Force Base near Lahore [41]. But the Clinton administration insists that only an admission by Pakistan or China, or a photograph of a missile outside its crate, will be sufficient proof to trigger sanctions. According to one administration official, "This is something we take seriously and that we have a high standard of evidence for" [41]. Such high standards of proof are admirable in courts of law, but they may not be appropriate for nonproliferation policy. Nor are they consistently applied. In the Reagan administration accusations were made in many cases on the flimsiest of bases, often going well beyond the evidence to score political points against the Soviet Union.[20] I will examine this problem from the policymakers' point of view in the next chapter. As for the analysts, they can be forgiven for feeling that they are damned if they do discover violations and damned if they don't. The delivery of analyses that challenge established policies can make consumers suspicious of the motives of producers [1]. The latter are obligated by professional responsibility to deliver the bad news, but they risk opprobrium and marginalization for their efforts.

A particularly unhappy producer-consumer relationship persisted for more than a decade between the Intelligence Community and ACDA. The Inspector General's report notes that ACDA's verification bureau "has been perceived as overzealous and lacking a sense of proportion," and that its "approach to verification uncertainties and compliance problems tends to obscure the relative signifi-

---

[20] For a detailed account of one such instance see Seymour M. Hersh, *"The Target Is Destroyed"* (New York: Random House, 1986).

cance of issues" [10, p. 16].   ACDA's relations with the Intelligence Community have been described as "tense," "strained," and "adversarial bordering on the dysfunctional," particularly with ACIS [10, p. 47].   The Inspector General's report recommended that ACDA "seek a more effective and constructive relationship as a consumer of intelligence, making use, as appropriate, of its role as chairman of the VCAWG."[21]

ACDA's problems with CIA appear to have been a temporary aberration induced by the heated political atmosphere surrounding arms control in the 1970s and 1980s. Prior to the mid-1970s, according to Duncan Clarke, ACDA's relations with the CIA were generally good [4, p. 213].   Problems arose in the mid-1970s and 1980s when "the Agency adopted the role of devil's advocate, taking issue with what it perceived to be the CIA's lax approach to verification and its chronic underestimation of Soviet deception and concealment activity" [5, p. 25]. In the Reagan administration, "ACDA officials championed the role of vocalizing Soviet misdeeds—both real and grossly overdrawn—while making little effort to negotiate solutions to the problems identified" [5, p. 64]. More recently ACDA's alienation from ACIS and NPC was "exacerbated by personality conflicts" [5, p. 70]. This suggests that ACDA-CIA difficulties may be a hangover from the political and ideological tensions surrounding arms control in the Carter and Reagan years. Terms such as "inflexible," and "hard-nosed" were more descriptive of ACDA's approach to verification and compliance issues then than they are today [10, p. 46]. The worst of the personality and ideological conflicts were apparently removed by personnel changes at ACDA under the Clinton administration. However, as long as ACDA remains outside the Intelligence Community and one of its smallest consumers, it will always be a very small tail trying to wag a very large dog.

TECHNOLOGY

Technology is undeniably important in monitoring arms control agreements. Without the remote sensing capabilities deployed on satellites in the 1960s it is unlikely that even a limited nuclear test ban could have been agreed to, much less the SALT agreements limiting strategic nuclear weapons and ballistic missile defenses. By the end of the 1970s national technical means had progressed to the point where treaties could place verifiable limits on missile throwweight, telemetry encryption, and the number of in-flight maneuvers of postboost vehicles carrying multiple warheads. As monitoring technology improved, treaties became more inclusive, more detailed, and more restrictive.

However, the end of the U.S.-Soviet competition, the increasing reliance on international treaties monitored by international organizations, and the increasing salience of nonproliferation relative to arms control have changed the requirements for technology in important ways. The usefulness of some kinds of remote sensing has been reduced relative to more traditional forms of intelligence gathering, and on-site inspection has created a demand for simpler, cheaper, and more rugged monitoring technologies. The rapid expansion of data exchanges,

---

[21] Verification and Compliance Analysis Working Group, an interagency committee that includes representatives from the IC and Defense, State, and Energy Departments. It provides tasking guidance for the NTM controlled by the IC and for the On-Site Inspection Agency (see figure 4.1).

notifications, and on-site inspections has also posed new problems for technology. Perhaps the greatest challenge is to manage the torrent of information generated by the monitoring process. In addition to the vast quantities of digitized imagery, communications, seismic, acoustic, and other data gathered by national technical means, there are now on-site inspection reports and debriefings, declarations and notifications, open source information, data on export license applications and other domestic and international commercial transactions, and covert and overt human intelligence. In principle, analysts ought to be able to draw on all this information to create an accurate picture of the arms control and proliferation activities of other states. In practice, producing a useful and reliable intelligence product from this mass of raw data remains a largely unsolved problem.

A number of agencies sponsor research and development for arms control and nonproliferation, but much of it is classified and not available in open sources. Some idea of the relative contributions of different agencies can be obtained by looking at their budgets, and this was done in chapter 5. Another way to do it is to look at the breakdown of research projects by treaty and agency, which can be found in a report produced by ACDA in its role as chair of the interagency Arms Control Research Coordinating Committee. Table 6.1 summarizes studies completed in 1993 [43]. It provides a reasonably accurate picture of the division of labor among ACDA, the Advanced Research Projects Agency (ARPA), the Central Intelligence Agency (CIA), the Defense Intelligence Agency (DIA), the Defense Special Weapons Agency (DSWA), and the Department of Energy (DOE). The categories defining the columns of the table correspond to the ones used in this book and are in most cases combinations of multiple subcategories in the ACDA report. The table lists only numbers of projects, which do not necessarily correlate with agency budgets.

Several comments will help to clarify the information in the table. First, the numbers for CIA and DIA are only for projects related to cooperative verification and some non-proliferation issues. The Intelligence Community has a considerably larger secret R&D effort associated with national technical means and other technology development that is not included here. Second, ARPA's research in 1993 was focused almost entirely on seismic detection and identification techniques for underground nuclear explosions in connection with the Comprehensive Test Ban. Third, the division of labor between DSWA and DOE is primarily based on DSWA's connection with the On-Site Inspection Agency (OSIA) [44]. DSWA has taken the major responsibility for R&D in support of OSIA, although DOE does contribute where nuclear weapons or nuclear measurements are involved [45, p. 21]. By far the largest number of projects are funded by the Department of Energy. Its major responsibilities are for nuclear testing and nuclear materials monitoring and management, where it has traditionally made important contributions to U.S. national technical means and to IAEA safeguards technology. DOE has also sponsored research on chemical and biological weapons (CBW) verification, but these projects were transferred to DSWA in 1994, presumably because of OSIA's role in monitoring the Bilateral Destruction Agreement. Much of the research on CBW verification is still being done at DOE's national laboratories, only with DSWA instead of DOE financial

Table 6.1
Arms Control and Nonproliferation Projects Completed in 1993

	Nuclear Weapons	Conven -tional	Nuclear Testing	Nuclear Prolif.	CW/BW	Regional Arms Control	Total
ACDA	4	0	1	5	8	2	20[a]
ARPA	0	0	24	1	0	0	25
CIA	13	13	0	12	2	2	42
DIA	23	3	2	4	4	0	36
DSWA	8	4	2	1	20	0	35
DOE	53	6	94	176	18	5	352
Total	101	26	123	199	52	9	510[b]

[a] ACDA's totals do not include its Annual Report to Congress and its Annual Report on Adherence to and Compliance with Arms Control Agreements, both of which encompass all of the categories except export controls.
[b] Some projects deal with more than one category and are counted more than once. No attempt has been made to separate out such multiple counting, since it does not appear to distort the overall picture significantly.

Source: Report to Congress on Arms Control, Nonproliferation, and Disarmament Studies Completed in 1993, U.S. Arms Control and Disarmament Agency, August 25, 1994.

support.[22] Finally, note that ACDA's effort remains only a small fraction of the other programs, reflecting its very small research budget (see figure 5.2).

The purpose of the arms control R&D effort is to put science and technology in the service of policy. Diplomats have objectives they want to achieve in negotiations, and scientists and engineers have ideas and devices that can accomplish certain tasks. The trick is to match capabilities to requirements—or, as is sometimes necessary, requirements to capabilities—in a timely and cost-effective manner. This requires a constant feedback between scientists and diplomats, two groups whose languages, values, and world views could hardly be more different. The interaction must be mediated by a bureaucracy capable of effecting communication between the lab bench and the negotiating table to produce results consistent with overall national security policy. In chapter 4 we looked briefly at the structure of that bureaucracy, and in chapter 5 at its cost. Now we must ask how well it is doing the job assigned to it.

The answer is mixed, but most would agree that there is substantial room for improvement. The most critical problem has been a lack of effective leadership, precisely the job that Congress had in mind in 1961 for ACDA to assume. ACDA's original mandate included requirements to:

• ensure the conduct of research, development and other studies in the field of arms control and disarmament;
• make arrangements for the conduct of research . . . by private or public institutions or persons;

---

[22] Personal communication, Livermore National Laboratory.

• coordinate research, development, and other studies . . . by or for other Government
  agencies. [46, p. 44]

The aim of Congress in making these requirements was to provide a bureaucratic
impetus behind arms control research that would be independent of the Atomic
Energy Commission and the Defense Department. But ACDA was never given
the status or budgets to allow it to exercise the coordinating and directing roles
that its founders intended. Despite an explicit Executive Order in 1964, and the
creation in 1984 of the interagency Arms Control Research Coordinating
Committee (ACRCC), of which ACDA was made the chair, ACDA never exerted meaningful control over the direction of arms control research [10, p. 43].
Control remained with the agencies that received the biggest budgets: CIA,
DOD, and DOE. As for the ACRCC, the Office of Technology Assessment
(OTA) found that "it appears to meet rarely, and . . . to be unknown even to
some of the principal officials involved in verification policy" [8, p. 5]. Its only
observable function has been to produce the annual report on completed research
projects cited above.
     Without a clearly defined leader, "U.S. technical research for cooperative
arms control verification regimes has been piecemeal rather than synoptic, and
oriented to the near term rather than the long term." It has evolved this way, "in
part because there is no one in charge—no one whose job is to make such a program happen" [8]. "Coordination of active and planned programs is supposed to
take place in a low-level interagency group called the Verification Technology
Working Group, but . . . this group's participants are still very preoccupied with
protecting their budgets and their research priorities" [5, p. 58]. Most succinctly,
"Research is controlled by the people who do the funding. Period" [5, p. 40].
This more or less free-running process has had many well-publicized successes.
There can be no disputing the impressive technical achievements of the
Intelligence Community's "black" R&D effort in producing sophisticated national technical means and other covert technologies. Yet this begs the important
question of whether the same results could have been achieved more quickly and
more cheaply if they had been subject to more competition and better-informed
oversight. One hears much about the successful programs but little about the
dead ends, misjudgments, and duplication of effort that are an inevitable part of
any R&D program. There is no basis for judgment, therefore, on whether the
problems encountered by these secret programs have been consistent with normal
expectations for a well-run research and development effort.
     The introduction in INF and START of on-site inspections, data exchanges,
and notifications began to change the character of treaty verification. The trend
has been away from hi-tech remote sensing technologies to simpler hands-on devices and techniques that can be operated in the field by military personnel rather
than highly trained technicians. One such technology, a portable fast-neutron
counter developed by the Department of Energy, was adopted in the INF Treaty
to distinguish between the Soviet Union's three-warhead SS-20 intermediate
range missile and single-warhead SS-25 strategic missile in on-site inspections.
Considering that development of the device did not start until after the treaty was
signed, it is commendable that the instrument was ready to be field-tested by the
summer of 1989, just one year after entry into force. It was formally accepted

into the inspection protocol in December 1989 and has proven to be both acceptable and reliable in the field [47, p. 145].

Another technology used in INF inspections has had a more controversial record. This is Cargoscan, an X-ray monitoring device used at the portal monitoring facility at Votkinsk (see chapter 3). The device is capable of seeing through the canister that holds a Russian missile emerging from the plant, and it has been a more or less continuous bone of contention between U.S. inspection teams and their Russian hosts, who are suspicious of its ability to see things it isn't supposed to see. Its cost of operation is high, and its benefit-to-cost ratio is less than fully persuasive. Some of its On-Site Inspection Agency operators see it as "an extravagant behemoth" [5, p. 38]. Cargoscan represents a level of technological enthusiasm and quantitative compulsiveness that is proving less and less tenable as cooperative verification measures find their way into more multilateral and international treaties.

Cooperative monitoring technologies must be politically acceptable, understandable, and affordable to all parties to multilateral treaties. Therefore, they cannot be too intrusive, too complicated, or too expensive. If a monitoring device sees too much or too clearly, it might gather collateral information or force the inspected party to take expensive precautions to avoid such collection. If it is too complicated, it may exceed the technical understanding of inspectors, require excessive maintenance or repair, or produce data too difficult to interpret. If it is too expensive, it will not be affordable to less wealthy treaty members and could discourage them from participating in the inspection regime. These pressures tend to reduce monitoring technologies to a lowest common denominator, one which is almost always far below the current state of the art in whatever technique is being applied. Examples of this phenomenon can be found in several of the treaties agreed to in recent years. During Open Skies negotiations the United States proposed the use of gravitometers and magnetometers on Open Skies aircraft. These instruments would have been useful in detecting underground structures or cavities and in providing information on what was inside closed buildings. But the proposals were withdrawn in response to objections from other states [48, p. 12]. In a similar concession the United States accepted a much less capable synthetic aperture radar (SAR) than it wanted to use. SAR is an airborne radar that can provide images of structures and vehicles with resolutions well under one meter, even at night and through cloud cover [49, pp. 45–49]. But it is expensive and technically demanding to operate and maintain, and few countries in the Open Skies regime possess the technology at all, much less the high-resolution form possessed by the United States and a handful of other technologically advanced states. The only SAR the United States could get accepted in the Open Skies Treaty was one that was commercially available to all parties [44, p. 25]. This limits resolution to no better than three meters (barely good enough to distinguish a tank from a truck) and also delays introduction of the equipment until several years after the treaty's entry into force. The United States actually had to reverse-engineer its own SAR to degrade its resolution to permitted levels.[23]

Another example of the pressures toward low or no technology in verification is the experience of tags and tamper-proof seals. Both technologies are used

---

[23] Personal communication, On-Site Inspection Agency.

by the IAEA in its safeguards program, and it was believed in the 1980s that they could contribute to monitoring some of the treaties then under negotiation. Unique identifying tags would be relatively cheap, and the devices to read and identify them could be compact, rugged, and simple to operate [50]. In START they could be used to guard against surreptitious modernization of controlled missiles by replacement of individual stages, or to help keep track of the numbers of deployed cruise missiles. In CFE, tags could be used like bar codes in supermarkets to identify equipment programmed for destruction and to automate the updating of inventory declarations. Many proposals for verified warhead dismantlement also called for tags and seals to maintain and verify the chain of custody for retired warheads [51, p. 29]. But in the end no tags were used in CFE or START, and little use has been found for them in other agreements. It has turned out to be acceptable to all CFE parties to use factory serial numbers as identifiers, and worries about clandestine substitution of rocket stages in START appear to have been exaggerated or monitorable in other ways.

According to the Office of Technology Assessment, "it would be a mistake to think of research and development of verification technologies as a quest for ever more sophisticated, high-tech devices. Rather, the challenge is to find the most appropriate ones" [8, p. 9]. This axiom needs to be more fully appreciated by the R&D community and by its supporters in Congress as well. Cooperative monitoring calls for an emphasis on the simple, cheap, and low-tech, while scientists and engineers, especially those accustomed to military and nuclear R&D, are drawn to the sophisticated, expensive, and high-tech. The latter is more professionally challenging and rewarding, especially to those who want to maintain high levels of financial support. Small may be beautiful to the inspector in the field, but it is not beautiful to a project manager or lab director trying to maintain a big payroll and a reputation for cutting-edge science and engineering. Superficially it seems like a wonderful idea to get all the talented people who used to develop nuclear weapons and other destructive technologies to develop new ways of implementing and verifying disarmament agreements. But the two kinds of work are fundamentally different. Verification R&D must be responsive to the evolution of negotiating positions and to the realities of international arms control. It is true that negotiating positions can occasionally be influenced by technological possibilities. But negotiating positions and inspection protocols evolve over periods of weeks or months, while the research process often requires lead times of years. A high-tech R&D establishment must also maintain a substantial technology base to ensure that skilled personnel are available for the long term [45, p. 57]. The maintenance of such a base is expensive, and that base is inevitably going to generate more ideas than can be used in actual treaties. This is not all wasted effort; it is an unavoidable aspect of any attempt to apply science to practical uses, and it sometimes produces unexpected benefits. However, it can become wasteful when the priorities and interests of the research community do not correspond closely to the needs and limitations of the potential users. Examples like Cargoscan and the on-site nuclear explosion yield measurement technique discussed in the previous chapter show that the United States has not escaped this problem, and continuing R&D budgets of over $200 million per year suggest that a lot of technologies are being developed that will never find their way into a cooperative monitoring regime.[24] The large amount still being spent on R&D for nuclear test monitoring (see figure 6.1), an effort that has already been heavily supported for more than 35 years, seems particularly inappropriate considering what is likely to be applicable to the international Comprehensive Test Ban.

The answer to the dilemma is to provide direction and guidance at a high political level to keep the R&D community focused on the real needs of negotiators and inspectors and on a practical and cost-effective approach to verification. In 1992 the Stimson Center strongly recommended both a reduction and restructuring of verification research, giving greater budgetary control to ACDA [5]. That did not happen, but in 1995 a new interagency group—the Nonproliferation and Arms Control Technology Working Group—was created to replace the old Verification Technology Working Group [11]. It is cochaired by ACDA, DOD, and DOE, with ACDA as Executive Secretary, and it was established "with a scope and charter that will empower [it] to provide the necessary coordination of arms control, nonproliferation, and disarmament R&D" [11]. This responds to many of the criticisms of weak and incoherent control of verification R&D that have appeared in recent studies.[25]

Figure 6.1
FY 1992 Funding for Arms Control Research

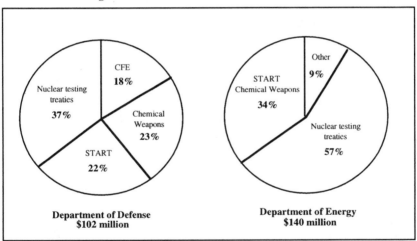

Source: Ref. 45, p. 12

---

[24] The great majority of R&D effort still goes into secret projects intended for the Intelligence Community and not into cooperative monitoring technologies. One Livermore scientist informed the author that only a "tiny fraction" of his laboratory's budget goes toward cooperative projects. Nevertheless, the R&D community often uses the promise of cooperative verification to justify continued high research budgets, and Congress has been quite receptive to this argument in recent years. As noted in chapter 5, DOE was given more money than it asked for in three consecutive years to encourage it to expand its verification research program, and a large increase in funding for the Defense Special Weapons Agency was seen as necessary to support R&D for on-site inspections in future treaties [45, pp. 14–15].

[25] Both the Stimson Center and Inspector General's reports single out R&D management as one of ACDA's most prominent shortcomings [5, 10].

As cochair with DOE and DOD, and in its role as Executive Secretary, ACDA may be able to exercise greater control over research priorities than it has in the past. It all depends on whether ACDA can influence the competition between DOD and DOE over priorities and budgets. The two large agencies have cooperated informally in the past, and in at least one area—chemical weapon verification technology—they have been reasonably successful in finding a rational division of effort [45, pp. 25–26]. ACDA could play a useful mediating role, helping to keep the effort focused on practical and politically relevant goals [29, p. 29]. However, it is difficult to see how just the creation of a new bureaucratic entity can give ACDA sufficient authority and power to gain any real control over two powerful agencies that have had things pretty much their own way for several decades.

REFERENCES

1. Mark M. Lowenthal, "Tribal Tongues: Intelligence Consumers, Intelligence Producers," *The Washington Quarterly*, Winter 1992, pp. 157–168.

2. Amy F. Woolf, The Future of U.S. Arms Control Policy, Subcommittee on Arms Control, International Security, and Science, House Committee on Foreign Affairs, July 30,1992 (Washington, DC: U.S. Government Printing Office).

3. Ronald F. Lehman, The Future of U.S. Arms Control Policy, Subcommittee on Arms Control, International Security, and Science, House Committee on Foreign Affairs, July 30,1992 (Washington, DC: U.S. Government Printing Office).

4. Duncan L. Clarke, *Politics of Arms Control: The Role and Effectiveness of the U.S. Arms Control and Disarmament Agency* (New York: The Free Press, 1979).

5. Michael Krepon, Amy E. Smithson, and James A. Schear, The U.S. Arms Control and Disarmament Agency: Restructuring for the Post-Cold War Era, The Henry L. Stimson Center, 1992.

6. Michael Krepon, "Can This Agency be Saved?" *Bulletin of the Atomic Scientists*, December, 1988, pp. 35–38.

7. Michael Nacht, testimony before the Senate Committee on Foreign Relations Subcommittee on International Operations, May 11,1995.

8. V*erification Technologies: Managing Research and Development for Cooperative Arms Control Monitoring Measures*, OTA-ISC-488, U.S. Congress, Office of Technology Assessment, May 1991.

9. Sherman M. Funk, The Arms Control and Disarmament Agency, Subcommittee on Arms Control, International Security, and Science, House Committee on Foreign Affairs, April 27,1993 (Washington, DC: U.S. Government Printing Office).

10. Sherman M. Funk, New Purposes and Priorities for Arms Control, U.S. Arms Control and Disarmament Agency, December 14, 1992.

11. *Threat Control through Arms Control*, U.S. Arms Control and Disarmament Agency, July 13, 1995.

12. Steven A. Hildreth, ACDA: Abolition, Reorganization, Cost, and Other Issues, Congressional Research Service, April 22, 1993.

13. Loch K. Johnson, "Strategic Intelligence and Weapons Proliferation," *The Monitor,* Center for International Trade and Security, University of Georgia, Spring 1995, p. 5.

14. James B. Busey and Clarence A. Robinson, "Facing Turbulence, Intelligence Community Revamps Internally," *Signal*, April 1995, pp. 48–51.

15. R. James Woolsey, World Threat Assessment Brief, Senate Select Committee on Intelligence, January 10,1995.

16. James Kitfield, "Looking for Trouble," *National Journal*, May 18, 1996, pp. 1094–1098.

17. "5 Are Named to Top C.I.A. Posts," *New York Times*, August 1, 1995, p. A10.

18. Walter Pincus, "Pentagon Gaining Turf From the CIA," *Washington Post*, November 16, 1995, p. A21.

19. Jay Taylor, "A Leaner, Keener CIA," *Washington Post*, December 22, 1996, p. C7.

20. Paula L. Scalingi, "Intelligence Community Cooperation: The Arms Control Model," *International Journal of Intelligence and Counterintelligence*, Winter 1992, pp. 401–410.

21. Sidney Graybeal, et al., Verification to the Year 2000, Arms Control and Disarmament Division, External Affairs and International Trade, Ottawa, February 1991.

22. Patricia Bliss McFate, et al., Constraining Proliferation: The Contribution of Verification Synergies; Non-proliferation, Arms Control, and Disarmament Division, Department of External Affairs, Ottawa, March 1993.

23. Patricia Bliss McFate, et al., The Converging Roles of Arms Control Verification, Confidence-Building Measures, and Peace Operations: Opportunities for Harmonization and Synergies; Non-proliferation, Arms Control, and Disarmament Division, Department of Foreign Affairs and International Trade, Ottawa, October 1994.

24. Bobby R. Inman, The Military Perspective, *Intelligence and Arms Control*, Thomas J. Hirschfeld, Ed. (Austin, TX: Lyndon B. Johnson School of Public Affairs, 1987), pp. 45–54.

25. Rick Atkinson, *Crusade: The Untold Story of the Persian Gulf War* (Boston: Houghton Mifflin, 1993).

26. *Sipri Yearbook 1991* (Oxford: Oxford University Press, 1992).

27. Annette J. Krygiel, "The Central Imagery Office Getting the Picture," *Defense 94*, 1994, pp. 30–34.

28. Paula L. Scalingi, "U.S. Intelligence in an Age of Uncertainty: Refocusing to Meet the Challenge," *The Washington Quarterly*, Winter 1992, pp. 147–156.

29. A Revitalized ACDA in the Post–Cold War World, House Committee on Foreign Affairs, June 23, 1994.

30. "IAEA Director Hans Blix: Keeping an Eye on a Nuclear World," *Arms Control Today*, November 1991, pp. 3–6.

31. Authorizing Appropriations for FY 1993 for Intelligence Activities of the U.S. Government . . ., Senate Select Committee on Intelligence, July 21, 1992.

32. Intelligence Authorization Act for Fiscal Year 1995, House Select Committee on Intelligence, June 9, 1994.

33. Michael Krepon, U.S. Government Organization for Arms Control Verification and Compliance, *Verification and Compliance: A Problem Solving Approach*, Michael Krepon and Mary Umberger, Eds. (Cambridge, MA: Ballinger, 1988), pp. 282–308.

34. Henry Kissinger, *Diplomacy* (New York: Simon & Schuster, 1994).

35. Henry Sokolski, "Fighting Proliferation with Intelligence," *Orbis*, Spring 1994, pp. 245–260.

36. *Export Controls and Nonproliferation Policy*, OTA-ISS-596, U.S. Congress, Office of Technology Assessment, May 1994.

37. Anne Hessing Cahn and John Prados, "Team B: The Trillion Dollar Experiment," *Bulletin of the Atomic Scientists*, April 1993, pp. 22–27.

38. R. Jeffrey Smith, "Pakistan Building Reactor that May Yield Large Quantities of Plutonium," *Washington Post*, April 8, 1995, p. A20.

39. R. Jeffrey Smith, "U.S. Waives Objection to Russian Missile Technology Sale to Brazil," *Washington Post*, June 8, 1995, p. A23.

40. R. Jeffrey Smith, "Iran's Missile Technology Linked to China, Report Says," *Washington Post*, June 17, 1995, p. A14.

41. R. Jeffrey Smith and David B. Ottaway, "Spy Photos Suggest China Missile Trade," *Washington Post*, July 3, 1995, p. A1.

42. "U.S. Waives Russia-Brazil MTCR Violation," *Arms Control Today*, July/August 1995, p. 27.

43. Report to Congress on Arms Control, Nonproliferation, and Disarmament Studies Completed in 1993, U.S. Arms Control and Disarmament Agency, August 25, 1994.

44. Program Plan for Research, Development, Test, and Evaluation For Arms Control, Fiscal Years 1995–96, U.S. Department of Defense, Office of the Under Secretary of Defense (Acquisition and Technology), May 10, 1995.

45. Arms Control: Improved Coordination of Arms Control Research Needed, GAO/NSIAD-92-149, U.S. General Accounting Office, April 1992.

46. Annual Report to Congress 1993, U.S. Arms Control and Disarmament Agency, March 28, 1994.

47. Joseph P. Harahan, *On-Site Inspections under the INF Treaty* (Washington, DC: On-Site Inspection Agency, 1993).

48. Peter Jones, "Open Skies: A New Era of Transparency," *Arms Control Today*, May 1992, pp. 10–14.

49. Allan S. Krass, *Verification: How Much Is Enough?* (Lexington, MA: Lexington Books, 1985).

50. A. DeVolpi, Status of Tags and Seals for Arms Control Verification, *Verification Report 1991*, J.B. Poole, Ed. (London, New York: VERTIC, Apex Press, 1991), pp. 131–138.

51. Frank von Hippel, Ending the production of fissile materials for weapons; Verifying the dismantlement of nuclear warheads: The technical basis for action, Federation of American Scientists, June, 1991.

7

NONCOMPLIANCE

More than 30 years of experience with arms control has made at least one thing perfectly clear: like the poor, noncompliance and the suspicion of noncompliance will always be with us. Ambiguities and suspicions are an inevitable part of the process, and every treaty considered in this book has had its share of compliance problems. The vast majority of them have been resolved in consultation forums that accompany each agreement, but some have not been resolved so quickly and have the potential to develop into disputes similar to those that poisoned U.S.-Soviet relations in the 1970s and 1980s. Compliance questions must be handled with a combination of patience, firmness, proportionality, and sensitivity to context that is often difficult to achieve in practice, especially where national security and domestic politics intersect.

There are two main areas in which compliance has been a chronic problem: formal arms control and disarmament agreements and informal export control regimes. I have not given much attention to the implementation of export controls in this book, but they form an important component of U.S. arms control and nonproliferation policy, and apparent violations of their restrictions are given at least as much attention in Congress, the executive branch, and the media as are violations of formal treaties. Both kinds of noncompliance will therefore be considered in this chapter, which will focus on the nature and motivations behind a variety of "violations" of treaties and regimes and the ways in which the United States has dealt with them.

WHAT IS A VIOLATION?

The distinction between compliance and noncompliance has a tendency to become less and less clear the harder one looks at it. If one drives 56 miles per hour in a 30-mile-per-hour zone one is clearly in violation of the speed limit, and that violation can be established by evidence that will stand up under scientific and legal scrutiny. The situation is less clear if one drives 56 miles per hour in a 55-mile-per-hour zone. From a technical point of view questions arise as to whether the accuracy of police measurements are reliable to plus or minus 1 mile per hour at that speed and whether the driver's speedometer is accurate enough to allow him or her to stay close to but still below the limit. From a legal and practical point of view, the "violation" in this case may be unprovable in court and not worth the effort of trying to prevent.

Abram and Antonia Chayes find in speed limit enforcement a useful example of the difference between strict compliance with laws and what they call "acceptable levels of compliance." They argue:

For a simple prohibitory norm like a highway speed limit, it is in principle a simple matter to determine whether any particular driver is in compliance. Yet most communities and law enforcement organizations in the United States seem to be perfectly comfortable with a situation is which the average speed on interstate highways is perhaps ten miles above the limit. Even in individual cases, the enforcing officer is not likely to pursue a driver operating within that zone. The fundamental problem for the system is not how to induce all drivers to obey the speed limit but how to contain deviance within acceptable levels. [1, pp. 197–198]

This is an excellent metaphor for what used to be called "adequate verification" in arms control. The phrase was coined in the Nixon administration and served throughout the 1970s to describe the U.S. concern that militarily significant violations be detectable in time to permit an appropriate response. This was not good enough for the Reagan administration, which set "effective verification" as its new standard. Former ACDA Director Kenneth Adelman described the difference between the two standards as follows:

"Adequate verification" had been defined as our ability to detect major violations early enough to respond in time to preserve our security. "Effective verification" now means having the ability to detect any Soviet violation, regardless of its military significance. [2, p. 145]

Not surprisingly, this standard was soon discovered to be impractical. It was more a device to prevent arms control agreements than to enforce them. An analogous situation would be to forbid driving of automobiles because the police could not guarantee that every speeding violation would be detected.

However impractical the Reagan standard may have been, the phrase "effective verification" has proven too attractive to abandon. Rhetorically and politically it is still the standard, but the reality looks much more like the old "adequate verification." Consider the most recent statement of the standard given by the Clinton administration's ACDA Director, John Holum:

The policy standard of "effective verification" is necessarily rigorous. We must retain the ability to detect militarily significant violations, with high confidence, in sufficient time to respond effectively with defense adjustments or other responses, as needed. [3]

To paraphrase the Chayes: The fundamental problem for the arms control and nonproliferation system is not how to induce all states to comply absolutely but how to contain deviance within acceptable levels.

Unfortunately this clarification of the objective does not make the problem easier to solve. The difficulty shifts to the phrase "acceptable levels," which can have as many interpretations as interpreters. The phrase also carries the same connotation of laxity or softness that many found objectionable in "adequate." Imprecision and uncertainty may be endemic to law enforcement and verification, but to admit it openly is to risk confusing both motorists and states parties about the real limits on their behavior. The highway patrol does not publicly announce that it is all right for drivers to exceed the speed limit by less than ten miles per hour. Such an announcement would simply raise the effective limit by ten miles per hour and encourage people to see how rigorously *that* limit was enforced. Instead, drivers remain somewhat uncertain of what will be enforced and what won't and can sometimes experience unpleasant surprises when they miscalculate. Uncertainty can serve as a deterrent, so occasional strict enforcement is useful. At the same time, sporadic enforcement can be seen as evidence of arbitrariness, discrimination, or incompetence in law enforcement. If such perceptions become widespread, they can engender contempt for the traffic laws and those who enforce them. In arms control as in traffic control there are costs and risks associated with enforcement that is either too rigorous or too lax. For arms control the goal of compliance policy is not only the direct protection of national security. It is also to maintain respect for the treaty and the norms it embodies. Violations at any level, if they become widespread and persistent, will eventually undermine a regime's authority and legitimacy.

WHY DO VIOLATIONS OCCUR?

There are two fundamentally different approaches to the question of why states do not comply with their commitments. One is the so-called "realist" model, which treats states as unitary rational actors who base their actions on calculations of risk and benefit. From this point of view violations are to be expected whenever the perceived benefits to the violator exceed the risks. The only way to prevent violations is with credible deterrent threats that change the risk-benefit calculation. An early Director of ACDA, Fred Iklé, distilled the essence of this point of view in his classic 1961 article (quoted in chapter 2):

A potential violator of an arms-control agreement will not be deterred simply by the risk that his action may be discovered. What will deter him will be the fear that what he gains from the violation will be outweighed by the loss he may suffer from the victim's reaction to it. [4, p. 208]

An alternative to the realist assumption takes compliance to be the norm and violations to be aberrations: "Almost all nations observe almost all principles of international law and almost all of their obligations almost all of the time" [1, p. 177]. From this point of view states are seen as complex, nonrational actors for whom international norms and institutions have important, many times decisive, influence on their behavior. In this view, "compliance problems often do not reflect a deliberate decision to violate an international undertaking on the basis of a calculation of interests" [1, p. 176]. This is true because states are made up of organizations, and for organizations:

standard economic analysis argues against the continuous recalculation of costs and benefits. The adoption of a treaty, like the enactment of any other law, establishes an authoritative rule system. Compliance is the normal organizational presumption. [1, pp. 178–179]

Nor are "interests" fixed or independently calculable; indeed they can at least in part be determined by the processes of treaty negotiation and ratification.

Modern treaty making, like legislation in a democratic polity, can be seen as a creative enterprise through which the parties not only weigh the benefits and burdens of commitment but explore, redefine and sometimes discover their interests. [1, p. 180]

Neither of the above starting assumptions is empirically verifiable [1, p. 177]. Most analysts choose between them on metaphysical or ideological grounds rather than on the basis of logic or evidence. The assertion that states only do what it is in their interests to do is tautological without an independent measure of "interests." Indeed, we usually learn a state's interests by observing what it chooses to do. Nor is the presumption of compliance as "normal behavior" provable by empirical means. Compliance is often measured in terms of actions not taken, and it is hardly ever possible to determine the degree to which the decision not to act was affected by positive compliant or negative deterrent influences. I will avoid making the choice between these two assumptions here and will treat them on an equal footing.

Rational choice by a unitary state actor then becomes one possible explanation for noncompliance. Some people break the speed limit because they have calculated that the benefits of earlier arrival at their destination are worth the risks of being caught and fined. Three other hypotheses suggested by Chayes and Chayes will be considered as alternative or complementary explanations.[1] One attributes noncompliant behavior to ambiguities in treaty requirements. Treaty language is always ambiguous at some level, and every provision is subject to varying interpretations in different contexts (is the speed limit precisely 55 miles per hour, or is it OK to do 60 if the traffic is light?). Such disputes are as much a part of domestic as international law and are the way lawyers make their living. A second justification for noncompliance can be a lack of capability—financial, political, or technical—to keep one's commitments (my speedometer is broken, officer, and I can't afford to have it fixed). Any number of things can happen to cause a state to lose or to be unable to acquire capabilities it assumed it would have when it ratified the treaty. Third, there is what Chayes and Chayes call the "temporal dimension" [1, p. 195]. It often takes time to create the domestic institutions and attitudes required to implement a complex treaty. (I'm new to this area, officer, and I thought this was a freeway.) "Wise treaty drafters recognize at the negotiating stage that there will be a considerable time lag after the treaty is concluded before some or all of the parties can bring themselves into compliance" [1, p. 195].

---

[1] Chayes and Chayes, from the perspective of lawyers, call them "defenses" instead of explanations. Defenses in this sense are "matters put forth to excuse or justify or extenuate a prima facie case of breach" [1].

These four "explanations"—rational choice, ambiguity, incapacity, and time lag—will form the basis for the following analysis of different states' compliance behavior. One that could use some clarification is "incapacity." I will include in this category violations that occur because of accident, inadvertence, or unauthorized behavior. All are indications of the incapacity of the state to control its own affairs, whether technically and administratively in the case of accidents and inadvertence, or politically in the case of unauthorized behavior by subordinate officials or citizens. Treaties are signed by states on the assumption that the parties have sufficient control over their own actions to guarantee compliance, just as adults are assumed to be competent to control their own actions in civil law. Sometimes this assumption is incorrect for citizens, and it has also been called into question by a number of analysts of state compliance behavior.

During ACDA's Reagan administration heyday as the chief prosecutor of Soviet misbehavior, its attitude was caricatured as "a violation is a violation is a violation," an attitude that "tends to obscure the relative significance of issues" [5, p. 46]. In such an extreme legalistic view, motivations and extenuating circumstances are irrelevant. The only question to ask is "Do the Soviets cheat?" [2, p. 145]. If they do they should be punished, and the punishment should be "condign," or at the very least "proportionate."[2] At the other end of the spectrum is the belief that motivation and extenuating circumstances are more important than the action itself; context matters more than content. In this view, until one understands why a violation took place one has no idea how to respond appropriately to it.

It is always possible to imagine scenarios in which a truly serious violation, one that significantly threatens the security of a state, is discovered or revealed as a *fait accompli*. In such a case one would be justified in arguing that motivations don't matter; one must shoot first (figuratively, of course) and ask questions about motivations and context later. But no such scenario has ever occurred, even during the darkest moments of the Cold War. The closest one can come to an example is the secret deployment of Soviet missiles in Cuba in 1962. However, this was neither a violation of a treaty[3] nor viewed by all policymakers as a threat that required an immediate military response. All other instances of actual or alleged Soviet violations have posed at most only minor threats to U.S. security (see chapter 2), have been observed by U.S. intelligence in a relatively early stage of their development, and have allowed plenty of time for analysis of their context and for consultations or diplomatic protests. None required or was ever used to justify a military response by the United States, although alleged Soviet violations of SALT were used by the Reagan administration to justify its renunciation of the treaty in 1986 [9].

The current U.S. policy is that "no violation, regardless of military significance is acceptable" [10, p. 23]. No other publicly stated policy would

---

[2] "Condign" punishment for violators was advocated by Bernard Baruch in his 1945 UN speech introducing the U.S. plan for international control of atomic energy. The word was synonymous in Baruch's speech with "immediate, swift, and sure" [6]. "Proportionate response" was the phrase defining the Reagan administration's policy toward alleged Soviet violations in the 1980s [7].

[3] It did violate private assurances by Premier Khrushchev to President Kennedy that no "offensive" missiles would be deployed in Cuba. But Khrushchev saw them primarily as "defensive" or "deterrent" missiles, so even in this case, if one wanted to stretch the point, one could see it as an example of differing interpretations of an ambiguous definition [8].

make sense, any more than it would make sense for the highway patrol to announce that it would overlook minor speeding infractions. The examples analyzed below will show, however, that the reality is less draconian than the policy implies. Nor is the United States exempt from suspicion of violations. States accused of noncompliance by the United States have not hesitated to make their own accusations in return, sometimes valid and sometimes not. Therefore, in the following I will look not only at the compliance record of Russia, China, North Korea, and others, but at that of the United States as well.

THE COMPLIANCE RECORD

The following analysis is not intended to be exhaustive. It would take far too much space simply to mention, let alone analyze, all instances of questionable or noncompliant behavior under the formal and informal regimes now in force. I will focus on a few examples in two general categories—export controls and formal treaties—that are either illustrative of some important point or particularly serious in their threat to the regime in general or the United States in particular. Commitments made under the two types of agreement have different standing under international law. Export control commitments are considered "politically binding" and treaty commitments "legally binding," which appears to imply that the latter are more "serious." But both are capable of producing suspicion and anger when violations are suspected, and either can become a major problem in a deteriorating political environment.

Export Control Regimes

World markets for high-technology goods are growing rapidly, and so is the number of suppliers. Competition in this lucrative and prestigious field is intense, as are temptations to cut corners on nonproliferation controls. These temptations were most flagrantly indulged during the long, bloody, and expensive war between Iran and Iraq. The war lasted through most of the 1980s, and high-technology weaponry and manufacturing technology were sold to both sides by most major industrialized states. Chemical weapons were manufactured and used by both sides, ballistic missiles were launched by both sides, and Iraq committed itself to an intensive nuclear weapon development program. Two of the major international export control groups were inspired by the Iran-Iraq war—the Australia Group by the use of chemical weapons, and the Missile Technology Control Regime (MTCR) by the use of ballistic missiles, including Iraq's Scud attacks on Israel and Saudi Arabia in the Gulf War. The Nuclear Suppliers Group (NSG) comes from an earlier time, when India's nuclear test alerted the industrialized states to the role of nuclear and dual-use exports in facilitating nuclear proliferation. The United States has long struggled to gain better control over its own exports and to convince other states to improve controls on theirs. For much of that time the big troublemakers from the U.S. point of view were in Western Europe: France, Germany, Italy, Belgium, etc. Now they are integrated more tightly into control regimes, and it is Russia and China who are causing most of the difficulties. Partly for geostrategic reasons but primarily for economic reasons, these states continue to sell nuclear and missile technology to states that the United States believes are aspiring or accomplished proliferants. Efforts to stop or retard these sales constitute a significant fraction of U.S. diplomatic activity with the two former adversaries.

Russia is a full-fledged member of the NSG, which "seeks to restrict the export of sensitive items that can contribute to the proliferation of nuclear weapons" [11, p. 16]. Yet Russia has made a deal with Iran to complete two nuclear reactors started by West Germany in the 1970s, to supply other kinds of nuclear technology, and to train Iranian nuclear technicians [12]. The Iranian deal represents a $1 billion shot in the arm for a Russian nuclear industry devastated by reduced government support and economic hardship. It was pushed through under the leadership of Viktor Mikhailov, Director of Russia's Ministry of Atomic Energy (MINATOM). In the state of political disarray that is likely to persist in Russia for the foreseeable future, Mikhailov has considerable independence from the central government. He has proven himself to be a tenacious defender of the interests of his ministry and the industry it serves [13, p. 11]. Mikhailov and the Director of Iran's Atomic Energy Organization signed a secret protocol to the reactor deal, committing themselves to negotiate additional contracts for research reactors, development of a uranium mine, training Iranian scientists at Russian facilities, and building a gas centrifuge uranium enrichment plant. It took a direct appeal from President Clinton to President Yeltsin at the May 1995 summit meeting to get the centrifuge plant canceled, but the rest of the deal will apparently go forward [12].

There is a substantial body of evidence suggesting that Iran is working clandestinely, much as Iraq did, to acquire a nuclear weapons capability. U.S. and Israeli intelligence have reportedly uncovered secret Iranian attempts to acquire enrichment technology [14], and there have been other reports of smuggling of advanced weapons and devices to Iran through many of the same channels used by Iraq during the 1980s [15]. Iran's nuclear program began in the 1970s when the Shah was in power with encouragement and assistance from West Germany and the United States. The program deteriorated after the 1979 revolution, with many Iranian nuclear scientists and engineers leaving the country. Recent agreements with Russia and China, and some fear with India as well, would train a new generation of Iranian nuclear technicians, ostensibly for civilian power projects, but also capable of contributing to a weapons program [14]. Iran does not appear to need a nuclear generating capability, much less enrichment and reprocessing plants. It is one of the world's leading producers of oil and faces no imminent energy crisis.

From the Russian point of view, the U.S. position is hypocritical and self-serving. In the 1970s, under the Shah, Iran had even less rationale for a nuclear energy program, yet at that time the United States and other Western powers supported Iranian nuclear development. More recently the United States has brokered a deal to supply light water reactors to North Korea on the grounds that such reactors do not pose a significant proliferation threat.[4] The reactors to be built by Russia for Iran are of the same basic type, and given that Iran is a member in good standing of the Non-proliferation Treaty (NPT) and that Russia

---

[4] It is also worth noting that Russia is anxious to sell nuclear reactors to North Korea and argues that this would be more logical than the U.S. plan because much of North Korea's nuclear complex is based on Soviet/Russian technology [16].

will insist on all required safeguards on the Iranian reactors, Mikhailov and many other Russians can see no reason why the sale should not proceed [12].

The United States may be correct in its suspicion that Iran has nuclear weapon ambitions. President Clinton is reported to have shared a detailed intelligence analysis with President Yeltsin summarizing the evidence for an Iranian weapon program [12], and there have been a number of leaks of intelligence information on Iran's efforts to obtain materials and technology overseas [14, 15]. Legally and politically, however, the U.S. case against the deal (except for the enrichment plant) is weak. This is especially true in light of the North Korean agreement, which makes the opposition to Iran's acquisition of similar kinds of reactors appear capricious and discriminatory to many international observers. From the U.S. point of view, the Russians appear to be violating their obligations under Article I of the Non-proliferation Treaty "not in any way to assist . . . any non-nuclear-weapon State to manufacture or otherwise acquire nuclear weapons." Russia sees itself as acting in full compliance with Article IV of the same treaty, which requires nuclear weapon states to "co-operate in contributing alone or together with other States . . . to the further development of the applications of nuclear energy for peaceful purposes, especially in . . . non-nuclear weapon States Party to the Treaty." President Yeltsin emphasized at the 1995 summit that the contract with Iran "was concluded legitimately and in accordance with international law and no international treaties were violated in the process" [17].

The possibility of contradictions between Articles I and IV of the NPT has long been recognized and has been seen by critics as one of the major weaknesses of the treaty [18]. The NPT and the International Atomic Energy Agency attempt simultaneously to promote and to regulate the worldwide development of nuclear energy, an inherent conflict of interests. At the same time, it is inconceivable that the treaty could have been so widely accepted if it had attempted to deny commercial nuclear technology to non-nuclear-weapon states. Only a promise by the nuclear weapon states of unrestricted access to peaceful nuclear technology could convince the non-nuclear-weapon states to renounce nuclear weapons forever and submit their entire nuclear establishments to IAEA safeguards. The ambiguity inherent in the requirements of Articles I and IV is at the root of the U.S.-Russian dispute over sales of nuclear technology to Iran. The United States and Russia disagree over the relative importance of the two articles to the Iranian situation, and Russia remains at least officially unpersuaded that its sales of reactors and other technology will contribute to Iran's development of nuclear weapons. Russian leaders certainly have no interest in helping Iran to acquire nuclear weapons, but they have a powerful interest in selling big-ticket items that will keep their nuclear establishment at work. There may also be a certain degree of "incapacity" on the part of the Russian government in controlling the actions of Viktor Mikhailov and MINATOM. The weakness of the Russian central government is apparent in many areas, and it took a direct exertion of presidential power by Boris Yeltsin to cancel even a small portion of the original deal Mikhailov signed with Iran.

China's sale of M-11 ballistic missiles to Pakistan (see chapter 6) has many of the same features as the Russia-Iran case, but also some important differences. China had promised the United States "informally" to adhere to the MTCR guidelines, which require "a strong presumption to deny" the transfer of "ballistic missile systems . . . capable of delivering at least a 500 kilogram payload to a range of at least 300 kilometers" [19]. China has never publicly acknowledged the missile shipments to Pakistan [20] but claims that, in any event, the M-11 falls outside the MTCR guidelines. It was designed, according to China, to have a range of only 280 kilometers with a payload of 800 kilograms [21]. The nominal range is therefore just under the MTCR minimum. But, as any freshman physics student knows, there is a simple tradeoff between range and payload. With a 500-kilogram payload, corresponding to the weight of a relatively unsophisticated nuclear warhead, the M-11 would have a range comfortably over the 300-kilometer minimum. Therefore, unlike the Russian claim for its reactor shipments to Iran, which has considerable legitimacy under the NPT and NSG guidelines, the Chinese defense of their missile transfer to Pakistan is transparently disingenuous.

A second similarity between the Russian and Chinese defenses involves their characterization of U.S. protests as self-serving and hypocritical. Where the Russians cite the North Korean reactor deal, the Chinese cite the U.S. sale of F-16 aircraft to Taiwan, which they claim was a violation of a U.S. commitment made in 1982 to reduce arms sales to Taiwan[5] [22, p. 156]. In the Chinese view, "When carrying nuclear warheads, BMs [ballistic missiles] are merely as effective as strike aircraft. Why should strike aircraft, not BMs, be permitted to be marketed?" [23, p. 173]. Some Western analysts agree that strike aircraft like the F-16 are at least as militarily effective as ballistic missiles [24]. Whatever the technical merits of such arguments, they do not address the suspicion and resentment of what many Chinese and Russians see as U.S. arrogance and capriciousness. For China these resentments derive from a long-term feeling of being discriminated against. The Chinese view of the MTCR is "[the] major powers negotiate a treaty behind China's back and then, after they sign it, 'invite' China to join it" [23, p. 175]. Such feelings do not yield easily to technical arguments, however disinterested and defensible.

Whatever the Chinese rationalization, it does appear that in this case "a violation is a violation is a violation," especially in view of the detailed intelligence evidence mentioned in chapter 6. Sanctions would seem to be warranted under U.S. law. But the administration hesitates, and there are understandable reasons for that hesitation. Sanctions against China would hurt U.S. exports and would set back efforts to integrate China more fully into international trade and arms control regimes. The violation does not pose a direct threat to U.S. security. Possibly most important of all, however, is the evidence that China is moving, however haltingly, in the right direction on export controls. In China, according to Zachary Davis, "Political and military officials regulate exports within the limits of their authority, and in effect, two export control systems have evolved—one of civilian commodities and conventional arms and another for sensitive exports. As China embraces nonproliferation norms and agreements, the continued evolution of its nonproliferation policy depends on bridging the gap between these two systems" [19, p. 587].

---

[5] For a clear and unapologetic exposition of the Chinese point of view see Hua Di, China's Case: Ballistic Missile Proliferation, *The International Missile Bazaar: The New Suppliers Network*, William C. Potter and Harlan W. Jencks, Eds. (Boulder, CO: Westview Press, 1994), pp. 173–177.

Using the Chayes' categories we might suggest both "incapacity" and "temporal dimension" defenses for China's actions. China's civilian authorities may want to adhere to international norms and commitments but may be unable to control the actions of military officials who want to sell missiles. It can also be argued that China is relatively new at the export control game and still has a lot to learn about how to administer and enforce such controls on a rapidly expanding and often anarchic economic system. In fact, the Clinton administration has accepted this defense in another case, the shipment by a Chinese company of thousands of ring magnets to the nuclear complex in Kahuta, Pakistan. The ring magnets are used in centrifuges that enrich uranium, and Pakistan's enrichment facility, which is not under IAEA safeguards, is suspected of being the source of the material used to produce nuclear weapons. The transfer was revealed in U.S. media in February 1996 [25], and after several months of charges and countercharges between the United States and China and of growing tension between the Clinton administration and Congress over the question of sanctions, the matter was finally settled at a meeting between the Chinese foreign minister and the U.S. secretary of state. The United States accepted the Chinese defense that senior officials were unaware of the transfer— the "incapacity" defense—and China promised to supply no more nuclear-related technology to unsafeguarded facilities [26].

Unfortunately, despite the U.S. willingness (some might say eagerness) to accept the incapacity defense in the ring magnets case, neither the temporal nor the incapacity defense is entirely persuasive. According to Zachary Davis, "Top leaders are not normally excluded from decision making on sensitive exports; they are in the loop."[6] He also sees "few signs that China is adapting its existing export control system to include nonproliferation objectives" [19, p. 597]. The Clinton administration's hope that it can constructively engage China and influence its export behavior in a positive direction is certainly understandable, and may even be the most logical and potentially effective approach to the problem. But as this is written there is still little evidence that it is actually working, and reports of new suspicious technology transfers from China to Pakistan and Iran continue to appear with depressing regularity.

We are pushed closer to the "rational actor" explanation: that China is consciously dissembling by promising to abide by MTCR guidelines and NPT requirements while simultaneously and knowingly breaking those promises. What should the United States do about it? There is no simple answer to this question. The United States is being forced to determine its own pragmatic way to "contain deviance within acceptable levels" [1, pp. 197–198]. No formula can determine where those levels are, nor is there any reason to expect that the problem will resolve itself any time soon.

Treaty Compliance

The best publicly available source of information on compliance with formal agreements is the report "Adherence to and Compliance with Arms

---

[6] At the same time it is worth noting that the value of the ring magnet sale was only $70,000, and the ring magnets are not specifically mentioned on the NSG control list. This makes it somewhat more plausible that top Chinese officials were not consulted.

Control Agreements," issued every summer by the Arms Control and Disarmament Agency [27]. The report comes in both unclassified and classified versions, and there are often significant differences between them. For example, the classified 1994 version reportedly accused Russia of continuing development of biological weapons, but the unclassifed version was far more circumspect [28]. From the latter we learn only that "some facilities, in addition to being engaged in legitimate activity, may be maintaining the capability to produce biological warfare agents," and that "the trilateral process that began in 1992 [see chapter 3] . . . has not resolved all U.S. concerns" [10, p. 14].

Both versions are the result of an intensely competitive interagency process. It can be compared to a war, in which bureaucratic armies fight for small parcels of ideological or political turf, intelligence evidence and estimates are the ammunition, and interagency meeting rooms are the battlefields. The evidence almost always permits uncertainty and divergent interpretations, which can be muted or amplified to serve different political agendas. If violations are politically inconvenient, even the smallest residual ambiguity can be exploited to preserve the presumption of compliance. The Clinton administration's treatment of China's missile shipments to Pakistan is an excellent example of this. On the other hand, if violations are politically convenient, the most tenuous scraps of evidence can be used to produce them. The Reagan administration relied on just such meager evidence in 1981 when it prematurely, and almost certainly falsely, accused the Soviet Union of using "yellow rain" as a biological weapon in Indochina (see chapter 3) [29].

All of the arguments over the evidence take place out of public view. By the time the final compliance report has been cleared for release to the public by all concerned agencies, it has the texture of overcooked oatmeal. It conceals far more than it reveals about the nature and causes of compliance disputes and the policy differences of concerned agencies. Nevertheless, for all its carefully crafted vagueness, the report does provide a general picture of the compliance process and how smoothly it is working. Since the issues that appear in the report are the more serious ones, or the ones that take a longer time to resolve, they provide a kind of upper limit of concern. It may well be that the classified version and "annexes" present more serious problems than the public version. But history has shown that anything truly alarming, or even moderately interesting, in the classified report will be leaked to the press. This is certainly true if the alleged infraction is serious enough to warrant a high-level diplomatic demarche or a change in military preparations.

The 1995 report (released in July 1996) is divided into several sections which focus on three major areas: U.S. compliance, compliance by former Soviet republics with U.S.-Soviet treaties, and compliance by all other states with multilateral or international agreements. As for U.S. compliance, the conclusions are unsurprising. The United States "continues to make every effort to comply scrupulously with all [its] obligations." The United States "has committed some errors . . . but has acknowledged them to our treaty partners and taken steps to correct them" [10, p. 6]. Unfortunately, almost all of these "errors" are discussed only in the classified annexes, so they can't be analyzed here. One exception is an incident in which U.S. escorts at the Vandenberg Test Range refused to allow Russian inspectors to directly measure the dimensions of a treaty-limited "object," presumably a missile. The Russians protested and the

United States ultimately admitted that "its implementation activities contravened the express terms of the START Treaty" [27, p. 64]. All other "errors" mentioned in the public report are those of other parties, so there is no way to find out to what degree U.S. compliance problems are comparable to or different from those of other states. We do know, however, that some states are not fully persuaded of U.S. good behavior. Perhaps the clearest example of this has been the U.S. attitude toward the ABM Treaty.

The United States and the ABM Treaty

The record of U.S. noncompliance or questionable behavior with respect to ballistic missile defenses goes back just about as far as the Soviet Union's. In 1983, even as the United States was publicly accusing the Soviets of their most serious and unambiguous treaty violation, it was planning to commit a similar violation of its own. The Soviets were building a large early-warning radar deep in the interior of their territory, in clear violation of the ABM Treaty's requirement to place such radars only on the boundary. The United States was building *two* large early-warning radars in Greenland and England, in clear violation of the treaty's requirement that no such radars be deployed outside its territory [30]. In 1984 the United States used a retired Minuteman missile against a target warhead in the so-called Homing Overlay experiment. With considerable justification the Soviets called this experiment a violation of Article VI of the ABM Treaty, which forbids giving any missile other than a specified ABM interceptor the capability to intercept warheads in flight [31]. Then in 1985 the Reagan administration announced a patently fallacious "reinterpretation" of the treaty to justify its Strategic Defense Initiative [32]. For their part the Soviets continually stretched the treaty's limits on simultaneous testing of interceptors and radars [33].

U.S. ambivalence toward the ABM Treaty has outlived the Cold War and shows every indication of continuing for the foreseeable future.[7] While the Clinton administration remained formally committed to the treaty, it sought to "clarify" the distinction between strategic and theater ballistic missile defenses in order to legitimate the Theater High Altitude Area Defense (THAAD) system under development by the U.S. Army and Navy [34]. In the view of many U.S. analysts, THAAD will violate the ABM Treaty's prohibition against mobile land-based and sea-based systems with the capability to intercept strategic ballistic missiles. It was just such attempts by the Soviets to develop their SA-10 and SA-12 ballistic missile defense systems that drew accusations of violations from the Reagan and Bush administrations [35, pp. 16–17]. Others argue that such comparisons are misleading and that THAAD and other tactical and theater ballistic missile defense systems can be accommodated under the traditional interpretation of treaty [36].

This is not the place to attempt to resolve this question. The point to be made here is that U.S. actions do not appear to others to be fully consistent with U.S. commitments, and that reasonable bases exist for those impressions. There are ways to resolve these questions by using the Standing Consultative Commission created by the treaty. Disputes about radars, Minuteman inter-

---

[7] For a review of the ABM Treaty debate in the mid-1990s see the September 1994 issue of *Arms Control Today*.

ceptors, and warhead speed limits are primarily technical and therefore subject to resolution by defining clearer limits and perhaps adding new monitoring and notification procedures. But actions like the Reagan administration's reinterpretation of the treaty are far more serious. A similar situation is brewing in the mid-1990s as the Department of Defense and the Republican-controlled Congress continue to exert pressure toward weakening or even renouncing the treaty. Republican plans announced immediately after the November 1994 elections promised to "create the base line of moving forward in subsequent years to undo the constraints that the ABM Treaty places upon us." Republicans were also committed to "removing interceptor speed limitations on theater components of the ballistic missile defenses imposed by the administration as a result of ABM talks" [37]. It was in this spirit that Senator Jesse Helms introduced legislation in February 1996 to withdraw the United States from the treaty [38], and that three Republican members of Congress moved the following December to cut off all funding for the Standing Consultative Commission [39].

The Pentagon wanted to maximize its freedom of action in developing theater ballistic missile defense systems and refused to accept Russian proposals to set quantitative limits on target speeds and interceptor ranges. Clinton administration proposals based on DOD's criteria were rejected by the Russians in July 1995. The Russian rejection note stated, "We cannot regard the testing of mobile systems to counter ballistic missiles, being conducted by the United States, as consistent with the ABM treaty" [40]. Some Americans attribute this attitude to a Russian desire to slow development of U.S. missile defenses that could compete with Russian systems offered for sale on the international arms market.[8] Others feel that the U.S. position is fully justified, and that Russia is being completely unreasonable. One administration official has been quoted as saying, "If they say this is a strategic system, and we don't think it is, we can pull out of the treaty" [41, p. 688]. Meanwhile, Russian commentators refer to "the inconsistency and contradictory nature of US policy," and warn that it threatens implementation of START I and ratification of START II [42].

A combination of the rational actor and ambiguous interpretation defenses can explain U.S. behavior. There are strong political forces in the U.S. Congress and military-industrial complex favoring development and deployment of a nationwide defense against ballistic missile attacks. To these groups the ABM Treaty is a Cold War relic that has outlived its usefulness, if indeed it ever had any. Most of the people now promoting ballistic missile defense never supported the ABM Treaty in the first place and see the end of the Cold War as a golden opportunity to get rid of it. If their point of view prevails, the United States will have consciously and intentionally violated or abrogated the treaty, and given the length and intensity of the public debate, no one will be able to claim that they were not aware of the potential consequences. At the same time there *are* ambiguities in the treaty that could be worked out in the Standing Consultative Commission if the motivation existed on both sides to solve the problem. This is not the place for a detailed discussion of the United States and Russian

---

[8] Interestingly, this is almost exactly the same theory many Russians advance for why the United States opposes their sale of nuclear technology to Iran.

positions on demarcation and clarification.[9] It is interesting to observe, however, that the United States and Russia have taken positions in the debate that are almost the mirror images of the roles they played during the Cold War. Then the Soviet Union favored vague general assurances while the United States pressed for specific and verifiable technical limitations on capabilities of systems. Now it is the United States that is offering vague and unverifiable assurances on the most technically capable systems and Russia that is insisting on clear quantitative demarcations between strategic and tactical or theater defenses.

In summary, U.S. actions are not the result of a single coherent policy but derive from hard-fought battles and tenuous compromises between constituencies trying to destroy or sustain the treaty. It is always easier to observe these internal struggles in the United States than in other less open societies. But it is certain that they are an important aspect of compliance policy in other states as well, including Russia and China.

Compliance Problems in the Former Soviet Union

Three bilateral U.S.-Soviet agreements are mentioned in the 1995 compliance report: the INF Treaty, START I, and the Wyoming MOU. All the problems mentioned are minor: the perennial Cargoscan disagreements at Votkinsk, "questions . . . on certain aspects of the Russian data declaration and inspections" under the MOU, and some confusion and uneven implementation in the early months of START I. One relatively serious problem mentioned in the 1994 report was resolved in 1995. According to the 1994 report, Russia used a converted SS-19 ICBM as a spacelaunch vehicle without giving proper notifications. This was only one incident in what had promised to become a significant compliance issue: the Russian insistence that they did not have to follow all of START's reporting and telemetry exchange requirements with missiles they converted to space launch vehicles. The problem was made public by ACDA Director John Holum in congressional testimony in 1994 [43]. In addition to converting SS-19s, Russia was reportedly using SS-25 stages, and even entire SS-25 missiles, to assemble space launch vehicles but not providing the United States enough data to maintain an accurate account of the numbers and locations of Russian ICBMs. The 1995 report notes that the dispute was resolved in September 1995.

None of the issues raised for these three agreements has significant national security implications or threatens the kind of political repercussions likely from U.S. actions under the ABM Treaty. But to focus on these relatively trivial matters is to miss the far more significant fact that the Bilateral Chemical Weapon Destruction Agreement (BDA) had still not entered into force more than six years after it was signed. An updated protocol for the BDA was agreed *ad referendum* in 1993, and according to the compliance report, it "is central to the implementation of the BDA" [27]. Unfortunately, there was still no agreement on this document at the end of 1996 or any public indication of when such agreement might be reached. This is not yet an official "compliance" problem, but the difficulties in reaching a final document and the increasing uncertainty

---

[9] The arguments are analyzed in Alexei Arbatov, The ABM Treaty and Theatre Ballistic Missile Defence, *SIPRI Yearbook 1995* (New York: Oxford University Press, 1995), pp. 681–696; and Jack Mendelsohn and John B. Rhinelander, "Shooting Down the ABM Treaty," *Arms Control Today*, September 1994, pp. 8–10.

facing Russia's CW implementation plans suggest that the United States should be prepared for many such problems if and when the agreement does enter into force. In 1994 the Senate Intelligence Committee showed impatience with Russian compliance problems under the Wyoming MOU, noting ominously: "In the absence of full compliance with the Wyoming MOU, neither the Committee nor the Senate can overlook the distinct possibility that Russia intends to violate the CWC" [44].

"Intends to violate" evokes the rational actor model, but incapacity provides the most plausible explanation for Russian difficulties in meeting their commitments. Financial problems are evident across the full spectrum of Russian implementation activities. To save money they abandoned their right to install continuous portal monitoring at the Promontory, Utah MX plant under START (see chapter 3), and they have conducted a disproportionate share of their INF quota inspections in Europe instead of the continental United States.[10] Russia has protested the imbalance of implementation costs in the Open Skies Treaty, and at least part of their motivations for challenging the CFE flank limits (see below) have come from the excessive costs of redeploying military units stationed in places that once made sense but are now anachronistic. For example, in 1995 an airborne division was stationed in the North Caucasus flank zone near the new southern border of Russia.[11] Airborne units are normally based several hundred miles from borders because of their capability for rapid deployment over larger distances than infantry or cavalry units. But when the United States suggested to Russia that this unit could be redeployed to help meet the flank limits, the Russians protested that it would cost too much to create a new base.

These problems pale in comparison with those associated with chemical weapons disposal and compliance with the reporting and inspection requirements of the BDA and Chemical Weapons Convention. The difficulties began with the data exchanges and on-site inspections required in Phase II of the Wyoming MOU (see chapter 3). Even though Phase I had been carried out "more or less as planned" by early 1992, negotiations on the Phase II data exchanges have dragged on for at least another five years [44, p. 27]. Russia declared a total stockpile of 40,000 agent tons stored at seven sites, but U.S. intelligence estimates were considerably higher, and several Russian scientists and technicians made public statements alleging that the stockpile was much larger. One whistleblower testified to a Duma committee that Russia had actually produced ten times the amount it had declared, i.e., 400,000 tons [41, p. 347]. It is always risky to rely on such testimony, but even allowing a substantial discount for exaggeration there is cause for concern that Russian authorities have not been totally candid in their declarations. For example, U.S. intelligence estimates, based in part on the reports of other Russian informers, suggest that Russia had, and possibly still has, a program to develop binary nerve agents. Russia officially denies it, and one of the original whistleblowers now claims that "to the best of my knowledge, the development, testing, and production of chemical weapons has

---

[10] Personal communication, OSIA official.
[11] Ibid.

stopped in Russia"[12] [45, p. 31]. Still other problems relate to Russian declarations of chemical weapon production and research facilities. Some production facilities that were declared by the Soviet Union in 1990 are no longer included on lists submitted by Russia. Russia claims that these have been converted to peaceful activities, but the United States is insisting that they must be declared anyway and subjected to routine inspections. Again, the Russian motivation for attempting to avoid inspections at these facilities appears primarily motivated by concern for costs.[13]

Along with Russia's financial problems go problems of interagency coordination, inefficient administration, official corruption, and weak central leadership. Russia's tradition of centralized decision making is not well suited to arms control implementation, where innovation and initiative at lower levels of the bureaucracy can resolve many minor problems. Cooperation among Russia's intelligence, military, and arms control bureaucracies was notoriously bad in the pre-Gorbachev years, and the persistence of the bureaucratic cultures of these agencies, coupled with the tenuous authority of the executive branch under Boris Yeltsin, has made it difficult to know who is really in charge of Russian arms control implementation. In many day-to-day tasks, such as conducting and escorting on-site inspections, providing notifications and data exchanges (at least under INF and START), and dismantling equipment and facilities, the Russian record is very good. But there appears to be much less coherence and effective authority in the chemical and biological fields [46]. Most Western analysts believe that if violations of the Biological Weapons Convention are occurring they are probably happening in spite of efforts by Yeltsin to stop them. In the area of control over nuclear materials there is great concern that the Russian bureaucracy is incapable of the rigorous control necessary to prevent theft and smuggling by dissident or criminal elements.

Finally, on top of all the technical, financial, and organizational problems there are serious disagreements over the benefits and risks of arms control within the Russian political system. START II and CFE are seen by many center and right politicians as overly generous to the West, and Open Skies is opposed by some Duma members as an unacceptable infringement on Russian sovereignty. The Russian military, severely demoralized by the breakdown of the Warsaw Pact, massive budget cuts, and a drastic drop in public respect, tend to be extremely defensive of Russian military legitimacy and sensitive to what they see as humiliating demands and interference by Western powers. The Nunn-Lugar program must be handled with great sensitivity, and compromises must often be made out of concern for Russian pride. The principle of reciprocity is particularly important to Russians, who have been stung by revelations of technological backwardness, environmental irresponsibility, and, most recently in Chechnya, military incompetence and brutality.

There is more than enough in this litany of problems to explain why Russia is having so much trouble living up to its arms control commitments. In particular, there is no need to imagine, as was so fashionable during the Reagan

---

[12] According to Vil S. Mirzayanov, a former high-level scientist in the Soviet CW program, the program has fallen into disarray and neglect as the result of massive budget cuts and the layoffs of as many as 50 percent of its scientific and technical personnel [45, p. 28].
[13] Personal communication, NSC official.

administration, that there is some nefarious conspiracy to gain military advantage by violating treaty commitments. Indeed, the disorganization and increasing pluralism of the Russian political system would appear to make such conspiracies nearly impossible to organize and keep secret. In testimony supporting U.S. ratification of START II, the CIA Deputy Director for Intelligence noted that "the increased openness of Russia and the other former Soviet republics make cheating increasingly difficult to conceal" [47]. The role of whistleblowers and informers in revealing details of the Russian BW and CW programs, and of investigative journalists in probing the nuclear weapons complex's handling of fissile materials [48], are examples of this new openness, which will continue to be a vital asset in future U.S. monitoring efforts.

Compliance with Multilateral Agreements

There were four major multilateral agreements in force in 1996: the Nuclear Nonproliferation Treaty (NPT), the Biological and Toxin Weapons Convention (BWC), and the Conventional Forces in Europe (CFE) Treaty and the closely related Vienna Confidence and Security Building (CSBM) agreements. Compliance issues have been raised under all of them, and the United States spends a sizable portion of its implementation efforts on keeping track of the behavior of its partners under these agreements and in negotiating to resolve ambiguities or apparent violations. Most of the issues are minor, but some, especially under the two fully international agreements (NPT and BWC), have been relatively serious and remarkably persistent.

By all accounts the most serious problems under the NPT involve North Korea and Iraq. Iran is another major concern, as was made clear in the earlier analysis of the Russian-Iranian nuclear deal.[14] But while the United States has gone to great lengths to persuade Russia, China, and other nuclear suppliers not to do business with Iran, it has not been able to make a solid case that Iran is in fact violating its commitment under the NPT not to seek to acquire nuclear weapons. The most that the United States could say in its 1995 compliance report was that Iran's nonproliferation credentials were "highly questionable," and that even so its "rudimentary" nuclear weapon program has met with only "limited" success. The Russian sale of technology is not even mentioned in connection with Iraq, and Chinese assistance "appears consistent with China's obligations under the NPT." In other words, the United States either cannot or will not make the case for Iranian violation of the NPT, and until it does, it appears that Russia, China, and possibly other suppliers as well will have considerable latitude to sell nuclear technology to Iran, which has so far remained in good standing with regard to its NPT safeguards obligations.

This is, of course, precisely what Iraq did for at least a decade while it was creating a nuclear weapon program that was far from "rudimentary." It seems likely that Iraq's program would have succeeded in producing a workable weapon by now if it had not been uncovered after the 1991 Gulf War and dismantled under supervision of the UN Special Commission for Iraq (UNSCOM). Iraq's nuclear weapon effort has been effectively terminated and will presumably remain so as long as UNSCOM can retain its authority to conduct intrusive inspections

---

[14] China is also cited for its assistance to Pakistan's nuclear program, but the Chinese promise to avoid future transfers to unsafeguarded facilities will, if kept, help to reduce this concern.

at times and places of its own choosing. But the process is difficult, and few imagine that UNSCOM will remain in Iraq indefinitely. Meanwhile, as in previous years, Iraq is cited in the 1995 compliance report for "continuing its effort to undermine the UNSCOM/IAEA inspection process by withholding relevant information, and to preserve as much as possible for a renewed nuclear weapons development effort" [27]. The problem of Iraq's violation of the NPT has therefore only been suspended, not resolved. Resolution will have to await major changes in the Iraqi government and/or the Middle East security environment.

North Korea signed the NPT in 1985 and took seven years to reach an agreement with the IAEA on application of safeguards to its nuclear facilities. The first IAEA inspection in May 1992 discovered discrepancies in North Korean declarations of the amount of plutonium it had separated from spent reactor fuel, and IAEA insistence on a special inspection to clarify the matter led first to North Korean refusals and then to a threat to withdraw from the NPT that was withdrawn only a day before it was to take effect in June 1993 [49]. More than a year of negotiations between the United States and the Democratic People's Republic of Korea (DPRK) finally resulted in an "Agreed Framework" (signed October 21, 1994), which provided assistance to North Korea in the form of fuel oil shipments and proliferation-resistant nuclear technology in exchange for the shutting down and dismantlement of North Korea's plutonium production reactors and reprocessing plant [50].

The Agreed Framework was still in force at the end of 1996 despite several periods of escalated tension on the Korean Peninsula, and as long as it remains in effect, fears of a DPRK nuclear weapon program will be greatly reduced. Nevertheless, the United States remains concerned about North Korean efforts to obstruct the implementation of full-scope safeguards, and points out in the 1995 compliance report that "until North Korea fulfills its safeguards commitments under the Agreed Framework, it will not be in compliance with [the NPT]." Whether or not the North Korean government retains a commitment to develop nuclear weapons cannot be determined on the basis of available evidence. But there is little doubt that they once had such a commitment and considerable uncertainty about how much progress they made toward their goal before 1994.

How do we "explain" Iranian, Iraqi, and North Korean behavior on the basis of our four criteria? The explanation is obvious: all three are examples of the rational actor explanation. All three were signatories of the NPT, and all three had negotiated safeguards agreements with the IAEA. None could claim ignorance of the rules, or inexperience or incapacity in implementing them. In the cases of Iraq and North Korea evidence of deception of the international community and obstruction of the IAEA are irrefutable. Iran's situation is much less clear, but if one accepts the hypothesis that Iran is trying to build a nuclear weapon capability, then the only explanation that makes any sense is that Iran is doing this consciously on the basis of a calculation that the security and political benefits of success will outweigh the costs of violating its international obligations. But while all three states may have set out intentionally to violate the NPT, none of them (with the remotely possible exception of North Korea) has succeeded in making a nuclear weapon. Both Iraq's and North Korea's programs have been brought to at least a temporary halt by United Nations and U.S. actions, and U.S. efforts to discourage nuclear cooperation with Iran have been, with a few notable exceptions, largely successful. In short, while there is undeniable evidence that some countries have violated their NPT commitments, there is also ample evidence that the regime is robust enough to survive occasional instances of even the most egregious noncompliance.

On the Vienna CSBMs the compliance report paints a picture that is considerably rosier than the actual situation. According to the report, "Compliance with the Vienna Document has been good," with only a few "mostly minor notification, data, and inspection problems." This assessment totally ignores the Russian deployment of troops to suppress the nationalist rebellion in Chechnya in the spring and summer of 1995. The invasion constituted a violation of the 1992 Vienna Document, which requires that military movements involving more than 9,000 troops or the use of heavy aircraft must be notified six weeks in advance [54]. This was not done in the case of Chechnya, which Russia has argued (and which the United States has agreed) is a purely domestic matter. But the Vienna Document makes no distinction between troop movements for domestic and international purposes; the requirements are based entirely on the size and nature of the operation, independent of its purpose.[15] There are some possible loopholes in the wording of the Document. For example, paragraph 39 states that activities carried out without advance notice to the participating troops are exempt from the 42-day advance notification requirement. Such exercises can be notified on the day they begin [55, p. 642]. But Russia has not attempted, nor is it likely to attempt, any such justification for an operation it believes to have been well within its rights as a sovereign state. Nor has any disciplinary action been suggested by the Organization for Security and Cooperation in Europe (OSCE). As the 1995 compliance report makes clear, the violation will almost certainly not be formally censured, much less punished. Russian combat troops were finally withdrawn from Chechnya, and a tenuous cease-fire was achieved by the end of 1996. However, none of this can change the fact that Russia displayed an utter disregard for its commitments under the Vienna regime in its Chechnya operation. The full implications of this incident for the regime remain to be played out.

The CFE Treaty faces the most uncertain future of all the multilateral regimes now in existence. The regime had been overtaken by events virtually from the day of its entry into force. The collapse of the Warsaw Pact and the disintegration of the Soviet Union rendered the basic East-versus-West structure of the treaty anachronistic, and political and economic problems in several of the former Soviet republics caused them to fail to meet their full reduction obligations by the November 1995 deadline. However, the most serious compliance dispute concerned the refusal of Russia and Ukraine to comply with the limits mandated by the treaty for the so-called "flank" regions in southern and northern Europe. This dispute was papered over at the May 1996 review conference and settled by formal agreement the following December. But the implementation period for the new limits was extended to May 31, 1999, by which time the entire treaty may be completely revised [51].

---

[15] See Article IV, paragraphs 36–38. For a text of the 1992 Vienna Document see SIPRI, *Sipri Yearbook 1993* (Oxford: Oxford University Press, 1993), pp. 635–653.

From the 1995 ACDA compliance report alone one would conclude that the CFE Treaty is doing very well. All but three of the 30 parties to CFE met their overall reduction quotas by the end of the third reduction period, although Russia and Ukraine, mainly because of their ongoing dispute over ownership of the Black Sea fleet, had not met their "related commitments" for reductions of naval infantry and coastal defense equipment. This equipment is formally exempt from the CFE Treaty but was included in a separate commitment assumed by Russia and Ukraine in the Tashkent and Oslo agreements following the breakup of the USSR. The numbers of tanks and artillery pieces involved are small, and it is not a major issue [52, p. 72]. The other problems are more serious but involve two countries, Armenia and Azerbaijan, that are not vital security interests of the United States. The two states have been at war for several years over the territory of Nagorno Karabakh, and neither has made a serious effort to declare its destruction liabilities under the CFE treaty or to actually destroy equipment. If two larger states were having this problem it would have serious implications for the treaty, but for Armenia and Azerbaijan it appears to qualify as an acceptable level of deviance. No disciplinary actions are contemplated against the two unfortunate states, who already have more than enough to worry about. Belarus' failure to reach its reduction quotas had both economic and political roots. Belarusian president Alexandr Lukashenko suspended reductions in 1995 because of their allegedly high cost, but more importantly in protest over the proposed expansion of NATO to former Warsaw Pact states in Eastern Europe. Belarus was over its quotas in three categories of weapons in its formal declaration of January 1996 [53] and remained in violation of its obligations at least through the review conference the following May [51].

The most serious compliance issue under the CFE Treaty involved Russia's decision to ignore limits the treaty placed on its deployment of heavy military equipment in the North Caucasus and St. Petersburg military districts, the so-called "flank zones" Russia had no difficulty meeting its overall reduction obligations [53], but in the North Caucasus, where its allotments are quite small, Russia is reported to exceed those limits by as much as a factor of three[16] [56]. A Russian official announced in April that deployments near Chechnya were being reinforced and assigned to a new army to be headquartered in Vladikavkaz, about 40 miles from Grozny. This sent a clear signal that Russia had no intention of bringing its forces into compliance by November. General Vladimir Semynonov was quoted by Interfax as saying, "The interests of Russia's security and integrity must come above the provisions set in this treaty" [57].

The Russian argument for relaxation of the flank limits had considerable logic, and this was finally acknowledged by the other parties in May 1996, when

---

[16] Article IV of the CFE Treaty divides the overall limits for the two alliances among four zones. The "flank" zones were farthest from the assumed front lines in a war between NATO and the Warsaw Pact. They comprised Iceland, Norway, Greece, and part of Turkey for the NATO side, and Armenia, Azerbaijan, Bulgaria, Georgia, Moldova, Romania, the southern part of Ukraine, and the Leningrad and North Caucasus military districts of Russia for the Warsaw Pact side. When the treaty was signed, Armenia, Azerbaijan, Georgia, Moldova, and Ukraine were all part of the Soviet Union. After the Soviet breakup the former republics met at Tashkent and divided the CFE limits among the new states. This left only the North Caucasus region (it includes Chechnya and borders on Turkey, Ukraine, Kazakhstan, Georgia, and Azerbaijan) and the Leningrad (now St. Petersburg) region (bordering on Finland and Norway).

the flank boundaries were redrawn, weapon allotments were adjusted, and some deadlines were relaxed to give Russia more flexibility in meeting the treaty's ultimate objectives [51]. It was agreed at the same conference to begin negotiations aimed at reforming the treaty to reflect the new European security environment, but this promises to be a long and difficult process, amounting in all likelihood to a complete overhaul of the treaty. The process will be enormously complicated by NATO's intention to expand its membership to include several former Warsaw Pact states. In September 1995, when NATO decided to offer its proposal to redraw the flank zones, it also committed itself to extending its "nuclear umbrella" to any former Warsaw Pact members admitted to NATO [58]. Whatever the attraction of the first proposal may have held for Russia, the second was anathema, not only to conservative nationalist forces but to moderate Russians concerned about the increased isolation an expansion of NATO into their former sphere of influence would bring. On the American side there were indications that even if the Russians were to accept the flank limits adjustment, the U.S. Senate would not. A spokesman for Senate Foreign Relations Committee Chair Jesse Helms called the NATO proposal "a mistake of the highest order, [that] plays into Russia's irrational paranoia that there's a threat to their security that doesn't exist" [59]. The May 1996 flank zone adjustment requires Senate approval to enter into force, so CFE will join the lengthening queue of arms control agreements awaiting the attention of Chairman Helms' Foreign Relations Committee.

The more the United States and its allies argue that the CFE Treaty and the expansion of NATO are not connected, the more Russia and other former Soviet republics are convinced that they are. Russia's noncompliance with the flank limits is clearly based on fundamental national security interests; there is no question of incapacity or differing interpretations or time lags. To many Russians the CFE Treaty is an anachronism that now threatens Russian security in ways that were unimaginable when the treaty was negotiated and ratified. In the words of Richard Falkenrath:

A substantial portion of the Russian national security elite detests the CFE Treaty, especially the flank ceiling. The treaty is forcing Russia to destroy valuable military equipment at great cost to itself; it permits Russia to maintain levels of conventional equipment that are only about one-third of those permitted of NATO and only about twice those permitted of Ukraine; it requires Russia to allow its neighbors—including the other former Soviet republics—to conduct highly intrusive on-site inspections at virtually any military facility they wish to visit; it constrains Russia's freedom of action on its own territory and on that of its neighbors; and it perpetuates a legal equality among the Soviet successor states that most Russians find abhorrent. [60]

To add the threat of an expanding NATO alliance to this litany of resentments and injured pride is like throwing gasoline on a fire. In the last analysis the question of whether Russian perceptions are "irrational paranoia," as they appear to Senator Helms, or prudent realism, as they appear to most Russians and many Western analysts,[17] is irrelevant. The perceptions are real and

---

[17] For a thoughtful analysis of Russian views on NATO expansion see Jonathan Dean, "Losing Russia or Keeping NATO: Must We Choose?" *Arms Control Today*, June 1995, pp. 3–7.

their potential consequences are disastrous for the CFE Treaty and the European disarmament process it began.

The final multilateral treaty dealt with in ACDA compliance reports is the Biological Weapons Convention (BWC). Again, Russia stands out as a prominent and troubling possible violator, although public allegations have been toned down relative to classified ones (see above). The evidence for Russian noncompliance is apparently quite strong, much of it coming from defecting scientists and technicians, at least one of them a "senior scientist in the [Russian BW] program" [61]. President Yeltsin acknowledged the Sverdlovsk anthrax incident as a violation in 1992, and at the same time promised that all prohibited research and development would cease. But two years later U.S. officials were still citing evidence that "large aspects" of an offensive biological weapons program were continuing. The working assumption in the U.S. government was that Yeltsin was sincere but that his "decrees have not filtered down to the working levels" [61]. This sounds a lot like the argument that the Chinese leadership is out of the loop where nuclear and missile deals are made. Neither argument is very persuasive, and the degree of knowledge and involvement of the Russian leadership in alleged violations of the BWC remains a mystery.

The trilateral agreement among Russia, Great Britain, and the United States has led to an exchange of inspections, or what the United States prefers to call "visits," to biological research and development facilities, but these had not fully satisfied the United States that all offensive BW work has stopped.[18] The compliance report takes the positive position that the United States is "actively engaged in efforts to work with the Russian leadership to ensure complete termination of the illegal program and to pursue a number of measures to build confidence in Russian compliance with the BWC." The Defense Department has even offered tens of millions of dollars of Nunn-Lugar funds to help destroy Russian BW facilities and equipment [61]. But Congress remains skeptical. In June 1995 a significant majority of the House of Representatives (244-180) supported a proposal to cut off Nunn-Lugar funding to Russia until President Clinton could certify that all Russian biological weapons work had been stopped [62]. The cutoff was revoked by the Senate and White House, but it does indicate a depth of congressional feeling about Russian noncompliance that will not be easily assuaged.

Seven other countries are mentioned as possibly engaging in BW activities, more than in any other section of the report. The heaviest concentration is in the Middle East, where Iraq, Iran, Syria, Egypt, and Libya are suspected with varying degrees of conviction.[19] For Syria it is "highly probable" that an offensive BW program is being developed; Iran "probably" has produced BW agents and "apparently has weaponized a small quantity"; it is "likely" that Egypt's capability "continues to exist"; and Libya "is seeking" to move its research program toward weaponization. According to the report, there is evidence for all of these accusations, although none is provided. From the carefully chosen

---

[18] Evidence that Russian BW research and development (if indeed it is occurring) is offensive rather than defensive must be coming from inside informants. As already noted in chapter 3, the distinction between work on prohibited offensive weapons and permitted defensive measures is difficult to make even with full access to the laboratories.

[19] Neither Syria nor Egypt has yet ratified the BWC, although both are signatories and therefore politically bound not to undercut the effectiveness of the convention.

wording of each indictment it is clear that the evidence is of variable quantity and quality, and it is likely that the great majority of it comes from human sources.

Iraq is in a wholly different category. Strong evidence for an Iraqi BW program was uncovered by both human intelligence and UNSCOM; inspections, and after several years of equivocation and obstruction Iraq finally acknowledged in July 1995 that it had an offensive BW program [63]. Thousands of Iraqi documents were turned over to UNSCOM after the defection of a son-in-law of Saddam Hussein, and analysis of them showed that Iraq had not only developed a wide variety of lethal biological agents, but had weaponized some of them in preparation for possible use in the 1991 war [64]. Iraqi Foreign Minister Tariq Aziz is also reported to have told UNSCOM Director Rolf Ekeus that it was the implicit threat of U.S. nuclear retaliation that deterred Iraq from using the weapons [65]. If this is true, and many U.S. military analysts and planners appear anxious to believe it, it could have extremely serious implications for the future of nuclear arms control and nonproliferation [66]. I will examine some of these implications in the final chapter.

The other two states mentioned are China and Taiwan. For China there are "strong indications" of a continuing offensive BW program, and despite China's accession to the BWC in 1984, it is "highly probable" that it is still not in compliance. As for Taiwan, it is unclear why it is even mentioned. All the report can say is that Taiwan has been upgrading its biotechnology capabilities by purchasing sophisticated technology abroad. At the same time, the evidence for a BW program is not sufficient to establish noncompliance. Nor has the evidence been any better in the previous three reports (1993 to 1995) in which Taiwan is mentioned. It seems unlikely that Taiwan is the only country shopping abroad for sophisticated biotechnology equipment, and Taiwan stands out in the report as the only one mentioned on the basis of evidence insufficient even to permit such qualifiers as "likely" or "probable" or "seeking." It is puzzles like these that make the annual compliance report simultaneously so interesting and so frustrating to read.

The most remarkable aspect of the assessment of BW activities is their persistence from one year to the next. Findings in the 1995 report are virtually identical to those of 1994, and some have remained unchanged for several years. This illustrates the difficulty of dealing constructively with noncompliance concerns under the BWC. The Verification Experts Group (VEREX) and its follow-on Ad Hoc Committee (see chapter 3) were created to attempt to improve this situation, but progress has been painfully slow, and the biological weapons control regime remains by far the most opaque of all the international regimes currently in effect.

THE COMPLIANCE DILEMMA

It is not surprising that arms control regimes are accompanied by chronic compliance problems. Any regime, whether for trade regulation, environmental protection, or law enforcement, is routinely challenged by problems of interpretation, incapacity, unfamiliarity, and sometimes outright defiance. To call noncompliance a "problem" suggests that it has a "solution." There are, of course, solutions to individual compliance problems, but there is no solution to the generic problem of noncompliance. The answer to Fred Iklé's famous and represented the triumph of rationality and common sense over an open-ended and terrifying arms race. Most of the treaties would look very different if they were to be renegotiated from scratch in the new situation, indeed if they could be renegotiated at all. The Soviet Union and later Russia were central to the achievement of the present arms control regime, and Russia's involvement and adherence is central to its continued viability. Russia's compliance problems stem from a combination of many causes, and the response of Russia's treaty partners must be to find the proper balance between firmness and understanding.

China is a newcomer to arms control and nonproliferation regimes. It did not join the BWC until 1984 and the NPT until 1992. It is not a member of international export control regimes, and it has often shown resentment at attempts by Western nations to enforce their standards on Chinese behavior. China's military, political, and economic power are growing rapidly. It faces a major transition to a new generation of leadership and aspirations to world as well as regional influence. It would be facile to recommend specific policies for dealing with China's unwillingness or inability to conform fully to Western arms control and nonproliferation norms. While it is clear that patience, sensitive diplomacy, and a recognition that our own house must be kept scrupulously in order will be necessary to gradually bring China into compliance with international regimes, it also seems clear that "such inculcation and integration will be extremely difficult at best, and will most likely be resisted for many years to come" [67].

Compliance behavior is just one aspect of the overall political relationship between states, so it is unrealistic to think that compliance can be dictated or coerced independent of the behavior of those doing the enforcing. Whatever the objective merits of developing U.S. ballistic missile defenses, or bringing former Soviet client states into NATO, or selling F-16s to Taiwan, it is utterly unrealistic to think that these things can be done without creating serious risks of Russian and Chinese retaliation. Already the threat of NATO expansion is being used in Russian domestic politics to challenge adherence to START I, ratification of START II, and compliance with CFE. Vladimir Lukin, chairman of the Duma's Committee on International Affairs (analogous to the position held by Jesse Helms in the United States), suggests that "it would be hard to explain to the Russian people why we are continuing to disarm while the world's biggest military machine is moving closer to our borders" [68]. On the American side we have government officials who feel it appropriate to say about the ABM Treaty negotiations, "Look, Russians, if you have a problem, let us know and we'll try to answer your question in good faith, but realize you have no veto over what we do" [69].

Whether intended or not, the United States sometimes conveys the impression that everyone else is supposed to adhere precisely to the rules while the United States retains full freedom of action. It is certainly true that the Russians and Chinese have no veto over what the United States does, but the converse is also true. Russia and China are powerful states whose continued participation in and compliance with arms control and nonproliferation regimes is vital to U.S. national security. Unilateralism, vindictiveness, or insensitivity in U.S. compliance policy could play directly into the hands of reactionary elements in Russia and China who could turn our worst fears into reality.

25. Bill Gertz, "China Nuclear Transfer Exposed," *Washington Times*, February 5, 1996.

26. R. Jeffrey Smith and Thomas W. Lippman, "U.S. Relents On Chinese Sanctions," *Washington Post*, May 11, 1996.

27. Threat Control through Arms Control, U.S. Arms Control and Disarmament Agency, July 26, 1996.

28. R. Jeffrey Smith, "U.S. Accuses China of Germ Weapons Work," *Washington Post*, July 15, 1995.

29. Matthew Meselson, "The Search for Yellow Rain," *Arms Control Today*, September 1986, pp. 31–36.

30. Peter Zimmerman, "The Thule, Fylingdales, and Krasnoyarsk Radars: Innocents Abroad?" *Arms Control Today*, March, 1987, pp. 9–11.

31. Allan Krass and Catherine Girrier, *Disproportionate Response: American Policy and Alleged Soviet Treaty Violations* (Cambridge, MA: Union of Concerned Scientists, 1987).

32. Sam Nunn, "ABM Reinterpretation 'Fundamentally Flawed,'" *Arms Control Today*, April 1987, pp. 8–14.

33. Gloria Duffy, *Compliance and the Future of Arms Control* (Stanford, CA: Center for International Security and Arms Control, Global Outlook, 1988).

34. John Pike and Marcus Corbin, "Taking Aim at the ABM Treaty: THAAD and U.S. Security," *Arms Control Today*, May 1995, pp. 3–8.

35. Soviet Noncompliance with Arms Control Agreements, White House Office of Press Secretary, February 23, 1990.

36. Keith B. Payne, Proliferation, Potential TMD Roles, Demarcation and ABM Treaty Compatibility, National Institute for Public Policy, September 1994.

37. Bill Gertz, "Republicans Eye ABM Treaty," *Washington Times*, December 7, 1994, p. A6.

38. "Helms Bill Seeks U.S. Withdrawal from ABM Treaty," *Arms Control Today*, February 1996, p. 29.

39. Bill Gertz, "3 GOP Lawmakers Halt Funds for Missile-Defense Talks," *Washington Times*, December 13, 1996, p. A3.

40. Bill Gertz, "Moscow Balks at ABM Proposal," *Washington Times*, July 19, 1995, p. A1.

41. *Sipri Yearbook 1995* (London: Oxford University Press, 1995).

42. Vladimir Belous, "ABM Talks Deadlocked," *Current Digest*, No. 11, 1995, p. 26.

43. A Revitalized ACDA in the Post-Cold War World, House Committee on Foreign Affairs, June 23, 1994.

44. U.S. Capability to Monitor Compliance with the Chemical Weapons Convention, Senate Select Committee on Intelligence, September 30, 1994.

45. Vil S. Mirzayanov, Dismantling the Soviet/Russian Chemical Weapons Complex: An Insider's View, *Chemical Weapons Disarmament in Russia: Problems and Prospects*, (Washington, DC: The Henry L. Stimson Center, 1995), pp. 21–33.

46. Igor Khripunov, "The Human Element in Russia's Chemical Weapons Disposal Efforts," *Arms Control Today*, July/August 1995, pp. 16–21.

47. Douglas MacEachan, Statement for the Record on the START II Treaty, Senate Foreign Relations Committee, February 28,1995 (Washington, DC: CIA Office of Public Affairs).

48. Kirill Belyaninov, "Nuclear Nonsense, Black-Market Bombs, and Fissile Flim-Flam," *Bulletin of the Atomic Scientists*, March/April 1994, pp. 44–50.

49. David Albright, "How Much Plutonium Does North Korea Have?" *Bulletin of the Atomic Scientists*, September/October 1994, pp. 46–53.

50. "Agreed Framework between the United States of America and the Democratic People's Republic of Korea," *Arms Control Today*, December 1994, p. 19.

51. Sarah Walkling, "CFE Treaty Review Completed; Parties Agree on Flank Resolution," *Arms Control Today*, May/June 1996, p. 18.

52. Threat Control through Arms Control, U.S. Arms Control and Disarmament Agency, July 13, 1995.

53. Sarah Walkling, "Final Weapons Reductions under the CFE Treaty," *Arms Control Today*, December 1995/January 1996, pp. 29–30.

54. Jane M. O. Sharp, "Let's Make a Deal: NATO and CFE," *Bulletin of the Atomic Scientists*, March/April 1995, pp. 19–21.

55. *Sipri Yearbook 1993* (Oxford: Oxford University Press, 1993).

56. Aleksandr Koretsky, "Door Slamming as a Means of Persuasion," *Kommersant-Daily* (translation in *Current Digest*, Vol 47, no. 8, pp. 25–26), February 21, 1995, p. 4.

57. "Moscow Reportedly to Maintain Large Armed Force in Caucasus," *New York Times*, April 27, 1995, p. A5.

58. Michael Dobbs, "Ex-Soviet Bloc Nations to Get NATO 'Umbrella'," *Washington Post*, September 29, 1995.

59. Steven Greenhouse, "Arms Treaty Restrictions on Russia Eased," *New York Times*, September 16, 1995.

60. Richard A. Falkenrath, "Resolving the CFE 'Flank' Dispute," *Arms Control Today*, May 1995, pp. 15–20.

61. R. Jeffrey Smith, "U.S. Officials Allege That Russians Are Working on Biological Arms," *Washington Post*, April 8, 1994, p. A28.

62. Bill Gertz, "House Bill Change Targets Aid to Russia," *Washington Times*, June 14, 1995, p. A14.

63. Barbara Crossette, "Iraq Admits It Produced Germ Arsenal," *New York Times*, July 6, 1995, p. A3.

64. Stewart Stogel and Ben Barber, "Iraq Entered Gulf War with Viral Weapons Ready," *Washington Times*, September 21, 1995, p. 1.

65. Theresa Hitchens, "U.S. Must Spell Out Bio War Response," *Defense News*, September 11–17, 1995.

66. Louis Jacobson, "Apocalypse Now," *National Journal*, September 9, 1995, p. 2245.

67. David Shambaugh, "Containment or Engagement of China?," *International Security*, Fall 1996, pp. 180–209.

68. Alexandr Sychov, "Nuclear Warheads as Deputies' Political Weapon," *Current Digest*, July 19, 1995, p. 30.

69. Bill Gertz, "Nuclear Talks Strategy Pondered," *Washington Times*, May 22, 1995.

8

THE CHALLENGE OF LEADERSHIP

The United States has devoted considerable effort, talent and money to construct the arms control framework described in this book. Other states have made real contributions, but a serious analysis of them would require a much longer and more comprehensive study than this one. My rationale for focusing on the United States is the leadership role it has played in achieving and implementing all of the treaties considered in this book and the necessity for sustaining that leadership if the regimes created by those treaties are to survive. Much has been accomplished in the past ten years, but much more remains uncompleted.

Several generalizations and trends emerge from the previous chapters. The first is that every U.S. administration since Eisenhower's has seen arms control and nonproliferation as essential components of national security policy. Progress was slow and uneven until revolutionary change took place in the Soviet Union. However, the often fruitless negotiations and tentative treaty making of the previous three decades provided a foundation on which much of the arms control revolution of the late 1980s was built. As a result of that revolution the United States finds itself committed to nearly a dozen major agreements with a wide range of demands for implementation, information exchange, monitoring, inspection, and consultation.

The U.S. national security bureaucracy has been reorganized in response to these new demands. New agencies have been created, along with new international organizations and new forms of multilateral cooperation. Technology, military policy, and diplomacy have become intertwined in unprecedented ways, and these interactions are reflected in bureaucratic innovations such as the Arms Control and Disarmament Agency, the On-Site Inspection Agency, the Cooperative Threat Reduction Program, interagency export control mechanisms, and Intelligence Community bodies such as the Arms Control Intelligence Staff and the Nonproliferation Center. The demands of arms control monitoring have helped to justify vast expenditures for sophisticated monitoring devices and the creation of powerful bureaucratic entities like the National Reconnaissance Office and National Security Agency to manage them.

Arms control has required substantial commitments of funds, and questions are being raised with increasing frequency about the costs and benefits of implementing and verifying agreements. Cost-effectiveness is emerging as perhaps the most important criterion by which future agreements will be judged. Still, arms control has not been fully successful in selling itself as a viable and economic alternative to traditional national security measures. Much more work needs to be done by arms control advocates to demonstrate to skeptical decision makers and legislators that national security can be more cost-effectively enhanced by expanding and reinforcing arms control and nonproliferation regimes than by increasing expenditures on military hardware.

For all its successes, arms control suffers from a number of chronic problems. The Arms Control and Disarmament Agency, originally intended to be the bureaucratic focus and lead policymaking agency for arms control and nonproliferation, lives from day to day under the threat of gradual starvation or sudden extinction. Problems persist in the interactions between the diplomats who negotiate and enforce agreements and the intelligence and research communities that support them. Compliance questions bubble up with unsettling frequency and tend to weaken domestic political support for agreements. It is inherent in all of these problems that none is fully soluble, but that all are manageable as long as a substantial majority of the U.S. public and leadership continue to see arms control as a valuable component of national security.

Progress in all areas of arms control has slowed noticeably since the United States signed the START II Treaty and Chemical Weapons Convention at the end of the Bush administration. Four years later these agreements had still not entered into force, and despite the Clinton administration's widely trumpeted achievement of an indefinite extension of the nuclear Nonproliferation Treaty, there are many indications that this "victory" papered over some fundamental contradictions in the NPT regime and may have driven threshold states like India and Pakistan into even more determined opposition to it. Much depends on the ability of the nuclear weapon states to deliver on their promises of a comprehensive nuclear test ban and a fissile material cutoff. To keep these promises, and to make these regimes truly international, the nuclear weapon states will have to demonstrate that the agreements are steps toward nuclear disarmament rather than devices to further constrain nonnuclear and threshold states while allowing the nuclear powers to retain their arsenals indefinitely.

It is not surprising that progress on arms control and nonproliferation has slowed. The remarkable progress made between 1986 and 1993 was the product of a pent-up backlog of agreements, many of them stalled for decades by Cold War military rivalry and diplomatic game playing. It was fundamental political change initiated by Mikhail Gorbachev in the Soviet Union that broke the logjam and made so many agreements possible in such a short period. The momentum of that breakthrough has now largely dissipated; Gorbachev is discredited and deposed, and reactionary nationalism is a potent force in Russian politics. China has shown some indications of wanting to be included in international arms control and nonproliferation regimes, but it is far behind the West in its ability to implement such policies effectively and still reluctant to restrict its freedom of action by full compliance with international norms. By the end of

1996 the Nonproliferation Treaty had captured 184 states, leaving only six outside its regime. But three of those six have traditionally been, and will remain, the most difficult to bring on board. The central questions facing the United States in this environment are how to provide effective leadership in preserving and extending regimes already in force and how to restore at least some of the positive momentum toward new and more comprehensive agreements.

REALISTS VERSUS INSTITUTIONALISTS

A basic premise of this book is that stable international arms control regimes are both effective in reducing the likelihood and severity of war and sustainable for the long term. But to the "realist" school of international relations such regimes are at best marginally effective and almost certainly temporary, in short a "false promise" [1]. In this view, arms control agreements, like all international institutions, "are basically a reflection of the distribution of power in the world. They are based on the self-interested calculations of the great powers, and they have no independent effect on state behavior" [1, p. 7]. Or as columnist George Will has more colorfully put it, "Treaties are like roses: they last while they last" [2].

Realists argue that although it may be convenient at this point in history to institutionalize the balance of power in a set of formal agreements, those agreements are no more permanent than the power balance they embody. National security remains the highest value for states, and treaty commitments are made and kept only as long as the costs to national security exceed the benefits to be gained by violating those commitments. Fred Iklé's approach to compliance (see chapter 7) is based on a realist analysis. In this view states constantly reassess the relative costs and benefits of compliance with agreements and rationally decide whether or not to comply based on the outcome of the calculation. When the balance shifts toward noncompliance, as it appears to have done in the attitudes of many Russians to the CFE Treaty and Americans to the ABM Treaty, the treaty becomes a national security liability. Realist rationality suggests that if it cannot be modified to reflect the new situation, the treaty must be abandoned. As Russia recovers from its political, economic, and military revolutions; as China's economy, military power, and hegemonic ambitions grow; as the competition for influence in Asia among Japan, China, Russia, and the United States intensifies; as Europe either does or does not find a common economic, political, and security structure; and as developing countries find themselves more and more in competition with regional rivals, a realist would predict that the present international security structure must give way to new and different forms. Such alterations cannot be prevented, or even significantly inhibited, by agreements signed and ratified under political and military conditions that no longer exist.

This is a powerful argument, and there is no shortage of evidence to support it. Russian attitudes toward existing and pending agreements have cooled noticeably under the Yeltsin government from the enthusiasm of Gorbachev and Shevardnadze. START II, the Chemical Weapons Convention, and the Open Skies Treaty face uncertain prospects in the Russian Duma, and Russian noncompliance with some provisions of the Conventional Forces in Europe (CFE) Treaty became a fact of life in November 1995. The United States continues to worry about Russian chemical and biological warfare activities, and Russia's willingness to sell nuclear reactors and other technology to Iran is a persistent irritant in U.S.-Russian relations. China's sales of missile and nuclear technology to Pakistan, Iran, and others also suggest a reluctance or incapacity to accept Western nonproliferation norms. Efforts by the U.S. Congress to undermine the ABM Treaty have come uncomfortably close to realization, and the 1996 election further weakened pro–ABM Treaty forces in the Senate.

France's resumption of nuclear testing in 1995, and its simultaneous effort to extend nuclear deterrence to other European states, call into question its commitment to nuclear disarmament, a pledge France made along with the four other nuclear weapon states to achieve indefinite extension of the Nonproliferation Treaty. But France is not alone in raising doubts about this commitment. None of the five nuclear weapon states is acting as if nuclear disarmament will happen any time in the foreseeable future, and the United States is openly, and at great expense, retaining the capability to resume nuclear testing and to reverse the reductions in deployed nuclear weapons mandated under START I and II [3]. How this behavior by the nuclear weapon states will affect the NPT and the actions of non-nuclear and threshold states remains to be seen. It has already helped India, Pakistan, and Israel, the so-called "threshold states," rationalize their refusal to join the NPT, and it is frequently used by Pakistan and India as a reason for their hesitation in joining a comprehensive test ban or fissile material cutoff.

Finally, U.S. concerns about chemical and biological weapon proliferation have become the rationale for a new counterproliferation program with a strong military emphasis, including suggestions that the United States might consider nuclear retaliation in response to chemical or biological attacks by non–nuclear weapon states [4]. Biological weapons have become the focus of growing apprehension in the Middle East, where at least five states rationalize their continued work on CBW by pointing to the Israeli nuclear weapon capability.

All of these examples could be seen as supporting the hypothesis that arms control regimes are fragile and temporary arrangements that merely paper over fundamental differences and begin disintegrating almost as soon as they are created. But there is another side to the story. "Institutionalists," or "liberal institutionalists," argue that institutions and norms can have significant and lasting effects on the likelihood and severity of war, especially if the major powers agree that war among themselves is not in their interests. In the view of Robert Keohane and Lisa Martin, the balance of power remains an important factor in world politics, but international institutions can "change the incentives for states to cheat" on agreements. They can also "provide information, reduce transaction costs, make commitments more credible, establish focal points for coordination, and in general facilitate the operation of reciprocity" [5].

Keohane and Martin base their analysis primarily on economic and legal institutions but point out that the role of institutions in providing information makes them applicable to security concerns as well. Data exchanges, notifications, and inspections built into all recent arms control and disarmament agreements are evidence for the importance of information and transparency in arms control. John Gerard Ruggie provides another example of the beneficial effects of international security institutions: the number of nuclear weapon states in the world, both acknowledged and "threshold," is far smaller than most experts predicted before the Nonproliferation Treaty came into force. "Indeed, in recent years more countries have left the list of problem cases—including Argentina, Brazil and South Africa—than have joined it" [6, p. 65]. Ruggie might have added Kazakhstan, Belarus, and Ukraine, who also found it in their interests to adhere to the institutional framework created by the NPT rather than attempt to turn their inherited Soviet nuclear weapons into security assets. Significantly, it was a leading realist who made the strongest case for Ukraine holding onto its nuclear arsenal [7]. His arguments were rejected by the Ukrainian President and Parliament, and there are good reasons to believe that the norms and institutions created by the NPT played a crucial role. They helped to legitimize the demand by other states that Ukraine abandon its nuclear option, to make clearer to Ukraine the benefits and costs of its different choices, and to move quickly to reward and support Ukraine's decision to join the treaty and accept safeguards on its nuclear activities.[1]

Evidence supporting the institutionalist argument can also be found in the role played by the CFE Treaty and the Stockholm-Vienna process in smoothing the potentially unstable transition from a bipolar Cold War European security system to the emerging post–Cold War structure. CFE and the Stockholm Document were negotiated under Cold War political conditions and designed to stabilize a seemingly permanent military standoff. Nevertheless, they proved extremely helpful in managing the revolutionary changes that accompanied the collapse of the Warsaw Pact and Soviet Union. Newly independent states, whether in Eastern Europe or the former Soviet Union, found themselves able to adapt to an established security framework with far less uncertainty than if it had not existed. The limits on large conventional weapons and the system of notifications, observations, data exchanges, and inspections in CFE and the Stockholm and Vienna Documents provided clear goals and guidelines, helped to structure negotiations among the newly independent states and between the former Warsaw Pact and the Western Alliance, and provided a degree of transparency that was reassuring to newly emergent states with little or no experience in providing for their own national security.

The fact that the great majority of states have joined the Non-Proliferation Treaty, ratified the Biological Weapons Convention, and signed the Chemical Weapons Convention suggests a growing acceptance of the value of arms control and disarmament agreements and of norms condemning the acquisition and use of weapons of mass destruction. The concept of nuclear-weapon-free zones that began in South America nearly 30 years ago has spread to the South Pacific, Africa, and Southeast Asia and is under discussion in the Middle East and Central Europe. That some states have violated these agreements and norms is not evidence that they are taken lightly or cynically by most states. Indeed, the handling of the Iraqi and North Korean situations is strong evidence for the willingness and ability of the international community to enforce them.

China's behavior in its disputes with the United States and the Missile Technology Control Regime also suggests a more important role for norms and institutions than the realists would predict. China is an emerging superpower with increasing influence and freedom of action in international politics. Yet

---

[1] This argument is made persuasively by Scott Sagan in "Why Do States Build Nuclear Weapons?" *International Security*, Winter 1996/97, pp. 54–86.

China has been eager to avoid the political opprobrium and isolation that violations of international norms could bring. It has signed the Comprehensive Test Ban even though that commitment will cap the technical sophistication of China's nuclear arsenal well below the levels achieved by the other four nuclear weapon states. China has also repeatedly pledged to abide by the full range of export control restrictions, and these pledges have become increasingly specific over time. No one expects a full meeting of the minds on these issues in the near future, but far from treating international norms and institutions with the calculating contempt of a confirmed realist, China has recognized their political power and has shown some willingness to adapt to their requirements.

All of the above examples provide support for the institutionalist argument, but they fall short of removing all doubts about the stability and longevity of international arms control. Despite ample evidence of its positive impact on the behavior of states in recent years, a confirmed realist can always argue that this evidence says more about inherently transient power relationships than it does about arms control. On the other hand, even though national security concerns and selfish interests are still causing some states to violate international norms and agreements, a confirmed institutionalist can argue that this behavior is rooted in attitudes and beliefs made increasingly obsolete by the growth of those same norms and agreements. Institutionalists believe that "state interests are in important part constructed by systemic structures, not exogenous to them" [8, pp. 72–73]. States may find their interests altered by existing norms and institutions, just as they can often clarify or discover their interests in the process of negotiating agreements (see chapter 7) [9].

U.S. LEADERSHIP

The jury is still out on whether arms control and the international institutions and norms it embodies will endure into the next millennium. One thing is clear, however: if arms control does have a future it will involve a continuing high level of commitment and leadership by the United States. Many other states have made important contributions to the process, and its ultimate success obviously depends on the continued adherence and cooperation of the five permanent members of the UN Security Council. Nevertheless, the United States has played a key leadership role in the negotiation and implementation of the agreements considered in this book, and it remains far ahead of other states in the priority it places on arms control and nonproliferation in its foreign policy, in the size and quality of its arms control bureaucracy and nongovernmental infrastructure, and in its willingness to devote human, technical, and financial resources to the process. These resources will continue to be essential if arms control is not to follow the path realists predict for it.

There are several ways in which the United States can demonstrate its commitment to sustaining international arms control regimes. The first and most important is to set an example of careful compliance with the agreements it has already signed. In most respects U.S. compliance has been excellent, but the ABM Treaty threatens to emerge as an important and dangerous exception. Debate over the efficacy, cost-effectiveness, and strategic benefit of ballistic missile defenses has been going on for more than 40 years. Far from being settled by the end of the U.S.-Soviet nuclear confrontation, it has emerged with even greater vigor as U.S. military policy has shifted to threats posed by so-called rogue states with emerging ballistic missile capabilities. The case for clarifying the ABM Treaty to incorporate new strategic and technological realities is a strong one, but so is the case for preserving its fundamental restrictions on the development and deployment of nationwide strategic missile defenses. There is an emerging threat of ballistic missile use by aggressive regional powers, and while this threat and the capabilities of defensive systems to counter it are often greatly exaggerated, there remains an essential kernel of validity in the argument for continued research and development on systems that can defend troops in tactical situations and counter small-scale regional ballistic missile attacks.

At the same time, the United States and Russia retain thousands of strategic nuclear weapons as deterrents against nuclear attack, and France, Great Britain, and China each deploy several hundred for the same reason. The development of even partially effective national defenses against long-range ballistic missiles would call into question the credibility of all of these deterrents and would make further progress toward their reduction and eventual elimination far more difficult, if not impossible. The Nixon administration's decision to sign the ABM Treaty was based on a determination that the costs of accepting its restrictions were outweighed by the benefits of having other parties accept them as well. While much has changed since the treaty entered into force in 1972, the essential elements of that calculation have not changed. It is still in the overall security interests of the United States to restrict its freedom of action in the development and deployment of ballistic missile defenses as long as others do likewise, and still in its interests to engage in the difficult and often tedious process of consultation and negotiation to update the details but preserve the essence of the ABM Treaty.

A second important aspect of U.S. leadership in arms control is a continued commitment to monitoring of compliance by other states. The United States possesses the world's most sophisticated arsenal of monitoring devices and the most extensive and competent intelligence capability devoted to arms control verification. These capabilities were developed during the Cold War primarily to watch the Soviet Union, but they have been adapted in the past several years to a much broader mission in support of U.S. nonproliferation policy. There are good reasons to reevaluate the priorities and missions of U.S. remote sensing and human intelligence efforts, and probably good reasons for reducing them from Cold War levels. But these assets still have a vital role to play in monitoring arms control agreements, a role that must be given a higher priority and status in the Intelligence Community.

Information gathered by U.S. intelligence assets has traditionally been protected at a high level of classification. There are good reasons for this, but at the same time it is often useful to share some of this information with allies, international agencies, or even rivals or adversaries after appropriate sanitization to protect sources and methods. In the emerging security environment there will be greater demands for the United States to share intelligence with foreign officials, international organizations, or even the general public. The International Atomic Energy Agency, the Organization for the Prevention of Chemical Weapons, the Comprehensive Test Ban Treaty Organization, the United Nations, and international export control groups will be particularly dependent on good intelligence. But while the United States must remain a leader in this process, it cannot do it alone. An exclusive dependence on U.S. intelligence could be damaging to the legitimacy and credibility of international organizations, and for both economic and political reasons, arms control monitoring must become more of an international effort.

A third requirement for continued leadership is a bureaucracy that more accurately reflects the high priority of arms control and nonproliferation in U.S. national security policy. The essential element here is the Arms Control and Disarmament Agency, which has never been given the budgetary strength or bureaucratic authority to provide effective leadership. It would be foolish to suggest that ACDA could or should be as big and powerful as State, Defense, or Energy, but it is only common sense to realize that if ACDA is to provide an independent and authoritative voice for arms control in the executive branch it must be freed from the constant harassment and restriction it has been subjected to in the past two decades, primarily by Congress. The Nonproliferation Treaty, the Chemical Weapons Convention, and the Comprehensive Test Ban provide evidence of what ACDA can accomplish when it has the support of the White House and is allowed to play a genuine leadership role. Future arms control agreements are going to be increasingly multinational, and these are precisely the kinds of agreements in which ACDA has shown itself most capable. A healthy, talent-rich, and authoritative ACDA will be essential if the United States is to play a leading role in future international arms control regimes.

Finally, the United States will have to resolve its own ambivalence about the future of nuclear weapons. During the Cold War nuclear arms control and nuclear nonproliferation evolved along separate tracks. The threats inherent in the U.S.-Soviet nuclear confrontation and those created by the gradual spread of nuclear weapons to other states were sufficiently different—strategically, technically, and politically—that they were dealt with by different bureaucratic actors with different priorities and objectives. Arms control was primarily bilateral, involving two superpowers with vast nuclear arsenals and an acknowledged mutual assured destruction capability. Nonproliferation was international, involving states with a wide variety of security concerns, regional ambitions, and technological and financial capabilities. It is increasingly clear that if the two programs are to continue they must converge to a single international process, one whose ultimate goal is total nuclear disarmament. As Russian and U.S. arsenals continue to decrease, those of Britain, France, and China will become increasingly visible. There will come a time when negotiations on further reductions must involve all five recognized nuclear weapon states. Meanwhile, the key NPT holdouts—Israel, India, and Pakistan—have the capability to produce nuclear weapons and have probably already done so. It is unlikely that they can be brought into the regime without simultaneously addressing their national security concerns and continuing the delegitimation of nuclear weapons begun by the INF and START treaties and the NPT regime.

The ability of the United States to influence this situation is limited but nonetheless significant. The United States can help to advance the delegitimation of nuclear weapons by unambiguously renouncing their first use, by initiating negotiations with Russia for further reductions beyond those mandated in START II, and by exercising leadership among the five nuclear weapon states to bring them into disarmament negotiations. The United States must also be more sensitive to the signals it sends from its own nuclear program. The expensive and sophisticated Stockpile Stewardship Program (see chapter 5) sends a strong signal that the United States intends to maintain a substantial nuclear arsenal and the option to resume nuclear testing, for the foreseeable future. The U.S. argument that a program of this size and expense is needed simply to preserve the safety and reliability of the existing stockpile has provided a convenient rationale for the Chinese and French (and possibly the Indian) test programs and appears to many nonnuclear states as a cover for a program to continue nuclear weapon development. Another ambiguous signal was sent by the Defense Department's Nuclear Posture Review, released in September 1994 [10]. While the review pointed with legitimate pride to many steps the United States has taken to reduce its arsenal and alter its doctrines, it also made clear the U.S. intention to hold onto thousands of nuclear weapons for many years to come, and to retain the option of stopping reductions and even reversing them if relations with Russia deteriorated. This sends a message to the world that the United States continues to see nuclear deterrence as the foundation of its national security policy, and influential U.S. analysts and policymakers continue to assert that possession of nuclear weapons by the five major powers is a key component, if not the *sine qua non*, of future world stability [11]. Far from delegitimizing nuclear weapons, such arguments reinforce the belief that they are essential to any state aspiring to world or regional power.

There is no reason to question U.S. sincerity in pursuing a comprehensive test ban and a fissile material cutoff. At the same time it matters very much to the threshold and non–nuclear weapon states whether these efforts are perceived as steps toward world nuclear disarmament or as devices to perpetuate an unequal nonproliferation regime. The ambivalence of the nuclear weapon states, and particularly the United States, became increasingly visible during the 1990s as many former supporters of nuclear deterrence began to question its relevance to the post–Cold War era. One of the first to do this in the United States was the late Secretary of Defense Les Aspin. As Chair of the House Armed Services Committee in 1993, he asserted that because of the fundamental strategic changes brought about by the collapse of the Soviet Union, "If [the United States] now had the opportunity to ban all nuclear weapons, we would."[2] Aspin's conclusion was not shared by many in the U.S. political establishment, much of which continues to hold that nuclear disarmament is either not feasible or that it would be undesirable even if it could be achieved.

Aspin's efforts were clearly premature, but by 1996 advocacy of nuclear disarmament was becoming increasingly mainstream. In July the International Court of Justice in the Hague determined unanimously that there exists a legal "obligation to pursue in good faith and bring to a conclusion negotiations leading to nuclear disarmament in all its aspects under strict and effective international control" [12]. In August the Canberra Commission, an international group of arms control experts and former policymakers convened by the Australian government, advocated "immediate efforts . . . to rid the world of nuclear weapons and the threat they pose to it" [13]. Finally, in December, an in-

---

[2] For a summary of Aspin's arguments and a wide spectrum of responses to them see Sean Howard, From Deterrence to Denuking: Les Aspin and New Thinking on Nuclear Weapons, The British American Security Information Council, Washington, DC: BASIC Report 93.4, September 22, 1993.

ternational group of 61 former high-ranking military officers joined in advocating substantial cuts in existing arsenals, progressive reductions in alert levels of deployed weapons, and nuclear policies "based on the declared principle of continuous, complete and irrevocable elimination of nuclear weapons."[3]

International pressures for nuclear disarmament are certain to increase in the next several years. The way in which the United States and the other nuclear weapon states react to these pressures will in great measure determine the degree to which existing arms control regimes can be preserved and expanded. Clearly, all five recognized nuclear powers will have to work together to make progress in this direction, and the monitoring networks and institutions created by the NPT, CWC, and CTBT would provide the foundation for a credible verification regime. The United States could exert significant leadership toward these objectives, but not until it is itself convinced that the goal is desirable and achievable.

The United States has recognized, albeit sometimes grudgingly, its responsibility for leadership in many parts of the world. The expansion of NATO, the Middle East Peace Process, and peacekeeping or peacemaking missions in Somalia, Haiti, and Bosnia have all been justified to varying degrees by the need for the United States to maintain its stature as a world leader. Such arguments have both a realist and institutionalist dimension. To a realist, continued recognition of U.S. power and leadership are vital strategic assets. An institutionalist would argue that the United States can in most cases act effectively only in cooperation with international institutions. The value of arms control and disarmament derives from the same combination of realist and institutionalist assumptions. This effort has gone too far and has been too universally identified with U.S. foreign policy for the United States to pretend it doesn't carry the major responsibility for its preservation.

The most important conclusion of this book is best expressed in the words of former national security advisor Brent Scowcroft. General Scowcroft was arguing in support of committing U.S. forces to the NATO peacekeeping mission in Bosnia. He was not referring to arms control, yet his words capture the essence of the position in which the many successes of the past decade have placed the United States. As Scowcroft saw it for Bosnia: "To the rest of the world, the United States is about as committed as it is possible to get in this enterprise. To turn our backs now would be a catastrophe for U.S. reliability, which I think is our most precious national security commodity" [14]. With respect to the U.S. commitment to biological, chemical and, ultimately, nuclear disarmament, I couldn't have said it better myself.

REFERENCES

1. John J. Mearsheimer, "The False Promise of International Institutions," *International Security*, Winter 1994/95, pp. 5–49.

2. George F. Will, "The Arms Control Fetish," *Washington Post*, September 21, 1995, p. A31.

---

[3] The group included 42 officers from nuclear weapon states and 19 from the United States, including the former commander in chief of U.S. Strategic Nuclear Forces, General Lee Butler. The quote is from the statement released at a National Press Club luncheon on December 4, 1996 by General Butler, General Andrew Goodpaster, and Admiral William Owens.

3. The Stockpile Stewardship and Management Program, U.S. Department of Energy, May, 1995.

4. Louis Jacobson, "Apocalypse Now," *National Journal*, September 9, 1995, p. 2245.

5. Robert O. Keohane and Lisa L. Martin, "The Promise of Institutionalist Theory," *International Security*, Summer 1995, pp. 39–51.

6. John Gerard Ruggie, "The False Premise of Realism," *International Security*, Summer 1995, pp. 62–70.

7. John J. Mearsheimer, "The Case for a Ukrainian Nuclear Deterrent," *Foreign Affairs*, Summer 1993, pp. 50–66.

8. Alexander Wendt, "Constructing International Politics," *International Security*, Summer 1995, pp. 71–81.

9. Abram Chayes and Antonia Handler Chayes, "On Compliance," *International Organization*, Spring 1993, pp. 175–205.

10. Nuclear Posture Review, U.S. Department of Defense, Washington, DC, September 1994.

11. Joseph S. Nye, Jr., "Conflicts after the Cold War," *The Washington Quarterly*, Winter 1996, pp. 5–24.

12. Legality of the Threat or Use of Nuclear Weapons, International Court of Justice, July 8, 1996.

13. Report of the Canberra Commission on the Elimination of Nuclear Weapons, Canberra Commission on the Elimination of Nuclear Weapons, August 1996.

14. Brent Scowcroft, Testimony before the Senate Armed Services Committee, November 28, 1995.

AFTERWORD

Two important events took place near the end of April 1997, as this book was being prepared for the printer. On April 25 the U.S. Senate ratified the Chemical Weapons Convention (CWC), allowing the United States to accede to the treaty before it entered into force on April 29. At just about the same time it was announced that the Arms Control and Disarmament Agency (ACDA) and the U.S. Information Agency (USIA) would be absorbed into the State Department. While it was officially denied that there was any connection between these two events, and while it is certainly true that there is no *logical* connection between them, it is understood by all knowledgeable observers that the loss of ACDA's independence was an important part of the price paid by the Clinton administration for Senate approval of the CWC.

Ratification of the CWC was a major achievement. It reconfirmed U.S. opposition to the production and deployment of weapons of mass destruction and its support for effective regimes for controlling them. U.S. participation and leadership are vital to the success of the treaty, and by acceding to it before its entry into force the United States is assured of a leading role in the treaty's implementation and verification. U.S. ratification also puts considerable pressure on Russia to ratify, and initial reactions from Moscow indicated that the Russian leadership was feeling that pressure. However, U.S. ratification has not changed the fundamental mismatch between obligations and resources that Russia would encounter by joining the CWC, and it remains to be seen how a cost conscious and politically reactionary Duma will respond.

Joining the CWC was unquestionably the right thing to do, but the price paid for it was very high. To the extent that ACDA's demise can be attributed to the Clinton administration's efforts to appease Senator Helms and his anti-arms control allies (none of whom voted for the treaty anyway), I am tempted to paraphrase the legendary U.S. army captain in Vietnam by saying that the Clinton administration decided it had to destroy arms control in order to save it. This would of course be an exaggeration; absorbing ACDA into State will not in itself kill arms control. But it does raise serious questions about the strength of the U.S. commitment over the long haul, and about how effectively the CWC—and all the other treaties discussed in this volume—will be implemented and verified. ACDA was a unique and creative effort to deal with the special problems posed by arms control and nonproliferation, and it is hardly a foregone conclusion that the arrangements that replace it will measure up to ACDA either in capability or commitment.

I have spent a good deal of time in this book discussing the trials and tribulations of ACDA, and now that the ax has finally fallen it is easy to conclude that it was inevitable. ACDA had many powerful enemies in the Senate and the executive bureaucracy, and with the 1996 congressional elections and the transition from the first to the second Clinton administration it lost a number of influential friends.[1] At the end ACDA had only one of its four bureau director positions filled, and Senator Helms had made it clear that no new appointments were going to be allowed past the Senate Foreign Relations Committee. An already small and marginalized agency was therefore faced with steadily weakening political clout and chronically inadequate funding. If this was in fact the only realistic alternative to integration with State, then integration must be seen as by far the lesser of two evils.

The irony of sacrificing ACDA to the CWC is striking—without ACDA there would almost certainly not have been a CWC. Nor would there have been a Non-Proliferation Treaty or a Comprehensive Test Ban. The State Department can take credit for many bilateral U.S.-Soviet arms control achievements, but it was always ACDA that led the fight for international disarmament and nonproliferation regimes, and always ACDA that played the key role in implementing, managing, and monitoring compliance with those regimes. Now, just as international regimes are assuming an increasingly dominant position relative to bilateral agreements, their most ardent and effective advocate has been driven from the scene.

It does not necessarily follow that international arms control regimes will wither and die; much depends on whether the new bureaucratic structure can preserve ACDA's unique combination of priorities, skills, and point of view. This is not impossible, but it will not be easy. The most positive aspect of the transition is that ACDA's Director has been given the authority to oversee the integration of ACDA with State's Bureau of Political–Military Affairs. The two entities have worked reasonably well together in the past, and there is no necessary reason why their integration cannot preserve the best aspects of both. No one doubts that the current secretary of state supports the goals of international arms control, and that support could manifest itself in her willingness to incorporate many of ACDA's values and much of its expertise into whatever new structure is created in State.

At the same time there is no indication that any of the persistent problems I discussed in chapter 6 have been or are likely to be resolved by the merger. The State Department remains a huge and poorly administered bureaucracy with a culture at best indifferent and at worst openly hostile to the technical expertise

---

[1] Retiring senators Sam Nunn, Claiborne Pell, Mark Hatfield, and James Exon, national security advisor Anthony Lake, secretary of defense William Perry, and secretary of energy Hazel O'Leary were all strong supporters of arms control in general and ACDA in particular.

that is an essential aspect of ACDA's mission. Every previous study of a possible merger has warned of the dangers inherent in this clash of cultures, and we will now have the chance to see if these warnings were prescient. The State Department also remains an agency with a broad spectrum of interests and priorities, and it will require strong and committed leadership to ensure that those other interests do not dominate international arms control and nonproliferation. While the current secretary may possess the right values and leadership qualities, there can be no guarantee that future secretaries will be either willing or able to overcome the traditional State Department tendency to compromise on arms control values when they conflict with economic or diplomatic interests.

There are a few specific areas where it will be particularly difficult for the new State Department entity to play the role that ACDA has played. One is ACDA's position as executive secretary of the Nonproliferation and Arms Control Technology Working Group. This group, which also includes the departments of Defense and Energy, oversees the research and development effort for arms control verification. It is hard to see the State Department in that role, and one consequence of the merger may be that the R&D programs of Energy and Defense will once again be freed from even the relatively weak control ACDA has been able to exercise over them. Another possible casualty of the merger will be the independent advocacy role ACDA has traditionally played with regard to rigorous enforcement of compliance with both formal treaties and informal export control regimes. Enforcing compliance has traditionally been one of State's most glaring weaknesses, and unless this weakness is corrected, the absorption of ACDA into State could undermine the legitimacy and effectiveness of international arms control regimes.

ACDA was created because of an understanding that arms control is not just another kind of diplomacy but a unique and vital activity in its own right. This understanding was influenced by the dangerous competition between two nuclear superpowers, and those who argue that ACDA was a creature of the Cold War make a valid point. Nevertheless, from its beginnings ACDA looked beyond the Cold War and the bilateral arms race toward the creation of international norms against weapons of mass destruction. Its first major achievement was the nuclear Non-Proliferation Treaty, and one of its most notable recent achievements was the indefinite and unconditional renewal and extension of that treaty in 1995. It has been ACDA people who have done the most to achieve the Chemical Weapons Convention, and ACDA people have done most of the tedious and frustrating work required to strengthen verification of the Biological Weapons Convention.

The Cold War is over, but the triple threat of chemical, biological, and nuclear proliferation will be with us for a long time to come. This is where arms control must now concentrate its major efforts, and it remains to be seen if the State Department, even granting the best of intentions by all concerned, can provide the political motivation, the technical expertise, and the bureaucratic focus necessary to make these efforts a success.

BIBLIOGRAPHIC ESSAY

There is a substantial literature on negotiation of agreements. Some classics of the genre are: George Bunn, *Arms Control by Committee: Managing Negotiations with the Russians* (Stanford, CA: Stanford University Press, 1992); John Newhouse, *Cold Dawn: The Story of SALT* (New York: Holt, Rinehart & Winston, 1973); Glenn T. Seaborg, *Kennedy, Khrushchev, and the Test Ban* (Berkeley: University of California Press, 1981); Glenn T. Seaborg and Benjamin S. Loeb, *Stemming the Tide: Arms Control and the Johnson Years* (Lexington, MA: Lexington Books, 1987); Gerard Smith, *Doubletalk: The Story of SALT I* (Lanham, MD: University Press of America, 1985); Strobe Talbott, *Endgame: The Inside Story of SALT II* (New York: Harper & Row, 1979); Strobe Talbott, *Deadly Gambits* (New York: Alfred A Knopf, 1984); Strobe Talbott, *Master of the Game* (New York: Alfred A. Knopf, 1988).

An excellent reference work that provides full texts of all treaties ratified before 1991, as well as some analysis of their negotiation history, is Jozef Goldblat, *Arms Control: A Guide to Negotiations and Agreements* (Oslo, London: International Peace Research Institute Oslo [PRIO], Sage Publications, 1994). Another valuable reference is the well-documented annual *SIPRI Yearbook* of the Stockholm International Peace Research Institute, published by Oxford University Press. The *Documents on Disarmament* series issued by the U.S. State Department is useful for historical research. The most authoritative sources of regular reporting and analysis on implementation, as well as all other phases of arms control, are *Arms Control Today*, published by the Arms Control Association in Washington, DC, and *Arms Control Reporter*, published by the Institute of Defense and Disarmament Studies in Brookline, Massachusetts.

The literature on ratification is much smaller. For a study of the ratification process in the United States see Michael Krepon and Dan Caldwell (Eds.), *The Politics of Arms Control Treaty Ratification* (New York: St. Martins, 1992). A useful study of Russian ratification politics is John W. R. Lepingwell, "START II and the Politics of Arms Control in Russia," *International Security*, Fall 1995, pp. 63–91. While the number of books devoted to ratification is small, the attention being paid to it in the arms control community is growing as one treaty after another joins the queues in Washington and Moscow awaiting approval by the Senate and Duma. *Arms Control*

Today and newspapers like the *Washington Post, Washington Times*, and *New York Times* are the best places to follow current developments in the ratification phase.

The literature on implementation has few books, and a researcher must dig a bit harder for information. One useful book is Richard A. Falkenrath's *Shaping Europe's Military Order: The Origins and Consequences of the CFE Treaty* (Cambridge, MA: MIT Press, 1995). Other sources for information on implementation are occasional studies by the General Accounting Office (GAO) and Congressional Budget Office (CBO). GAO reports are listed in a monthly catalogue that is available to the public, and individual copies of reports can be obtained free of charge from GAO's publications office in Gaithersburg, Maryland. Some excellent studies of arms control and nonproliferation implementation were done by the U.S. Congress Office of Technology Assessment (OTA). Examples include: *The Chemical Weapons Convention: Effects on the U.S. Chemical Industry*, August 1993; *Dismantling the Bomb and Managing the Nuclear Materials*, September 1993; *Proliferation of Weapons of Mass Destruction: Assessing the Risks*, August 1993; and *Nuclear Safeguards and the International Atomic Energy Agency*, April 1995. Unfortunately, OTA was abolished in 1995 and there will be no more of its useful studies. But the older ones are still valuable to researchers in arms control and nonproliferation and will likely remain useful for several more years.

An important reference on implementation is the annual report of the Arms Control and Disarmament Agency, *Threat Control through Arms Control*, which focuses on the activities and accomplishments of ACDA during the previous year. Another useful source is the "Nuclear Notebook," prepared every two months by the Natural Resources Defense Council (NRDC) and published in the *Bulletin of the Atomic Scientists*. The Notebook keeps track of the weapons stockpiles of all five nuclear weapon states, and in the days when nuclear weapons were being tested it kept a running count of all nuclear weapons tests. NRDC, based in Washington, also publishes occasional reports on specific aspects of arms control implementation, especially nuclear arms. Chemical arms control has been a special focus of the Henry L. Stimson Center in Washington, and it has conducted or sponsored studies of all phases of the CWC and the U.S.-Russian bilateral agreements.

There is an extensive literature on verification. Several books were written during the 1980s, when verification often seemed to be the central problem of U.S.-Soviet arms control. A few of these are: Allan S. Krass, *Verification: How Much Is Enough?* (Philadelphia: Taylor & Francis, 1985 and Lexington, MA: Lexington Books, 1985); Richard A. Scribner, Theodore J. Ralston, and William D. Metz, *The Verification Challenge* (Boston: Birkhauser, 1985); and William F. Rowell, *Arms Control Verification: A Guide to Policy Issues for the 1980s* (Cambridge, MA: Ballinger, 1986). Some valuable edited collections are: William C. Potter (Ed.), *Verification and SALT: The Challenge of Strategic Deception* (Boulder, CO: Westview, 1980) and *Verification and Arms Control* (Lexington, MA: Lexington Books, 1985); and Kosta Tsipis, David W. Hafemeister and Penny Janeway (Eds.), *Arms Control Verification—The Technologies That Make It Possible* (Washington, DC: Pergamon-Brassey's, 1986). A more recent work that covers the full range of conventional arms control—the CFE Treaty, confidence- and security-building measures, and the Open Skies Treaty—is Sergey Koulik and Richard Kokoski, *Conventional Arms Control: Perspectives on Verification* (Oxford/SIPRI: Oxford University Press, 1994). Two useful studies of verification from the perspective of the On-Site Inspection Agency are Joseph P. Harahan, *On-Site Inspections under the INF Treaty* (Washington, DC: On-Site Inspection Agency, 1993) and Joseph P. Harahan and John C. Kuhn, III, *On-Site Inspections under the CFE Treaty* (Washington, DC: On-Site Inspection Agency, 1996). A useful reference on the U.S. Intelligence Community, which plays a key role in arms control verification and nonproliferation monitoring, is Jeffrey T. Richelson, *The U.S. Intelligence Community*, 3rd ed. (Boulder, CO: Westview Press, 1995).

The increased concern with nonproliferation in the post–Cold War world is reflected in a growing number of books, articles, and reports on the subject. One of the best analyses of U.S. nonproliferation policy during the Cold War is Peter A. Clausen's *Nonproliferation and the National Interest: America's Response to the Spread of Nuclear Weapons* (New York: Harper Collins, 1992). Less analytical, but excellent for reference purposes, are Leonard Spector, *Going Nuclear* (Cambridge MA: Ballinger, 1987) and Leonard Spector and Mark G. McDonough (with Evan S. Madeiros), *Tracking Nuclear Proliferation* (Washington, DC: Carnegie Endowment, 1995). Proliferation of weapons of mass destruction, especially nuclear weapons, is monitored by a number of nongovernmental organizations. Most active in this regard is the Monterey Institute of International Studies, which publishes the quarterly journal *Nonproliferation Review* and other more focused reference works. One of the more useful of the latter is Roland M. Timerbaev and Meggen M. Watt, *Inventory of International Nonproliferation Organizations and Regimes*, February 1995. A useful quarterly called *The Monitor* is published by the Center for International Trade and Security (CITS) at the University of Georgia. Other organizations that publish occasional reports and papers on nonproliferation are the Nuclear Control Institute, the Nonproliferation Policy Education Center, and the Henry L. Stimson Center, all based in Washington, DC.

The compliance phase involves the long-term maintenance and adaptation of a regime as well as dealing with the noncompliance of individual parties with treaty obligations. The latter subject is dealt with in three works that focused on the U.S.-Soviet compliance disputes of the 1980s: Allan Krass and Catherine Girrier, *Disproportionate Response: American Policy and Alleged Soviet Treaty Violations* (Cambridge, MA: Union of Concerned Scientists, 1987); Michael Krepon and Mary Umberger (Eds.), *Verification and Compliance: A Problem-Solving Approach* (Cambridge, MA: Ballinger, 1988); and Gloria Duffy, *Compliance and the Future of Arms Control*, Center for International Security and Arms Control, Stanford University, Global Outlook, 1988. The best reference for more recent compliance information is ACDA's annual report to Congress, *Threat Control through Arms Control*. Since 1994 it has included a chapter entitled "Adherence to and Compliance with Arms Control Agreements," which summarizes the unclassified information on compliance behavior of parties to all treaties currently in force. Finally, there are two journals, *International Security* and *International Organization*, that frequently publish scholarly articles on arms control, nonproliferation, and the international regimes created to deal with them. Both journals have provided important sources for this book.

For students doing research on current issues in arms control there are a number of valuable sites on the Internet. A few of the most useful are:

Arms Control and Disarmament Agency (http://www.acda.gov)
Arms Control Association (http://igc.apc.org/ACA)
Henry L. Stimson Center (http://www.stimson.org:80)
Monterey Institute of International Studies (http://cns.miis.edu:80)
Natural Resources Defense Council (http://www.nrdc.org).
Stockholm International Peace Research Institute (http://www.sipri.se)
Union of Concerned Scientists (http://www.ucsusa.org)
University of Georgia CITS (http://www.uga.edu/~cits)

INDEX